Morrison.

King's Quiver

By the same Author

Breakers
Solitaire
The Gowk Storm
When The Wind Blows
The Strangers
These are my Friends
The Winnowing Years
The Hidden Fairing
The Keeper of Time
The Following Wind
They Need no Candle
The Other Traveller
Mary Queen of Scots
Thea
The Private Life of Henry VIII
Haworth Harvest: the Lives of the Brontës

King's Quiver
The Last Three Tudors

N. Brysson Morrison

J. M. Dent & Sons Ltd London

First published 1972

© N. Brysson Morrison, 1972

Made in Great Britain
at the
Aldine Press · Letchworth · Herts
for
J. M. DENT & SONS LTD
Aldine House . Bedford Street · London

ISBN: 0 460 03902 4

Contents

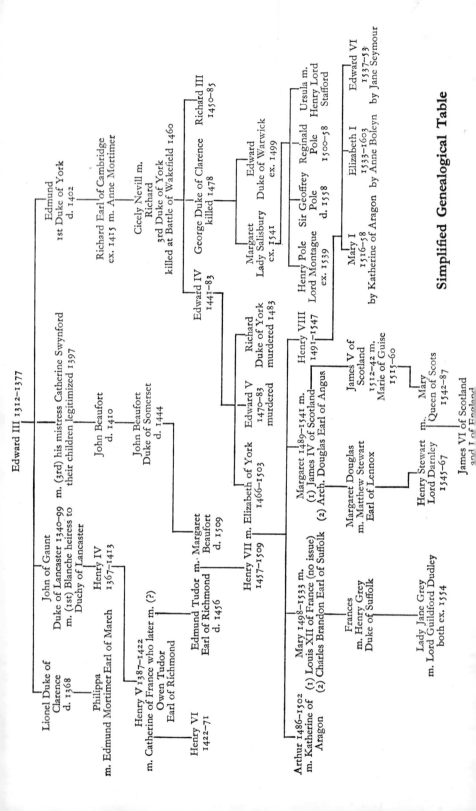

Simplified Genealogical Table

Edward III 1312–1377

Lionel Duke of Clarence d. 1368

Philippa m. Edmund Mortimer Earl of March

Henry V 1387–1422 m. Catherine of France who later m. (?) Owen Tudor Earl of Richmond

Henry VI 1422–71

John of Gaunt Duke of Lancaster 1340–99 m. (1st) Blanche heiress to Duchy of Lancaster

m. (3rd) his mistress Catherine Swynford their children legitimized 1397

Henry IV 1367–1413

John Beaufort d. 1410

John Beaufort Duke of Somerset d. 1444

Margaret Beaufort d. 1509

Edmund Tudor m. Earl of Richmond d. 1456

Henry VII 1457–1509 m. Elizabeth of York 1466–1503

Edmund 1st Duke of York d. 1402

Richard Earl of Cambridge ex. 1415 m. Anne Mortimer

Cicely Nevill m. Richard 3rd Duke of York killed at Battle of Wakefield 1460

Edward IV 1441–83

Richard III 1450–85

George Duke of Clarence killed 1478

Margaret Lady Salisbury ex. 1541

Edward Duke of Warwick ex. 1499

Henry Pole Lord Montague ex. 1539

Sir Geoffrey Pole d. 1558

Reginald Pole 1500–58

Ursula m. Henry Lord Stafford

Edward V 1470–83 murdered

Richard Duke of York murdered 1483

Henry VIII 1491–1547

Mary I 1516–58 by Katherine of Aragon

Elizabeth I 1533–1603 by Anne Boleyn

Edward VI 1537–53 by Jane Seymour

Arthur 1486–1502 m. Katherine of Aragon

Mary 1498–1533 m. (1) Louis XII of France (no issue) (2) Charles Brandon Earl of Suffolk

Margaret 1489–1541 m. (1) James IV of Scotland (2) Arch. Douglas Earl of Angus

Frances m. Henry Grey Duke of Suffolk

Lady Jane Grey m. Lord Guildford Dudley both ex. 1554

James V of Scotland 1512–42 m. Marie of Guise 1515–60

Margaret Douglas m. Matthew Stewart Earl of Lennox

Henry Stewart Lord Darnley 1545–67

Mary Queen of Scots 1542–87

m.

James VI of Scotland and I of England

List of illustrations

Between pages 72 and 73

1. Henry VII, the first of the Tudors and Henry VIII's father, holding the red rose of Lancaster. Painting by an unknown artist, reproduced by kind permission of the National Portrait Gallery.

2. Elizabeth, Henry VII's Queen and mother of Henry VIII, holding the white rose of York. Painting by an unknown artist, reproduced by kind permission of the National Portrait Gallery.

3. Mary, probably twenty, in the year she was reconciled to her father. Drawing by Hans Holbein the Younger, reproduced by gracious permission of Her Majesty the Queen (from the royal collection at Windsor Castle).

4. Edward painted in his third year (1540) by Hans Holbein the Younger as a Christmas present for Henry VIII. Reproduced by kind permission of the National Gallery of Art, Washington, D.C.; Andrew Mellon Collection. Verse translated by Marion Lochhead, M.B.E.

5. Family picture painted *c.* 1545 by an unknown artist. Henry VIII has Edward on his right side and Jane Seymour, Edward's mother, on his left. Her likeness is believed to have been taken from the wax effigy carried at her funeral. Mary is seen entering on right of picture, Elizabeth on left. Reproduced by gracious permission of Her Majesty the Queen (from the Hampton Court collection).

6. Mary at twenty-eight, by an unknown artist. The year 1544 was a happy one for Mary when she was living with her stepmother Katherine Parr. Reproduced by kind permission of the National Portrait Gallery.

7. Edward painted when he was nine (1546), by an unknown artist, shortly before his accession. Reproduced by gracious permission of Her Majesty the Queen (from the royal collection at Windsor Castle).

8. Elizabeth painted at thirteen at the same period as Edward at nine and almost certainly by the same unknown artist. Reproduced by gracious permission of Her Majesty the Queen (from the royal collection at Windsor Castle).

9. *Top:* Elizabeth I, as depicted on a silver sixpenny coin; *Centre:* Edward VI, gold coronation medal; *Bottom:* Mary I, silver-gilt medal by Jacopo da Trezzo, 1555. Reproduced by kind permission of the Trustees of the British Museum.

10. *Top:* Signature of Edward. Reproduced by kind permission of the Trustees of the British Museum.
Centre: Signature of Elizabeth. Reproduced by kind permission of Mr Ray Rawlins.
Bottom: Part of document supposed written by Mary. Reproduced by kind permission of the Trustees of the British Museum.

11. Elizabeth, painted probably in the early 1580s, when in her late forties, by an unknown artist. Reproduced by gracious permission of Her Majesty the Queen (from the royal collection at Hampton Court).

Book One

King's Quiver
February 1516–January 1547

'Unfledged arrows cannot fly far, and are greatly affected by the wind.'

Quoted in *The Book of Archery*, 1840, George Agar Hansard

Chapter One

She was born in February, before winter had loosed its hold or spring broken through hard earth, the shortest month of the year, heralded by the ringing of church bells and lit with the aspiring flames of candles.

Once more the silver font travelled from Canterbury. All royal children were christened the third day after birth, and the highest in the land trod the carpets spread from Greenwich Palace to Grey Friars, where jewels winked and gleamed in the church hung with tapestries.

The trumpets of heralds blazoned forth her titles. She was called Mary after her father's favourite sister who had been Queen of France when she was the loveliest woman in Europe, content to be known as the Duchess of Suffolk now she had been allowed to marry her brother's jousting comrade.

The highest in the land attended the Princess on her short first journey except for the two highest. Custom decreed that neither parent should be present, in the unlikely event that the mother were well enough. Now the King waited beside his consort for the procession to return, when the baby would be handed to her mother that she might be the first to call her by her Christian name.

In 1516, at the birth of his daughter, Henry VIII was in his twenty-fifth year, the handsomest man in the country, standing head and shoulders above lesser men, fair-skinned and bright-complexioned. The woman he, boisterous with good health, waited beside had been his wife for the seven years he had reigned.

He could not contain his pride in his daughter. He called her this girl of mine and declared she never cried. Nor would he have any of it when ambassadors (the French were the most needling) tempered their congratulations with commiseration that the child was a daughter not a son. 'We are both young,' he assured them, strong with conviction. 'If it is a daughter this time, by the grace of God the sons will follow.'

But were they so young? Certainly he was in his prime but she, the bearer, was six years older, and the list of her pregnancies like a toll: a stillborn daughter and a son who had lived only a few sickly weeks; at least two more occasions when foreign ambassadors reported to their respective countries the secret christening of the King's new son—all the record known of lives short as sighs.

The new child, with a female's tenacity, thrived. She had her father's rosy cheeks, and like him was merry and joyous, her hair retaining its baby silvery fairness even when she was a child.

Her hair had been her mother's chief beauty, when auburn meant light yellow rather than reddish brown. The Londoners remembered it streaming over her shoulders in the wind when they saw her first as she rode across London Bridge on her mule that November day in the year 1501. They had taken her to their hearts from that hour, bellowing their appreciation as though loudness would convey to her what might be unintelligible in words. This was the Infanta, whose father was King of Aragon and mother Queen of Castile, who had come from a far land to make her home amongst them, to wed their Arthur, Prince of Wales, and bear his sons and so make secure for ever the throne of England.

It was too far back for them to mind what their fathers had lived through, but no one wanted a return of those evil days when for thirty years, from 1455 to 1485, their country had been laid waste as two Houses wrestled for the crown. The Wars of the Roses the contest was called, as the ding-dong of battle favoured now the white rose of York, now the red rose of Lancaster, a murderous struggle between two Houses both sprung from the one branch.

But Bosworth Field in 1485 had put an end to all that when the plundered naked body of the defeated Yorkist king, Richard III, the last of the Plantagenets, was carried from the battlefield. His battered crown, found hidden in a hawthorn bush, was placed on the head of the Welshman who had little hereditary right to it, while his victorious army, half the size of that it had vanquished, hailed him as Henry VII.

It mattered as little to his subjects as it had mattered to his soldiers that the man who sat on the throne was there because his royal Lancaster grandmother had had a clandestine union with her Welsh clerk of the wardrobe. He grasped the sceptre with a

4

strong hand, established peace within the realm, and with peace came prosperity to the people.

Within an hour Henry VII, the first Tudor king, won victory, crown and bride. He married Elizabeth of York, daughter of Edward IV, whose two young brothers had been murdered in the Tower of London by the king defeated on blood-stained Bosworth Field. Some said behind their hands that she, a king's daughter, had better right to the crown than her husband, but England had never been ruled by a queen, and they prayed God it never would be. His people needed no surer sign that Providence had arranged the union of their sovereign when they flocked in their hundreds to see what had never been seen before: red and white roses, the rival colours of Lancaster and York, miraculously produced by the one bush.

No wonder that she had been called 'the good Queen', providing the royal nurseries with princes and princesses in goodly numbers, of which four survived the shocks of infancy; Arthur, Prince of Wales, the Princess Margaret, Prince Henry and Princess Mary. And their father had been a real good king. There was no gainsaying that. When trade had increased with the stability of the reign, he had negotiated a favourable treaty with the Netherlands. Instead of shipping wool to feed foreign looms, the cloth itself was now woven and exported, and the clothier flourished where the weaver had waxed and waned. A careful man, he accumulated and amassed, did not part with property— least of all with land—bringing back to the crown estates that had passed to subjects and adding to them the wide domains of his beaten opponents.

But after he had been twenty-four years on the throne, they were due for a change. Enshrined in his own chapel, embalmed by stone, was a fitting place to think of him—and leave him. God would rest his soul, for he had been devout. So was his son Henry who had succeeded him. He heard mass three times a day, but as well he could draw a bow with greater strength than any man in England.

Scarcely had the stir of the old king's funeral settled when the people heard their new king, Henry VIII, was to marry the Infanta, she who had been the bride of their Prince of Wales for six months before he died. It was common talk that his father on his deathbed had adjured him to fulfil the marriage treaty, but this was no marriage he had been pushed into by a parent's dying wish, but one he made of his own free choice and rejoiced in for all the world to see. As for the bride, her love for him made her at one with the people, and they held jubilee with her.

As befitting their royal state, each prince or princess had an elaborate household of his own, circling round the small personage like constellations round the sun, and the luminary to lead them was customarily of royal rank.

Margaret Plantagenet, Countess of Salisbury, daughter of George, Duke of Clarence, the brother of Richard III, filled the position in little Mary Tudor's establishment known as state governess. This was the female equivalent of the comptroller or governor of the princess's household and was the closest association she had.

Mary's mother had treated Lady Salisbury tenderly from the days when she became both bride and consort of the King of England. Dead men did not usurp, and Queen Katherine knew well that her father would not allow her to leave Spain to marry the sixteen-year-old Prince of Wales until the best qualified pretender to the English throne had been destroyed. One grim November day in 1499 King Henry VII's subjects learnt that the White Rose, the young Earl of Warwick, Margaret Plantagenet's brother, had been executed for treason. As the Tower, where he had been incarcerated at the age of ten, had been his home since Bosworth, his opportunities for treason were few and far between; but that he had been allowed to grow to manhood proved that the first Tudor king preferred imprisoning his competitors to murdering them.

But no long shadow from Tower Green fell between his sister and her queen or her queen's daughter. Mary knew her from her cradle days, so that by the time she began to walk Lady Salisbury was familiar as part of her existence. The very solitariness that separated a royal child from his or her fellows lent a significance to those who were allowed to approach within a certain distance, and of Lady Salisbury's grown sons it was the fair-haired Reginald Pole with his oval face and debonair grace who was separate from his brothers. He did not marry, but took minor orders that were no bar to marriage, a kindly, gentle man, cultivated like the gardens he loved, whose religion was his life.

Her parents saw more of their small offspring than was customary where different households tended to separate families. Often enough a boat was sent across the Thames to bring her from her residence to theirs, and for months it would not carry her back again, so that she grew accustomed to be made much of by her father, and to be taught how to form her letters and her first words of Latin by her learned mother.

At the age of two, in the presence of her parents before the throne, she listened to Bishop Tunstall address her on the honourableness of the marriage state, there was an exchange of speeches between men who seemed very tall and far above her, she was lifted up and a small ring with a very big diamond slipped over her tiny finger. Now she was affianced to the Dauphin of France, who had been suggested as her bridegroom, should he be a boy, before he was born.

The betrothal was anything but popular with her father's subjects; they did not hold with it at all. They had never taken to foreigners, but any foreigner was better than a Frenchman. An Englishman inherited his hatred of him as he inherited his father's blood.

The story of 1066 is told by an English artist on the Bayeux Tapestry for his Norman patron. 'God help us!' the Normans cried as battle joined round the hill at Hastings. The unremembered past was rolled up tightly, like a length of tapestry, for the descendants of the English, who had replied 'Get out!' All they were left with was the scrap that time could not fray: at some time in their history an invader had come from across the seas, conquered them and made them serfs, and that invader was a Frenchman.

The French name Agincourt passed into the English language when their Henry V won the battle there in 1415 with such decisiveness he could dictate the terms. He became Regent of France, married the daughter of the defeated king, Charles VI, and would have succeeded to the throne of France after him had he not died first. His young son Henry VI was proclaimed king in Paris at the same time as Charles VII was proclaimed at Bourges. The French states united to drive out the national foe and by 1453 Calais alone and the countship of Guines remained in the hands of the English king. But in the minds of the English Agincourt spread over centuries, obliterated Hastings, whose Norman invaders were now Plantagenet Englishmen, and gave English rights of tenure to enemy country of which Henry VIII's coronation proclamation declared he was king.

And so he was. He had been King of England for but four years when he took his army over the sea and gave the French such a fright that they were glad to pay him a high price in the form of pensions for a peaceful settlement.

That was when the Scots came storming over the Border, the Scots whose French allies were England's enemies. But the English were ready for them. Their king was left dead on Flodden field, he who was brother-in-law to King Hal. The baby in Queen Margaret's arms was James V before he was weaned.

They were two nations, two different races of men, sharing the one small island. The nearer the neighbour the deadlier can be the feud; it was now of such long standing that on the Border fighting between them was looked upon by both sides as a pastime. Scotland was a poor country with a population approximately one-tenth of England's, but poverty and defeat did not make her people tractable. Inquisitive, combative and noisy with talk, their independence was the breath by which they lived.

Henry's subjects were a lusty folk, who came of healthy stock, bold, hardy and keen to do business. Even the English commons fed well on light-coloured bread and beer and quantities of meat, unlike the half-starved French peasantry. Such a diet tended to make a people swift to act with both tongue and hand. There were no half-measures where their passions were concerned.

They gathered to watch hangings and floggings, shouldering one another for a better view, feeding their eyes on spectacles such as a royal progress, at one with the clamour of life that filled street and market-place; but not quite at one with the ecclesiastical processions that wended to or from cathedral or abbey. They were unaware of that themselves as they stood there looking on with speculative eyes. It was not the crucifix, the crosier, the canopy they were to deride; it was the men who bore them, 'Pope's men'. To the English the Pope was a foreigner.

In 1520 they were told their king and his queen were crossing the water to greet in friendship his contemporary, the French king Francis I. It was stressed that although their king was making the journey, he was convening with his French counterpart at Calais, on English soil, the ground between two castles still manned by English soldiers.

Three French gentlemen called on their four-year-old daughter while her parents were abroad She held court in the magnificence of Richmond Palace, intricate with carving and ablaze with gold and azure, spangled with stars. Its great Hall had glazed windows and coloured tiles, and its courts were peopled with fantastic beasts blazon bright. Every tower had its weather-vane flashing with the king's arms, filling the air on a windy day with the whirl of their sound.

The Frenchman, who took a proprietary interest in their small hostess betrothed to their Dauphin, were captivated by a child of her tender years who could greet them with such pleasantness and entertain them by the nimble grace with which she played the virginals.

In France the King of England started from English-held Guines at the same time as the French king started from Ardes, to meet in the valley between the two towns on a site which became known as the Field of the Cloth of Gold. As French and English converged, suspicion of French designs broke over the English ranks, but it was overcome.

For sixteen gilded days the two retinues remained together, entertaining each other, exchanging compliments. The two kings, of an age, held the field against all comers, no one could say which outshone the other. They breakfasted together, gave gifts to each other, professed eternal amity, for all the world to see the fastest friends in Christendom. 'These sovereigns,' commented a penetrating Venetian, 'hate each other very cordially.'

After the painted spectacle and display of chivalry, transactions and acts. Henry, on his way back to England, met Charles, the young King of Spain, at the Flemish town of Gravelines, and together they repaired to Calais. The Emperor was unlucky with weather; a great wind blew the roof of the conference hall away, but negotiations were satisfactorily completed. Henry bound himself to proceed no further in the marriage between Princess Mary and the Dauphin, and Charles bound himself to proceed no further in that between himself and Francis's little daughter. Not included but implicit in the treaty was the proviso that Charles should marry Henry's daughter himself.

Of the three reigning monarchs, Henry VIII of England, Francis I of France and Charles V of Spain, Charles was the youngest, but, self-contained as an oyster, he might well have been the oldest. Henry and Francis were to be lifelong rivals in exuberance, parade and extravagance; Charles, so grave it was said he had never been seen to smile, with indefatigable energy, was to become a soldier of genius.

Katherine's nephew and Duke of Burgundy, he had succeeded her parents as King of Aragon and Castile. As well as King of Spain and its South American colonies, he was now King of Sicily and Naples, and Emperor of Austria and the Low Countries, which included England's best customer, the Netherlands.

Such predominance made Francis uneasily aware of the encircling of his country by realms over which his enemy held sway, while the duchy of Milan was a centre of contention between the two kings. The very extent of Charles's far-flung territories was disadvantageous, for trouble in one meant a weakening in others to deal with it. Henry was courted by both powers, for whichever had not England as its ally was perilously outbalanced.

Treaties could be signed and countersigned, secret bonds entered into, promises made and vows exchanged, offspring pledged as surety for their parents' bounden word, but in this game of kings each played a solo hand. Charles kept his cards close to his chest, whereas Francis was a rash player, while the ace Henry kept up his capacious sleeve sometimes did not turn out to be the winner he had imagined.

The marriage between her daughter and her sister's son was the marriage her mother wanted for her above all others, Mary to live in the land of pomegranates and myrtles where she herself had been born.

Her father himself brought the Emperor to Greenwich, to that favourite palace where the river wound. They landed by barge, climbing the water-stairs. Waiting for them, framed in the principal doorway, stood Queen Katherine, holding by the hand Charles's future bride, the Princess Mary.

She was six years old, tiny with brown eyes and the Tudor fairness of skin. Already she could talk to foreigners in their own tongue. Henry thought the world of her. He was fond of children, and this clever little girl was his own, did not belong to someone else. Children for their part felt at home with his uninhibited personality; to Mary everything that was big, warm and splendid all happened in his presence at the one time.

The bridegroom was twenty-two, with the protruding Hapsburg underlip, his face animated only by bright and intelligent eyes. He and his small pleasing bride, who had been wearing Spanish dress to accustom herself to it, drew together in a kind of mannered courtship.

Before he left England he signed the matrimonial treaty in

which he bound himself to marry Henry VIII's daughter when she was twelve. The agreement provided that if Henry had no son to succeed him, the eldest male child born to Charles and Mary should become King of England. It was a very full moment for Henry: his daughter to marry not a king's son but the Emperor of the Holy Roman Empire himself, his grandson maybe not only to rule England but the empire.

Charles was anxious for his bride to be sent to Spain where she could be educated as his bride, but every time the point was raised in the years to come Henry adroitly turned it aside. The Princess was too young as yet to stand a sea journey, or be moved from her native air, and where in all of Christendom could the Emperor find a more fit mistress to bring up his future wife after the manner of Spain than her own mother?

She was, however, subjected to a rigid education when Vives, a learned Spaniard, was made director of her studies, and the lilting hours were cut and dried into a rigorous time-table. The 'right merry and joyous' infant with her father's rosy cheeks grew into a pallid, spare, short-sighted scholar before she was twelve, although not all the Spaniard's stern dictums were put into practice, such as that cherishing, which marred sons, utterly destroyed daughters. Also he did not approve of cards, dice or splendid dress, all three of which were much in evidence at the court of Mary's father.

She was intelligent, but had not the grasping mind of the intellectual, so that from the beginning she had to apply herself to her studies rather than to reach out to explore and enjoy.

The silver font did not travel again from Canterbury. Her mother's face had begun to wear the sorrowful look of one who accepts that her prayers will go unanswered. Not all the physicians brought from Spain, nor her father's vow to lead a crusade against the infidel if God would but grant him a son, worked the miracle. The grace of God did not extend to her mother. The harvest of eight pregnancies was one small daughter, pale as an ear of wheat, and no heir.

God did not grant him an heir by his lawful wife, but in 1519 Henry had fathered an illegitimate son. The mother was Elizabeth Blount, a girl who had taken gleeful part in all the revels and romps of the young court. She had beauty, for the child was said to be goodly, like his parents. He was christened Henry.

The King ordered the affair with the greatest circumspection.

No ambassador or envoy knew of it, or had wind of the birth. He was jealous of royal prestige, and to foreigners, inured to the palace excesses and scandals of their own courts, his was a model of discretion. He himself was not licentious. The King of France was so libertine his profligacy was scarcely news; the King of England's only known liaison, with Mary Boleyn, one of his queen's ladies-in-waiting, was so discreet as to raise no comment.

Henry, now allied to Charles, declared war on Francis in what was to be a concerted invasion of France. It was pleasant to believe that the overtaxed French wanted to change their king and were crying, 'Vive le roi d'Angleterre!' But nothing was more costly to mount, and for the first time in his life he was short of money. When Parliament was summoned in the spring of 1523, to provide the resources for the campaign, he had reigned fourteen years, and in these fourteen years he had exhausted with his extravagance his father's patrimony, which has been estimated at thirty million pounds.

The war was unpopular in the country. His subjects grumblingly wondered why they should be asked to burn their fingers taking chestnuts out of the fire for the Emperor. Could they not or would they not see that through war with France their all-wise king would recover his right to the French crown? They saw it was bad for trade, and the moment an English army left its island base the Scots would be across the Border in their hordes. Parliament voted with the greatest reluctance only part of the colossal sum demanded.

The largest army to leave England for a hundred years sailed for Calais before the end of August, hindered until autumn by the emptiness of the coffers and the usual administrative delays. It advanced to within forty miles of Paris, capturing all towns on its way, when it had to fall back on Calais, for the Emperor's joint invasion did not materialize and the dead time for war was setting in. Only the dread of a second Flodden kept the Scots from pouring over the defenceless Border.

The following year Charles made up for his inactivity, and invaded France, laying siege to Marseilles. No attempt was made to help him from the English side. Henry, playing tit for tat, had neither the heart nor the resources. The new Pope, Clement VII, in an effort to redress the imperial preponderance, threw his weight on the French side. No longer was England the crucial balance between two forces: to keep any position at all she had to shift from side to side. Very tentative overtures were made to France.

The French defended Marseilles with such stubbornness it did not fall and the imperial army were forced to retreat towards Italy before the onslaught of winter.

All would have been well for Francis had he been content to defend his kingdom, but he had ever been over-ambitious. He had had victories and conquests in the past when he had taken the offensive; this time he would regain the glittering prize of Milan. He crossed the Alps with his army. As he sat down to besiege Pavia, the Lombard capital, astrologers read from the stars what any general should have known from the ground, the disastrous outcome of such a campaign undertaken in winter with the Alps between Francis and his own territory.

Mary's father was in bed when an excited courier arrived to tell him the startling news that imperial troops had annihilated the French army at Pavia and taken the French king prisoner. Mary's mother began to smile again; she dreaded when English policy veered towards Francis from the nephew she longed to see her son-in-law. Henry ordered London to celebrate the capture of the French king, bonfires were lit and free wine dispensed to the citizens. Mary's parents attended a jubilant Te Deum in St Paul's with the foreign ambassadors.

The historic victory was won on 24th February 1525, the Emperor's birthday. Charles received the news of the complete defeat of the French and the capture of their king with none of Henry's triumphant exuberance, but with a self-restraint that awed the world into admiration. At twenty-five years of age he was a Caesar astride the globe, in a position to dictate to Christian and infidel alike.

Henry, riding the crest of his ally's conquest, dispatched envoys to Spain, proposing that the Emperor should depose Francis and invade France with England to satisfy their just claims. But Charles had not defeated his enemy to exalt his prospective father-in-law, and showed no disposition to share a victory he had won alone while his ally had stood idly by.

Mary was seen to whiten when she heard court gossip that her suitor might take another cousin for his bride, not a little girl for whom he had to wait but the grown up Infanta Isabella of Portugal who was not only beautiful but had a dowry of a million crowns.

The meeting between the English ambassadors and the Emperor was uncomfortable. His Imperial Highness knew all about the overtures their king had made to the French. When he was asked for the return of the 5,000 crowns Henry claimed he had borrowed, they were told the Emperor too was short of money. The Englishmen saw it was useless to blow any longer at a dead coal, but reeled when they heard that if they wanted him to marry their lady princess she must be brought to Spain at once with her dowry of £80,000.

Coldly Henry acquiesced when Charles asked to be freed from his engagement with his daughter that he might marry the Infanta Isabella, which he was to do, the following year. By the time Francis had bought his freedom at the price of promises he had no intention of keeping, England had negotiated a treaty of amity with France. Now Henry was no longer in the Spanish camp, he naturally felt safer in Francis's: after all, France could boast four times the inhabitants that England had. But instead of an emperor who held the corners of the earth in his hands, Henry had for his allies Clement VII, a pontiff who trembled with irresolution, and a Lucifer who had fallen from heaven, cut down to the ground.

No longer was Mary treated as the Empress of Spain. Imperceptibly the tenor of her life was changing, conflicting strains creeping into a score that had been all of a piece before.

The French queen Claude had died, and Mary's father, to revenge himself on the Emperor, had set his heart on Mary's marriage to the French king He sent pointed messages to the widower to turn over a new leaf and wax a good man. His brother sovereign accepted his advice in good part, and riposted gaily. He had purchased his release by giving his two eldest sons as hostages to Charles, whose widowed sister Eleanor he had undertaken to marry, but to none of the three sovereigns were such undertakings, however solemn, inviolate.

Mary was sent to Ludlow Castle on the marches of Wales in August 1525, luckless Ludlow Castle to her mother, who had travelled there with her boy husband Arthur a lifetime ago, and where he had died. Mary, as Princess of Wales, was provided with a more handsome court than was even Arthur, Prince of Wales, because her father deemed it necessary for her to have the state of a future Queen of France.

Her mother sorely missed her little daughter, and asked for her exercises to be sent to her now and again for the comfort of seeing how she was progressing with her Latin and writing. No longer had Katherine any say in the plans for her child's marriage. If she had, it was thought she favoured Reginald Pole now the bridegroom she had desired above all others had married elsewhere. Her first marriage had been sealed with the innocent blood of his uncle. She had not forgotten that in the joyous days of her second marriage, she did not forget it now as she felt the climate of her life begin to chill around her. Mary's marriage to one of the Countess of Salisbury's sons would surely go some way to expunge an old wrong, and the union of Tudor with Plantagenet restore an ancient House. But such a bridegroom for his daughter never entered her husband's calculations.

Lady Salisbury accompanied her charge, to make familiar the unfamiliar, and returned with the eleven-year-old Princess to Greenwich, through the green of early spring, when the cavalcade of litter and wagon wound back from the marches of Wales. The rambling palace beside the river had always been used as a family home, and the additions succeeding generations had built on gave the impression that the residence was still unfinished. Here her father had been born, as she had been, and had married her mother in the heyday of summer, here jocund court was held for the Twelve Days of Christmas, when amidst all the splendour and glitter the Lord of Misrule presided with his vaulting mummers and their rough and tumble revelry.

Everyone knew why Mary's return was timed to correspond with the feast of St George, the season which celebrated the highest order of knighthood in the land. This spring there were envoys from France to impress, to feast and toast.

The King himself presented them to Mary's mother and to Mary herself, whom he hoped shortly would be their queen. The Venetian ambassador always thought it absurd that the little girl from her baby days received more honour than her mother. Now Henry prompted his guests to speak to the child in French, Latin and Italian, and Mary did not shame him. The Frenchmen thought she was the most accomplished child they had ever seen, but agreed amongst themselves that she was so small and spare it would be impossible for her to be married for another three years at least.

The festivities lasted until well into May, the King's daughter the star of every spectacle, the cynosure of every masque, her little person clad in cloth-of-gold and carrying so many jewels they dazzled even the sophisticated Venetian ambassador.

In the same year the Infanta Isabella of Portugal, now empress and queen of Charles, was confined. Her labour was so arduous that her doctors urged her to cry out lest the effort of repression prove fatal. 'Die I may,' she told them, 'but call out I will not.'

Her child was a son, with the long head that betokened a protracted birth; it was covered with golden down. He was christened Philip.

Chapter Two

It is not known when Mary first learnt there was something amiss between her parents; probably it was nothing clear-cut and decisive, but an implication brushed aside before it could settle, a vague awareness of things not being as they were, the uneasiness of what was not uttered before the sinister happened.

What is known is that during her formative years what she had to face blighted her for life, and robbed her of her flowering. It told on her health; from now onwards she suffered, not from consumption, the bane which stalked the Tudors, but from recurrent headaches and indigestion caused by strain acting on a highly strung temperament. Amenorrhoea (failure of menstruation) took its toll, and her strength was further depleted by the frequent bleedings in which the physicians of her day placed such trust.

The restraint of royalty had early been inculcated in one whose descent on both sides was from kings and queens, but what she was subjected to now had to be endured with a passivity that only the faith of her religion made possible. Her nature was not resilient, but it had a strength pressure could not bend. Neither for short-term exigency nor long-term advantage would Mary commit the sin against the Holy Ghost and say what she believed to be wrong was right, or what she knew to be right was wrong.

In her single-mindedness and the honesty of her character she was like her mother; she had little of her father in her, and none of his deviousness. It was now second nature with him to believe he could do no wrong, which is more than half way to the stage when one believes everything one does is right. He was never to realize that though his wife might and did look upon him as her husband, king and lord, she never regarded him as God; and he was outraged to discover his people championed not him but his queen.

It is unlikely that had his wife borne him a prince Henry would have contemplated separation, for his marriage to her in the golden days of his youth had been happy. But she had failed to give him a son to secure the succession, a legitimate heir whose rights could not be disputed after his father was dead as the rights of a natural son could be disputed, a son not a daughter whose accession would only breed strife and rebellion whether she married a subject or a foreign prince.

Only one Being was strong enough, powerful enough, omnipotent enough to lay this rod upon a sovereign He had favoured in every other way, and that one Being was God. The rod pointed at his marriage to his brother's widow, and Katherine's little waxen babies were the token of His displeasure at their union.

They rose before him, a ghostly small train, the seven-month daughter born dead, the son he had held in his arms whose catafalque had so soon taken the place of his cradle, the boy he had never seen born to him between the victories in France and at Flodden, the baby fleetingly referred to as 'the King's new son' who lived only long enough to be christened, the miscarriages, the premature births—every one proved the wrath of Omnipotent God. Only Mary had He allowed, Mary who was a daughter not a son.

Since it was impossible for him to do wrong, he must in his innocence have committed an unlawful act by taking Arthur's widow as his wife. And as there was no such thing as unlawful marriage, a marriage that was not lawful was not marriage at all.

All Katherine had to do was admit she was Arthur's widow and not the wife of the reigning monarch, when she could live in the greatest honour and reputation, possess her dower and have the guardianship of her daughter. But Katherine would not believe she had been living in sin for close on twenty years, which made their daughter a bastard, and the simplicity of her case could stand the broad glare of daylight. Her marriage to her dead husband's brother had been allowed by the Church. Also her first husband, the sixteen-year-old Arthur, had left her as he found her, a virgin—which her second husband must know full well.

Hearsay can become battened into history, and Anne Boleyn, the younger sister of his former mistress Mary, has been held responsible not only for the King's change of heart towards his wife but for his break with Rome. Yet as far back as 1514, before Mary's birth and before she he called his great folly danced across his path, it was rumoured he was about to repudiate his wife, his brother's widow, because he was unable to have live children by her and 'will obtain what he likes from the Pope'. Katherine certainly believed her one-time lady in waiting edged him into heresy and disobedience to the Pope. But Henry went his own way without edging, and Anne's adherence to the new religion was not from any devotion to its gospel, but because the Pope failed to provide the King with a dispensation that he might marry her.

Those living in a century violent with upheaval and disruption are not aware when the lava first rises in the volcano, only of the changes to their own landscape. Mary was born at a time when the climate of Europe was changing, as a wave of what was known as the new learning rose to flood France, Germany and the Netherlands. It was in the far-flung realms of her cousin the Emperor that men first began to dispute the indisputable, the Holy Roman Catholic Church.

In England a corrupt Church had loosened its own hold, and secularization spreads in a thriving community. It might be a theological age, it was also an irreligious one. The Reformation did not come to England as it was to come to its neighbour Scotland, as it did to Germany and Switzerland, through men whose blazing heat to redress wrongs forged Protestantism. There was no John Knox in England, no Martin Luther or John Calvin. When the English Reformation came it came through the State and not a counter Church, and the State was Mary's father. Its impulse was not a matter of conscience but a grievance about money, when the 'Peter's Pence', the rich revenues the English Church paid to Rome, were withheld. It would have come about without the dissolution of the King's marriage; the wand of the arrow had been fashioned for some time amongst an insular people who were no ardent Pope's men, but the abortive annulment was the goose's feather that winged it on its way.

It was in 1527 the rumours from Rome reached France that the King of England was about to put aside his queen because he had discovered his eighteen-year-old marriage was not valid, since she had been his brother's widow. How then, inquired the Bishop of Tarbes, a member of the French delegation come to England to treat with the Princess's suggested betrothal, could his daughter Mary, whom he wished to marry to their king, be legitimate?

No longer was Mary the pearl of the world. The King of France married the Spanish Eleanor, and the Dauphin, his eldest son, to whom Mary had been betrothed in the past, was trysted to a

Portuguese princess. That left his second son for Henry's daughter, but the half-hearted negotiations came to nothing.

Only His Holiness the Pope could grant a dispensation to annul the royal marriage, everything therefore depended on Clement VII as far as the King and Queen of England were concerned. Henry had no doubts. Did not the law of Moses in the Book of Leviticus forbid a man to take his brother's wife, calling it an unclean thing, and warning those who broke the law they would be childless? Surely, Katherine prayed, no Vicar of Christ would annul a marriage a predecessor had legalized and blessed; and did not Deuteronomy actually enjoin a man as his duty to take his brother's wife, and raise seed? God had blessed them with Mary.

In May the lurid news that Rome had been sacked by the Emperor's Spanish and German mercenaries, to make good their arrears of pay, spread like conflagration through Christendom. The very ground on which the Church stood crumbled beneath it. The Pope had been taken prisoner. When horror reached saturation point and had to subside, one fact stood out stark as a solitary landmark on a riven landscape. No Pope would grant the King of England an annulment from his Spanish wife when he was a prisoner of the Spanish wife's nephew. Even when he was allowed to escape, disguised as a domestic, from the Castle of Sant'Angelo that December, everyone knew he might be nominally free again, but he was still in the hollow of the emperor's hand.

Opposition, however, only hardened Henry. He was as determined to make the Pope shoulder his responsibilities as the Pope was anxious not to accept them. The King of England must have a sentence that would ensure the legitimacy of his children by a second marriage. The world must be shown that the King of England's second marriage was unassailable. Only the Pope, whose decrees were the laws of the Church, could supply the necessary warrant.

Henry had never envisaged that the people of London should stand solidly behind the queen, not himself. The women waited for her to pass, shouting out their encouragement, telling her to care for nothing and not to give in to her enemies. If the matter were to be decided by the women, the French ambassador reported, the King would lose the battle. But the Spanish ambassador noted sadly they had no leader, 'So this people will probably content themselves with only grumbling'. It was Eustace Chapuys, the Emperor's new ambassador who arrived in London in 1529, who said that. Already he knew the English.

He was to prove himself a trusted servitor to the King's daughter and her mother, a man upon whom they could depend. Avid he went about his imperial master's business. He was young and voluble, and so cunning at scenting out information, tracing in the explosion of rumours the pinch of gunpowder which had sparked it off, that he was known as the Fox at the English court, where he was highly unpopular. It was the French ambassador who was made much of, prized as the representative of the French king. If the protracted dispute with Rome over the annulment led to Charles making war on England, Henry must have as strong an ally as he could find. *177663*

Chapuys made a point of cultivating the acquaintanceship of doctors because they came and went unsuspected amongst their patients. And he needed every contact he could find, any go-between of whom he could make use, to link him with his master's cousin and her mother the Queen who, forced from familiar palace and castle, was moved from place to place, each more inaccessible than the last.

From the days of her early girlhood to the daybreak in grey November when she died at forty-two, the condition of Mary's health is charted by what was happening to her. When she was fifteen, in the year her father finally abandoned his queen and Mary was separated from her mother, she was seriously ill. Dr Butts, her father's favourite physician, attended the girl through these months. He was a big man with a strong, calm face and the steadying presence of the born doctor, who placed on the Princess's attendants the responsibility that she ate nothing they did not oversee.

She still had her attendants round her, her princely establishment of 150 servants and officials in the manor of Newhall in Essex, some thirty miles from London. It was a property her father had purchased and had 'incomparably adorned and beautified', so that he contentedly called it Beaulieu, but it was still known in the neighbourhood as Newhall.

News of what was happening beyond the gardens, lake, orchard and greens of the manor still reached her, news to turn over with Lady Salisbury, ever closer as the horizon darkened.

Her son Reginald was no longer in England, he left quietly after

he had been offered the archbishopric of York. Such advancement his forward-looking brothers had been hungry for him to accept but he declined, for he knew the price of the promotion was the holder's sanctioning of whatever the King did to have his marriage annulled. The refusal incensed Henry, and Pole was summoned to his presence to answer for it. His tears at having aroused the King's wrath did not in any way water down his arguments against the putting aside of the Queen and the degradation of their daughter.

Mary once saw her father by chance in October the following year, when she was walking in the country with her attendants and was surprised by the King's party. The harvest had been reaped and the fields shorn. He spoke to her apart, asking her how she was and telling her soon he would see more of her, moving away when two of Anne Boleyn's servants came up to listen to what he said that they could repeat it to their mistress.

So Chapuys reported, who referred to the one-time lady in waiting as 'this Anne', or the 'she-devil of a concubine', or 'a common stewed whore'. For six years the King had called her his own Sweet Heart and still they were not married. Frustration made her waspish and, sure of her hold upon her royal lover, she had become tyrannical, so that he had been heard to complain she was not like the Queen, who never in her life used ill words to him. Her jealousy of the King's daughter was even stronger than her jealousy of the ageing, demeaned, plain woman she had displaced, because she could not compete with Henry's affection for his child or his pride in her attainments.

Anne could have a larger court round her than her queen had ever had, wear the jewels her one-time mistress had been forced to surrender, have family titles heaped upon her to make her royal, be raised to the peerage although she was a woman, and created Marquis of Pembroke in her own right, receive a thousand pounds a year to maintain her new dignity, but to the people of London, who loved their queen, she was still Nan Bullen, the merchant's daughter. 'No Nan Bullen for us!' the women screeched when they saw the Lords of the Church pass through the streets under their swaying canopy. 'Ha! Ha!' they jeered as they watched her initials, entwined with the King's with a true lover's knot, set up in the city.

The weather that winter was tempestuous and the wind blew

the new year in with unabated fury. A curious item has been noted about this time that the Princess Mary ate so much meat for breakfast that she terrified her physicians. She was small and thin, her beauty a skin so fair it dazzled foreigners. The hair her father used to tumble about her shoulders to tease her had lost its silvery fairness and was reddish, the colour of her blond father's beard when he began to grow one; and her voice, sweet as a robin's when she sang, began to deepen as a boy's does into a man's. Her eyes were small like her father's, and she whom he had once boasted never cried wept easily.

There was much to weep about as she waited for the news which travelled tardily on winter roads, so that at times she might have been living amongst the echoes of events that had already happened in all their ominousness. In January they were saying in London that the King and Nan Bullen were already married and that she was bearing him a son. The Bishop of London demanded when he heard that, 'The King's Grace, ye say, shall have another wife and she shall bear a prince. Who hath promised him a prince?'

Who indeed, unless Mary's father himself. He was boasting that as far as his own country was concerned he was king, emperor and Pope. To any Catholic worthy of the name it was blasphemous to say what was being said in England that the Pope, the Holy Father, the mirror image of eternal Truth, was no more than the Bishop of Rome. But Mary's father, since the days he with boy's ardour had enlisted himself as the Pope's knight errant, had witnessed the Vicar of Christ, for the return of his earthly territories, grant absolution to those guilty of the sack of Rome, had seen the men who held the keys of heaven prepared to barter them for unholy gain, to peddle their divine office like merchandise. Why should those who supplied annulments and licences on the flimsiest pretexts refuse to provide on lawful grounds for him, King of England, for whom Leo X in 1521 had promulgated a Bull, which conferred on him the unprecedented superb title Defender of the Faith? The Defender of the Faith would never stoop to what was illegal or unorthodox—every step he took must be sanctified by the Church and ratified by law.

If any proof were needed that God was on his side it was in the death of the Archbishop of Canterbury. William Warham had not been a courageous man, he had whispered in Queen Katherine's ear four Latin words which signified that the wrath of a king meant death, but he had been unwilling to judge the King's suit, which was tantamount to declaring the King's marriage to Queen Katherine invalid, when the Pope had forbidden him to do so. Now his office was empty it could be filled by the King's nominee, and the King's nominee was 'a wonderful and grave wise man', who had written a book, founded on Leviticus (the Pope favoured Deuteronomy), proving that the King's marriage was against God's law, and so no Pope could make it lawful by dispensation. His name was Thomas Cranmer, whose patroness was Anne Boleyn.

At once he was recalled from abroad, and English ambassadors were no longer allowed to chivvy and harry the Vicar of Christ but were instructed to use all gentleness towards him. No hint of his most secret marriage to the woman who was bearing his child must get abroad. It was vital that the consecration of his new archbishop should be recognized by the Pope, essential that the highest Church dignitary in the land should have papal authority for his position so that everything could be expedited and the prince be born legitimate in the eyes of the world.

Thomas Cranmer, when he was taking his first tentative steps towards the new Lutheran teaching, was sent abroad to Germany to win men over to the King's matter. He left England believing what his master believed, that his union to Queen Katherine was against the word of God, and expediently closed his priest's eyes to the knowledge that his patroness, Anne Boleyn, was living in sin with their sovereign. Abroad he came in contact with men who did not view the King of England as the King of England viewed himself. They saw him as a man trying to to be rid of a faithful wife that he could marry his concubine. These scholars did not believe in gleaning the Bible for convenient texts to prop up a dubious point of view, but searching it for the truth by which the Church could be purged of erroneous doctrine. Under their influence, Cranmer began to disapprove of what his master was doing against Queen Katherine and Princess Mary.

When the summons came from King Henry to return, his ambassador lost no time in starting, but once on the road he delayed his journey. Did he really want to become Archbishop of Canterbury? What about his grave doubts on the propriety of the King's conduct? Did he wish to be associated with another's actions, even if he were king, which he as a priest knew to be wrong? But surely it was the duty of a subject to obey and serve his prince. He could not turn now, he had gone too far on the road back. Never would he desert his prince in the middle of a foreign mission. After all his king was appointing him to the highest position in Church and State. If he held it, he could advance the new Lutheran teaching in England.

'Never man came more unwilling to a bishopric than I did,' Cranmer could say. But he came. The impress of Henry's forcible mind was to be stamped upon Cranmer's pliant one. If scruples, hesitations or doubts ever troubled the new Archbishop of Canterbury they did not rise to the surface but wavered and floated in those wan regions of the mind where, like fronds of seaweed pulled and distorted with unseen tides, they appear to be what they are not—rootless.

Chapuys sent warning messages to Rome not to believe that the King had given the Lady Anne the marquisate to compensate for not having received the throne—the coronet had been conferred on her as an earnest of the crown, not by way of compensation. Urgently he wrote that His Holiness must be persuaded not on any account to issue Bulls recognizing Cranmer as Archbishop of Canterbury unless he swore not to interfere in the King's great matter. Bitterly he remarked that His Holiness would not be so eager to admit Thomas Cranmer as archbishop if he knew he was a Lutheran and belonged to the new sect.

But it all seemed so harmless to the Pope, basking in the unusual sunshine of a bland King of England whom he was heard to say was wiser and had a better nature than the King of France. He had refused him so much, and this opportunity to please appeared heaven-sent. With astonishing and uncharacteristic alacrity he issued eleven Bulls authorizing Thomas Cranmer's consecration, and dispatched the pall to England.

Henry was saved. In May of the year 1533 Cranmer as papal legate pronounced the King's marriage to Katherine of Aragon to be void *ab initio*, and his secret marriage in January to Anne Boleyn valid.

Mary heard of the celebrations when 'the King's dearest wife Queen Anne' was crowned in June. She wore a golden dress which made her look as though she were clothed with the sun and the pearls round her slim neck were bigger than chick-peas. Everything had been done to amuse and divert the citizens as they crowded on the banks of the Thames to watch her borne from Greenwich Palace to the Tower with all honour and might, and with music all the way. But few heads were bared as she went by, and few voices raised to cheer.

Chapuys believed the King himself was not ill-natured, that it was the vindictive woman at his side, bragging she would make the Princess Mary her waiting-maid, who had changed and alienated him from his former humanity. But one person and one person alone was responsible for his actions and that was Henry VIII.

The difficulty of procuring an annulment marked a watershed in his life, and undoubtedly hardened him. Much of his pleasantness receded as he steeled his will to brook neither opposition nor resistance. His new Archbishop of Canterbury had declared his union with the Spanish Infanta incestuous and proclaimed another as his lawful wife, who had been crowned as his queen, yet the Spanish Infanta continued to thwart him by asserting she knew herself to be his true wife, refusing to accept her new title, and chose to live in poverty and isolation rather than to be dowered as Princess Dowager.

His animus against the recalcitrant mother rubbed itself off on her daughter, not only in the hope of bringing the mother to heel but because his new queen was bearing him a lawful heir.

Mary was forbidden to write or send messages to her mother, and Lord Hussey, her new chamberlain, was instructed by the King to hand over the Princess's jewels into another's keeping. Unhappily he declared he had never seen the jewels except when the Princess was wearing them, and asked Lady Salisbury for an inventory. As no inventory could be found, the jewels were brought forth while he had one made, but they were not handed over, nor would they be until the Princess received a letter from her father commanding her to do so. The chamberlain wished to God the King knew what task he had set him as he tried to procure possession of all the royal plate that had been granted to his daughter to use, but the clerk of the Princess's jewel house declared he had never seen it, and Lady Salisbury when approached said shortly it was in use when the Princess was ill, and could not well be spared.

Never had the King been merrier as he waited for the reward of his queen's happy hour. The circular to be sent to the nobility announcing the birth of a son was already prepared. He was to be christened Henry after his father or Edward after his kingly great-grandfather, and the King of France had consented to be his sponsor.

Throughout the summer months Mary waited to hear what God would grant to the woman who had supplanted her mother. The news reached her after the first week in September, news that was of so little consequence to Chapuys he merely mentioned in his dispatch that the King's concubine had borne a bastard.

Spitefully a smiling foreigner declared when he heard the giant bonfires in London crackle as they were lit and the city bells ring out that it was for joy at the King's disappointment, for *ss* had to be added to the word prince on the circular to indicate the new royal child was a princess.

She was born on the Eve of the Virgin's Nativity, on Sunday, 7th September 1533, and christened Elizabeth after her father's mother. Mary had a half-sister and her father a second daughter.

Chapter Three

Within a week of her birth, the illegitimate child of her father's paramour was proclaimed Princess of Wales at the Cross in Cheap, where the crowd listening to the proclamation received it in dead silence. They knew Mary was the true Princess of Wales as they knew her mother was the true queen. But the true princess saw her own device cut from her servants' coats and replaced by that of the King's, heard the man who was her chamberlain tell her it was not befitting she had so large an establishment as she was no longer Princess of Wales, and that her household was to be reduced.

No longer was she living amongst the echoes of events that had already happened, she was caught in the cavity of the whirlpool, not reverberation but thunder itself was splitting her life into pieces.

When she demanded to see such an order in writing, she read her own name stripped of its titles: the Lady Mary, the King's daughter. She turned on her heel then and went to her room to write to her father. She could not believe, she wrote, that he was aware of the contents of such a letter, for he must know in his conscience, as she did, that she was his lawful daughter. 'If I agreed to the contrary,' she wrote on that October day, 'I should offend God: in all other things your obedient daughter.'

But the King of England was not going to take from a seventeen-year-old offspring what he would take from no man, be he Pope or Emperor. God and his conscience, he once told Chapuys, were on very good terms, and instructed him to inform the Emperor that the King of England took himself to be right not because so many said so but because he, being learned, knew it. A man, he believed, should rather endure all the censures of the Church than offend his own conscience.

A commission of lords, headed by the Dean of the King's Chapel, arrived at Beaulieu to correct the Lady Mary once and for all regarding the King's conscience. It was impressed on her that she had deserved her sire's high displeasure and punishment by law but that 'on conforming to his will he might incline, of his fatherly pity, to promote her welfare'.

As conforming to her father's will entailed believing, for Mary would not say what she did not believe, she was the child of an incestuous union and her half-sister the fruit of a legal marriage, the King's daughter refused, and was removed to a smaller residence with a reconstituted and reduced household. Her manor of Beaulieu was lent to Viscount Rochford, Anne Boleyn's brother. The cornucopia of the Boleyn family, which had provided two mistresses for the King, brimmed over with benefactions.

The letter Mary received from her mother, passed by faithful hands, read like the sailing-orders to one about to embark on an uncharted voyage. It breathed with the love of the sender, was charged with warning, tempered with advice and heightened with the heroic faith of its writer. 'When they have done the uttermost they can, then I am sure of the amendment.'

Londoners knew what was about to happen to the King's elder daughter. They had watched his new baby carried through their midst with the pomp of fanfare on her way to a residence of her own. Her maid of honour was to be her half-sister.

The Duke of Norfolk, Anne Boleyn's uncle, rode through the twilight of that December day to carry out his master's commands and ordered her to make ready at once to attend the Princess of Wales. Roughly he cut her protests short, telling her he was not there to dispute: all he would grant was half an hour's delay before she left with him on her journey.

No one knows how she spent that half-hour in her room; it may have been on her knees, it may have been secreting certain papers on her person.

The members of her household had always meant much to her, and when she came downstairs she asked Norfolk to beg the King to be good to her servants. When she inquired how many of her ladies were to be allowed to go with her, he told her there would be plenty where she went—she could take two of inferior rank. The Countess of Salisbury cried out then she would go with her and take servants at her own cost, but Norfolk would have none of that.

Through the hostile winter landscape the girl was carried in a clumsy, leather-covered litter to her destination, the manor of

Hatfield standing amongst trees on the slope of a hill. All her life she had been accustomed to acclamation on arrival. None greeted her here. Norfolk suggested she would wish to pay her respects to the Princess, to which she replied she knew of no other princess in England but herself—as for the daughter of Madame of Pembroke, she was no princess, but if the King acknowledged her as his daughter Mary would call her sister. When he asked on his departure if she had any message for him to take to the King, he received the answer, 'None, except that the Princess of Wales, his daughter, asks for his blessing.' Norfolk told her he dare not carry such a message. 'Then go away and leave me alone,' she wept.

Alone amongst enemies, utterly alone. Her half-sister's establishment was governed by two of Anne Boleyn's aunts, scolding Lady Anne Shelton and Lady Alice Clere. Mary's own household had naturally always revolved round her, the most commonplace function made an order of the day, dressed by her ladies in waiting in the morning, undressed by them at night, every meal a celebration because she was partaking it. Here she was allotted the worst room in the house where, by bidding of the woman who had supplanted her mother, her meals were not permitted to be served but in the jostling Great Hall. She, used from her baby days to the rich gowns and costly ornamentation of her wardrobe, had neither ladies of the chamber nor anything for them to guard or set out. She who loved walking and riding was not allowed even to go to the church adjoining the dwelling for mass—lest outsiders saw her.

Once some rustics caught sight of her in a gallery and waved their caps, hailing her as princess. That happened only once, but although never again could she walk in that gallery, the incident must have meant something to Mary. She might be incarcerated but she was not forgotten; and the knowledge of why she was incarcerated must have given her an inverted sense of power. Because she was the true princess they dare not let her be seen in case there was a rising on her behalf. All over England they were talking about her, wondering about her. All over Europe they were asking for her, English ambassadors parrying as best they could the pass of barbed questions.

Before Christmas the two ladies she had been allowed to bring with her were dismissed and the common chambermaid who took their place did not even taste her food. The fear that she would be poisoned was very real, and the dread of what was happening to her mother lay like a pall over dismal days.

The baby who had taken her place, who had everything she had once had, was a healthy child. The house was bursting at its seams with her courtiers and attendants, and sometimes the whole establishment was put in a stir of preparation as they waited for the bugle call to herald the King or Queen on a visit to their off-spring. Her father's displeasure with his elder daughter was such that he would not permit her to enter his presence, but he sent Master Cromwell to her room to discover if she, who he said inherited her obstinacy with her Spanish blood, were more amenable.

He stood before her, the one-time money-lender now Chancel-lor of the Exchequer, the merchant soon to be Secretary of State, the trooper promoted to Vicar-General who could recommend bishops and clergy. It was to this blacksmith's son one referred if one desired access to the King, he who in his strong, short-fingered hands the reins of government resided—for the King.

It was all plain as a pikestaff to him. The Lady Mary had only to agree she was no longer Princess of Wales, that the marriage between her father and Queen Anne was lawful, and their off-spring the legitimate heirs to the throne, when she could be brought *in bona fide parentium*—he was proud of his Latin. After all, her parents had been honestly ignorant of the invalidity of their marriage. Where was Mary's obstinacy leading her when the very act bastardizing her was even now passing through Parlia-ment? But he was talking to the daughter of the Spanish queen Katherine, and came no speed.

When the act was sealed by Parliament the courtiers in Hatfield became bolder towards her. Several gentlemen put hands on her royal person, lifted her bodily and pushed her into the litter she had refused to enter because it followed instead of preceded that of her half-sister. The money she had brought with her was exhausted now, and she was deprived of the little support it had lent her. Norfolk ordered the Queen's aunts to treat her more harshly, as the bastard she was. Mistress Shelton needed no bid-ding, telling her that only yesterday the King had said he would have her beheaded for disobeying the laws of the realm. But Mistress Clere replied that if she were a bastard, aye, even of a poor gentleman, the girl deserved respect and kind treatment, for she was a good girl.

The Parliament that pretended to make legal her bastardization brought in another Act vesting the succession to the crown in the heirs of the King by Anne Boleyn. It was known as the Act of Supremacy, and the King's prominent subjects and all clerics were called upon to subscribe to it.

It was put before Mary, as it was put before her mother, to swear that her father's former marriage was invalid and against the teachings of the Bible. How could they claim that when the Holy Father had granted the royal bridegroom a dispensation to marry his brother's widow, and thus overruled Leviticus? She read the words: 'Ye shall swear to bear faith, troth and obedience only to the King's Grace, and to the heirs of his body by his most dear and entirely beloved lawful wife, Queen Anne.'

Only—to subscribe to such was blasphemy: that the King, her father, was not only King, not only Pope, but God. Mary refused as her mother refused. Never must either sign such an article, if they did they would betray the Holy Church, the Holy Father and He who had died to save them, as well as all their fellow believers in England. They were the nucleus round which Roman Catholics could secretly gather, their hope in a sagging world.

For a time they were let be on that count; not so others who refused to sign. Queen Katherine's confessors were burnt alive. Priors and vicars who would not take the corporate oath for their religious houses were hanged, drawn and quartered. Many of their followers remained 'unmoved, unshaken, unseduced, unterrified' in the face of torture and death for refusing to deny the authority of 'the Bishop of Rome' in England. Sir Thomas More, who had walked with Henry and his Queen as their friend in earlier sunlit days, made the short journey from Tower to block affirming he was the King's good servant but God's first. John Fisher, Bishop of Rochester, the only one of the Lords Spiritual to stand stiff in her cause, went to his death, calmly as though he were taking the air, for asserting that the King could not possibly take the place of St Peter's descendant the Pope, their only link with Christ. After their deaths Queen Katherine's failing health never again rallied. And a foreigner wrote home: 'In England, death has snatched everyone of worth away, or fear has shrank them up.'

Mary fell ill, and Queen Katherine wrote to Master Cromwell, begging him to tell the King that what she desired above all else was to see her daughter: 'A little comfort and mirth she would take with me, would be a half health to her. For my love let this be done.' But the King dare not let mother and daughter come together. He had two fears, one that his subjects might rise in their cause—together that danger was doubled, separate it was halved; the other that Charles might declare war to redress his aunt's wrongs. He knew that his one-time wife had the power to wage as fierce a war against him as ever her mother Isabella had waged in Spain, but Katherine had no hate in her except that of being the cause of bloodshed and suffering. She had always steadfastly refused to countenance hostilities against her husband or her adopted country. It was only now, towards the end of her life, when the sickening thud of axe on block was heard in the land that she believed her nephew's sword should be unsheathed to redeem England.

Chapuys managed to pass to Mary a protest she learnt by heart and used often, as when she was made to watch the King's baby daughter usurp her precedence. The wily Fox found ways and means of smuggling letters to her, avenues she was sometimes able to use herself to send scrappy notes to him written in haste and fear, telling him her only hope was to die, begging the Emperor to provide remedy for what was happening in England. Chapuys was the only man she could trust in her own country, and he was not an Englishman. He gloried with her when she was able to balk having to follow after her half-sister, and in disguise watched her journey up the river and reported to his master such excellent beauty and heroic bearing were a pleasure to see.

He waited on the King to make the fruitless request that he, a Spaniard, should appear before the English Parliament to state the case against the Bill that made her a bastard and tried to work on the Machiavellian Master Cromwell on her behalf. In this play of circumvention and forestalling, with its intricate pattern of gyration, it was impossible to tell which was cat and which mouse, for that subtle relationship, akin to familiarity, bound stalker to the stalked.

The ambassador was for ever appealing to his imperial master to declare war on England. 'You never saw prince nor man who made greater show of his horns or wore them more light-heartedly,' he exclaimed when the King of England, threatened with excommunication, snapped his fingers and prepared another buffet for the Pope. What Chapuys, Katherine, Mary and the Roman Catholics of their day failed to realize was that people only fear what they believe in. The English Church still paid the tribute it had always paid to Rome, but now the rich revenues, their Peter's Pence, jingled in the pocket of their sovereign, their Supreme Head, the Defender not of papal Faith but of his own. The Pope, forced to take notice of such defiance, solemnly pronounced in Rome, seven years after the English King's case had begun, that the marriage between Queen Katherine and the King of England was valid. And when the terrible sentence of greater excommunication did at last fall, the court sported, gamed and danced as though it had never been.

But God was not mocked. There was no privacy in a royal household with its ladies and gentlemen in waiting, their attendants and hangers-on. Within six months of the secret marriage everyone knew things were not as they had been between the King and his new queen. They were not lovers' tiffs that were overheard, when she took him to task for allowing his fancy to rove from her, but a master silencing his maid, telling her he could degrade her as easily as he had raised her.

Periodically each overcrowded dwelling had to be emptied of its occupants that it could be cleansed and purified. Mary might still have to follow after her sister, but the litter that carried her now was lined with velvet and she was allowed one or two women to wait on her. Some of Lady Pembroke's maids of honour even came to her room to pay their respects when they arrived with their mistress, and Lady Pembroke's uncle, the Duke of Norfolk, came. It was common talk that his niece's vituperative tongue had driven him from court. Lady Pembroke herself made a significant gesture towards her.

Always when her stepsister's mother came to visit her daughter, Mary stayed in her room to avoid any chance of seeing her. Only in the chapel was common ground. Anne Boleyn could be described by Roman Catholics as a spleeny Lutheran, but she went to mass and adhered to the usages of the old religion. She was identified with the new reforming sect only because Roman Catholics rejected her as the wife of a man who had married her when his first wife was still living, and who looked upon her daughter as a bastard.

A well-meaning lady in waiting told the Queen that she had seen the Lady Mary do obeisance to her before she left the chapel. 'If we had seen it,' the Queen replied swiftly, 'we would have done as much to her.' Eager to take so opportune an opening, she sent a message to the King's elder daughter: 'The Queen salutes you, and she desires that this may be an entrance of friendly correspondence which your Grace shall find completely to be embraced on her part.'

The King's daughter chose to misread her words. 'It is not possible that the Queen can send me a message,' she replied blankly. 'Her Majesty being so far from here. You would have said "the Lady Anne Boleyn", for I can acknowledge no other queen but my mother, nor esteem them my friends who are not hers. And for the reverence I made, it was to the altar, to her Maker and mine.'

The dolorous news reached Mary that her mother was dead, tidings that at any time would have made her bereft but that now left her inconsolable, unable to be with her at her passing, to perform for her those last services and rites and keep vigil as chief mourner.

Chapuys as he moved about in high places listened to courtiers saying that the Lady Mary was ill and like to die with grief, the same suspicious prognostications he had heard before Queen Katherine's death. He believed, particularly after he heard the report of the physician who helped to embalm her body, that she had been poisoned—what Mary believed.

Her mother was fifty-one when she died, in January 1536, an old ailing woman, sick with dread that the Oath of Supremacy would again be placed before her and her daughter. She had been taken forcibly a year ago, when December winds raged and wailed over the dreary marshlands, to be hidden away in the stronghold of Kimbolton Castle. It was winter now when she lay on her deathbed and the air clanged with cold; it was always winter now with the sun so low on the horizon it shed neither light nor warmth and might as well not be there at all.

Chapuys was allowed by the King to visit her but not Mary. The sight of her trusted young compatriot cheered the sick woman. Now, she said, she could die in his arms and not all alone like a beast, but she improved so much, smiling as she talked as she used to do, able even to comb and tie up her own hair, that it was not thought the end had come and Chapuys left after some days. She died suddenly a day or two later.

To Mary, strung with anxiety, played upon by sorrow, plucked with despair, her only salvation appeared to be escape from her father's domain. She wrote Chapuys she would cross the Channel in a sieve if only he would advise it, and he dare not advise it. He knew both the King and his Council had been aware of the earlier abortive schemes and plans for her flight to her cousin's country. The ambassador was caught between her feminine inopportunity and the deliberation of his master the Emperor, so cautious and wary he waited for time to play his hand for him.

Like a spider in the network of his far-spread empire, the last thing Charles wanted was to mount war against England, particularly now his aunt was dead. Instead of clash of arms, he was envisaging alliance with the English king—as long as he recognized his elder daughter's legitimacy. Mary as potential heir to the throne of England was of much more significance to her cousin than her mother had been and, instead of flight, every diplomatic card in the pack must be played.

'She is my death and I am hers,' Anne Boleyn said of Mary, and vowed it would not be Mary who would have the last laugh. But after her mother's death she made one more overture to the King's elder daughter. Anne was with child again, and the exultation of pregnancy brought its trepidation. Now there was no one-time mistress to gainsay her title, she could believe she was indeed queen, but so much depended on the child she was bearing being a prince that she felt the necessity to make some gesture of oblation.

She chose not her shrill aunt Shelton to deliver her message but the kindlier Mistress Clere. Mary was told that if she would only obey the King's will, the Queen herself would be a mother to her, and Mary should come to court again, not to carry the Queen's train as she had once boasted, but to walk at her side.

From the depths of her grief, Mary made formal answer to Mistress Clere that no daughter could be more obedient than she was to the King's Grace, saving her honour and her conscience.

Not one word to or of the sender of the message. That Anne Boleyn could neither overlook nor forgive. Mistress Shelton was used this time to convey to the Lady Mary that if the Queen had a son, as she hoped shortly, the Queen knew what would happen to the Lady Mary. No one knew that Mary's scornful laugh at the reception of these words belied Anne Boleyn's prediction about which would have the last laugh.

She was brought to bed before her time in January, the month Katherine died. Palace talk attributed the premature birth to the shock she received when she surprised Jane Seymour, one of her ladies in waiting, sitting on the King's knee. The child she nearly lost her life to deliver was a dead son.

London was busy with the gossip filtering from the court. Never again did the King share bed or board with her. There was often much scratching and bye-blows between her and her maid, who was the eldest of Sir John Seymour's family of eight. It was said she was back now in her father's house, Wolf Hall, with her tall brothers, waiting and watching—as all the world was waiting and watching.

Master Cromwell, smiling behind his hand, chatted to Chapuys at a window; they understood each other without words. Never would the world, which meant of course the Emperor, recognize the concubine as the King's wife, but now Queen Katherine was dead another could be put in her place and accepted without question.

They said Nan Bullen's singing-man was in the Tower—the rack and thumbscrew soon made him babble out the whole song, and three more, knights all, were clapped in along with her brother. There was no end to the wickedness in high places—they were charging him with incest with his sister. But she should never have been in high places—the King himself was saying she had bewitched him.

No confessions could be wrung from any them—'She has a stout heart,' the King said, 'but she shall pay for it'—except of course from her singing-man. He was promised his life if he confessed he had committed adultery with the Queen. He confessed all right; but was hanged as well. They said Nan Bullen had sent a message to the Princess Mary by the lady wife of the Lieutenant of the Tower to ask for her forgiveness, as well she might. Ay, she was in the Tower now, not waiting for her coronation as last time but for her execution, and the King going to and from Wolf Hall, and feasting with his friends.

With her father's concubine dead, there was no barrier to Mary's reconciliation with her parent, who had recently sent her a present of a hundred crowns, the first present she had received from him since he used to caress her, load her with gifts and give her money to disport herself with. If he were not already married to Jane Seymour he soon would be. And Jane Seymour, who had been lady in waiting to Mary's mother before in service to the merchant's grand-daughter, was no wanton Nan Bullen. It was believed she had told the King unless he did justice to his elder daughter Englishmen would never be content.

Mary's half-sister can have had little if any memory of her mother, who was dead before she was three and whom she had seen only on rare visits. In looks the child did not take after her, whose hair had been the blue-black of a blackbird's wing. She inherited the Tudor hair that was neither red nor butter yellow, an active child with eyebrows and lashes so fair as to be almost invisible, which gave her face an eggshell look.

Her first reported words reach us when she was informed by Sir Francis Bryan, governor of her household, of the King's decision that from now on she was to be known merely as the Lady Elizabeth.

'Why, Governor,' the child took him up sharply, 'how hap it yesterday Lady Princess, and today but Lady Elizabeth?'

Chapter Four

Lady Bryan, governess to the infant Elizabeth, was at her wits' end to know what to do about her charge. She heard that the motherless child was no longer princess but nobody told her how she was to be treated now. She no longer knew what position she herself held in the household, or how to order the Princess's women and grooms. Everyone appeared to have forgotten about the child in her care, who had grown so fast she now had neither gown, nor slip, nor petticoat, no manner of linen, nor day chemises, nor kerchiefs, nor sleeves, nor mob-caps, nor night-caps—ruthlessly she detailed each item for Master Cromwell's benefit that he would see such shortage was made good.

The loss of her mother, transient as a shooting-star, did not affect the little girl since she had never been a part of her life. In this existence of shifting from manor to palace and from palace to castle it was those who moved with her who lent the stability of background, and Elizabeth never outgrew her affection for the few who cared for her in her young days. Her lady governess, appointed when the child was four, was called Katherine Champernowne, which her little charge lovingly shortened to Kat. She was a young woman, with a young woman's faults and attributes, lacking judgment but loyal, who delighted in the little girl's precocity and her winning ways, and who believed there was no one to hold a candle to her.

Then there was Elizabeth's half-sister Mary of whom the child was fond, so much older she belonged to another generation and might have been an aunt. As these early years spun by Elizabeth came to associate her with presents, necklaces and brooches, yellow satin for a dress, money for playing at cards and, gift of gifts, a golden ball to hold scents and inside a clock.

Both sisters shared the royal manor of Hunsdon as Mary waited for Master Cromwell to reply to her letter. She was told she need no longer call Elizabeth princess, and showed becoming gratitude for permission to address her as she had done all along, but when the child appears in the elder sister's accounts, which she kept herself, she is always detailed with the forbidden designation 'my lady Elizabeth's grace.'

Mary was twenty years of age now, not unpleasing in appearance, with her clear skin and the gloss of youth still upon her reddish hair, but small and without the endearing attraction to captivate and charm that some small women do possess.

She received the sanction she desired and wrote to her father, acknowledging and repenting of all her offences and promising that after God she did and would submit to his goodness and pleasure in everything. As his marriage to Jane Seymour was now known, she was able to congratulate him on the comfortable news and to tell him that daily she prayed God to send his Grace shortly a prince.

But 'Your Majesty's most humble and obedient servant, daughter and handmaid', had put in the two words 'after God', which made her letter totally unacceptable. Cromwell refused to forward it. Sternly he exhorted her to do better and, to make sure she did, enclosed the draft of a letter he ordered her to copy out.

Through the hot summer days and nights she was nagged with toothache, racked with headache and unable to sleep as she tried to keep at bay the realization that nothing less than the Oath of Succession was demanded from her.

Word for word she copied out Cromwell's grovelling draft, inserting four words of her own—'next to Almighty God'—enclosing it along with a troubled letter in which she assured him by the faith she owed to God she had done the uttermost that her conscience would suffer her to do, and that she neither desired nor intended to do less than she had done.

Back came another draft and a stinging letter from the Vicar-General whose position became more dangerous the longer her submission was delayed. She realized from its tone she dared not make any insertions of her own and obediently copied his pattern letter word for word. She could not bring herself to make another copy of it.

Her father was not deceived. A commission arrived, the Duke of Norfolk, the Earl of Sussex and the Bishop of Chichester, to discover how far her submission went and with the articles for her to sign. Did she recognize the King as her sovereign and submit to his laws? Did she acknowledge the King as Supreme Head of the Church? Did she admit the nullity of her mother's marriage? To all three she answered No.

She heard herself called an unnatural daughter, told that she was not even so much as the King's bastard, that she should be beaten to death and her kead knocked against the wall till it was soft as a baked apple. Four days she was given to think it over, during which time she would be allowed to speak to no one and the harpy Lady Shelton would not leave her day or night.

Chapuys sent her a message to submit. He knew if she refused to sign she would be proceeded against under law, and he feared what had happened to Anne Boleyn might well happen to her. He believed if the King died, England would accept his elder daughter as queen and, trained in statecraft, he realized her lack of submission was dangerous to her father, for she could well supply, even inadvertently, a rallying point for his potential enemies. If she continued her resistance, he wrote to the Emperor, many would die because of it.

God, his message to her ran, did not look so closely at the actions of men as at their intentions, and she could absolve her conscience by remembering that the oath was exacted under duress. Some believe that, present when her mother was dying, he carried a message from Queen Katherine telling her to yield. She must save her life that she be preserved to do a good work.

Cromwell's final word reached her late in the evening, telling her that her folly would undo her and all who wished her good. He took God as his witness that she was the most obstinate and obdurate woman that ever was. Unless she signed the book of articles he was enclosing and wrote a letter declaring that she thought in her heart what she signed with her hand, he would make no more effort with the King to effect a reconciliation.

She sat alone in her room in the silent house, the paper before her headed 'The Confession of me, the Lady Mary'. It was June, when the air was thick with moths. She signed by candlelight that the King was Supreme Head of the Church in England, that she utterly refused the Bishop of Rome's pretended authority, and that the marriage heretofore made between his Majesty and her mother was by God's law and man's incestuous and unlawful. Each clause she attested separately and wrote her name as 'Marye'.

The girl who rose after she had done was not the same as the girl who had sat down. Never again could or would she feel the same. Her remorse was such that nothing could ease it, even the secret absolution she craved Chapuys to write for her to the Holy Father. She had done what she had sworn she would never do, she had put her name to what she knew to be wrong, she had surrendered her conscience, she had broken her troth, she had shattered what was and should have been more precious than life itself.

Three weeks later she was taken in the darkness to the manor of Hackney where she spent the night. The King and Queen arrived that afternoon, he a jocose bridegroom, she a retiring, attentive bride.

It was four years since father and daughter had come face to face, in the stubble field, and each must have seen a difference in the other. He had just turned forty-five and his bland boy's face had stoutened round his watchful small eyes, while his magnificent physique had begun to reveal its human origin rather than the god-like immunity which had protected it heretofore. And she might prostrate herself at his feet but she was no longer 'this girl of mine', she was a grown woman withdrawn into herself, keeping her secrets close.

The presence of the gentle queen softened the meeting into reconciliation. Her preference had probably always been for her first mistress and the longer she served the second the more loyal was she likely to become to the memory of the first. Also the treatment Mary had suffered from Anne Boleyn went a long way to justify the King's marriage to her successor. Jane had been at court until after the Queen's miscarriage and knew all there was to know about the scandal, intrigue and titillating gossip of that enclosed, inbred world.

The new queen was twenty-seven at the time of her marriage. She had not the decided personality of her predecessor, and her docility made her the happier wife; nor had she pronounced opinions on any subject, but the whole tenor of her character inclined her to be true to the old order rather than embrace the new. Instinctively she was drawn to the King's elder daughter as the King's elder daughter was drawn to her.

The royal couple left the next evening, when Mary rode back to Hunsdon through the blue summer twilight, the Queen's diamond ring on her finger, the King's written promise of a thousand crowns in her pocket and his word she would have what she wanted for the asking.

Master Cromwell, now Lord Privy Seal, sent her the gift of a magnificent horse as well as other costly presents. Not unnaturally some of the gold and silver rubbed off on the man who was channelling it into the royal coffers. The lesser religious houses throughout the land were being systematically suppressed and their lands confiscated because of the corruption, slackness and sin Cromwell declared to have uncovered in them. Superstition was being plucked out by the roots and everyone knew religious houses were the strongholds of superstition as well as the most influential centres of papacy in the country. Pilgrimages and the celebration of saints' days were forbidden, relics destroyed and wonder-working images pulled down, their jewels and gold directed through Cromwell's hands to the King.

The act bastardizing Elizabeth did not make Mary legitimate, but no one could deny she was the elder daughter, and until the King had a son by his queen, or daughters, or any other legitimate daughters he might have, she held prior position. Her father saw to it there was to be no unseemly scramble for his crown after his death. Parliament gave him full authority to give, dispose, appoint, assign, declare and limit the Imperial Crown of the realm 'to such person or persons as shall please your Highness', a unique Act framed by a unique king to give himself unique powers. Even from the dead he would pronounce what was to be done by his servant Parliament.

With her household re-established, Mary's days could have passed with that rewarding orderliness that was so much in tune with her temperament, but always there was some violent dissonance from without or some jar, like a snapped string, to break the harmony and undermine her health.

The rattle of revolt came from the north, and in the autumn, an inconvenient season for warfare. But those who gathered under their crimson banner sewn with the Five Wounds of Christ did not look upon themselves as rebels but pilgrims. They were bent not to destroy but to restore, a crusade that was called the Pilgrimage of Grace.

Thirty thousand men suddenly realized what was happening in their very midst when they saw monks turned out of the priories, abbeys and monasteries, familiar as landmarks, and the places where they had served despoiled and desecrated. Thirty thousand men demanding with one voice the dismissal of low-born men in high offices, shear-man Cromwell and tavern-keeper Cranmer for two, the burning of heretical bishops who favoured the Reformation, reconciliation with the Pope and the restoration of their monasteries. Thirty thousand men claiming that the act bastardizing the Lady Mary, rightful heir to the throne, be repealed.

Her father had never heard anything like their presumption: rude and ignorant men, the most brute and beastly of all his subjects, taking upon themselves to amend his laws, as if, after being their king for twenty-eight years, he did not know how to govern his own realm. To pardon or parley with rebels he considered would stain his honour, but he had no standing army and to treaty was necessary while one was mustered.

Their leaders, chief of whom was a lawyer, Robert Aske, were soothed with skill and vague promises. Their king was a benignant prince and would grant a free pardon to all who had taken up arms if they would only disperse. Their demands would be conveyed to and considered by the King himself. Aske must prepare a full statement of them. The King would visit the northern counties, and Parliament would be asked to reconsider the liberties of the Church. On such assurances Aske dispersed his well-disciplined troops while the King's army gathered in York.

Mary was made to blazon her submission to the nobles at home, that no secret flag of hope could be nailed to an abandoned ship, and abroad to the Pope and Emperor. To her cousin Charles she was forced to add the rider that, for her sake, he should not trouble England, or reduce her to her late unhappy condition by bringing up her case at a General Council or anywhere else. Only then was she allowed to join the court for Christmastide.

In the same month of December Aske was summoned to London to place his statement of the northerners' grievances before their sovereign who, affable with goodwill, lent him the favour of his ear. Their complaints about the Faith were so general they were hard to be answered; the King intended always to live and die in the Faith of Christ. When the Queen was crowned, he would like nothing better than that her coronation should take place in York—in spring or summer next year when the roads were passable.

At Greenwich the festivity, glee and excitement of other years stirred Mary's memory. In the gay whirl of the court there were remembered faces as well as newcomers, all anxious to show their friendship now she was reinstated in her father's good graces. The courtiers marked as proof of his affection how he would sit apart conversing with her.

44

Mary found these private audiences with her father wellnigh unbearable, cloistered alone with his overwhelming personality, listening to his monologue on how he held the balance between France and Spain, telling her that although she had erroneously trusted Spain would help her, Spain would never dare to do so as long as he lived.

The Queen's friendship added a depth to these strange days, for she had Mary often with her. Jane Seymour never forgot that her stepdaughter was of the blood royal, and in the absence of the King it was noticed she would take the girl's hand when they came to a doorway that they could pass through it together rather than let Mary follow her.

In the New Year Mary visited her favourite house of Beaulieu to take possession of it once again. The man to whom it had passed was dead now, his body with his sister's hastily thrust away in the garrison chapel on Tower Green. Seymours walked at court where Boleyns had trod. Mary liked Jane's eldest brother Edward, a handsome man with the steady qualities she admired, and grew fond of his wife, to whom she wrote as 'My good Gossip' and 'My good Nann'. She became godmother to one of their daughters. Then there was the Queen's youngest brother Thomas, always the centre of his own coterie, dazzling, bold, talkative.

Aske returned to Yorkshire secure with promises. All would be well, he told his fellow leaders, if only their monarch's just conditions were fulfilled. But all those who bore the Badge of the Five Wounds were not single-minded pilgrims; many were men with political and economic scores to settle. When these extremists saw no signs of the government fulfilling their promises, they broke the truce.

This was the chance and now was the hour to recall the free pardon. Mary heard of the dread execution that fell upon every town, village and hamlet that had offended in the rebellion. All the leaders, including the innocent Aske, were put to death. Instead of a queen's coronation in the white city of York, courts were set up throughout the northern counties. Even those who laid down their arms and fulfilled the royal obligations were not spared, and no pity shown to abbots and monks who had joined in the Pilgrimage. Once and for all her father would stamp out revolt in his realm and make rebels a terrible example to the rest of his subjects.

Mary was ill during June and July as the trials and executions reached their height. London learnt the Queen was with child when Te Deums were sung in its churches. As the city was sick with a visitation of the plague she was moved to rose-red Hampton Court for her lying-in. The King, remembering her predecessor's miscarriage, remained near his consort lest she should hear any sudden or unpleasant rumours blowing about—she was but a woman, and women were prone to idle fancies. Nearer her time his queen asked for Mary as a companion and her husband promised, 'She shall come to thee, darling.' When Mary came, she brought Elizabeth with her. Their father was interested in his bright little four-year-old, while to Elizabeth this glorious being was like a whole world in himself.

Two daughters in his quiver, but no heir. Even his illegitimate son, whose charm and grace and love of letters reminded everyone of his father, had not been spared to him but had died the previous year at the age of seventeen of consumption. Even the solitary son of his favourite sister, after whom he had called Mary, had succumbed in his twelfth year to the sweating sickness. Yet her two daughters had survived, as his two daughters survived, and the elder was brought to bed in the same month as her queen with the first child—but with a daughter, not a son, the Lady Jane Grey.

Jane Seymour's labour was a martyrdom of suffering, she endured thirty hours of travail, but she gave to her husband the crown of his life, a son, a prince, an heir. There were no doubts whether he should be called Henry or Edward: arriving on the vigil of St Edward, 12th October 1537, the child decided for himself it was to be Edward.

Chapter Five

The country went wild with delight when it heard the news and London was delirious with joy. Never was there such an explosion of bell-ringing, gun-firing, singing, cheering, feasting and music that brayed with triumph. Never had there been such a lighting of bonfires in praise of God for granting them a prince.

Mary, as godmother to her brother, was clad in cloth of silver sewn with pearls at his christening, which took place three days after his birth and at night. The chapel royal at Hampton Court was made a worthy scene for such a spectacle, for it was hung with cloth of gold and costly tapestry.

They entered two by two, the esquires and knights, each bearing an unlit torch, their feet rustling in the fresh rushes as they came through the gallery that led from the great chamber into the chapel. The King's chaplains followed, with abbots and bishops, and the members of his Council, each secure of his position in this scene. The nobles entered according to their rank. Foreign ambassadors were there to witness this goodly sight which many of them hoped they would never see—the christening of England's heir. Each of the lord chamberlains carried his symbol of office, and the Lord Chancellor walked with my Lord Cromwell, after his master the most powerful man in the land, now father-in-law to the Queen's sister. The two godfathers came together, Thomas Cranmer, Archbishop of Canterbury, and the Duke of Norfolk; and, important in the arms of the Queen's tall eldest brother, was little Elizabeth holding the white cloth the priest would lay on her brother after he had been anointed.

The ceremony lasted hours in air sweet with scent and laden with the perfume of the anointing oil. Mary, as godmother, presented the precious baby at the font, in which he was immersed, to his sponsors, Cranmer and Norfolk. Not until he was christened were the torches lit, when Garter King-of-Arms proclaimed:

'God, of His Almighty and Infinite Grace, give and grant good life and long to the right high, right excellent, and noble Prince, Prince Edward, Duke of Cornwall and Earl of Chester, most dear and entirely beloved son of our most dread and gracious Lord Henry VIII.'

Big-browed amongst his cushions, the newly baptized baby was made ready to be borne back to his parents. The congregation went with him, the gentlemen, knights, heralds, and sergeants-at-arms, their faces swept with light and shadow as the moving torches flared, trumpeters flourishing and minstrels announcing their approach at every step, until they entered the room where the father awaited his son beside his mother. She, wrapped in crimson velvet furred with ermine, had been lifted from her bed to a pallet sewn in gold thread with the crown and arms of England.

Mary did not go with them. It was after midnight, and she led her small sister back to bed to the quiet of their own quarters. Elizabeth had had enough excitement for one day.

The Queen was so ill the day after the christening that all the rites of the Roman Catholic Church were administered, but rallied sufficiently to raise hopes of recovery. The betterment, however, proved to be the delusive pause that sometimes precedes death, and she died between sunset and sunrise twelve days after the birth of her child.

The widower took his bereavement heavily and would not be spoken to, withdrawing from Hampton Court and leaving Mary as chief mourner, who performed for her friend and stepmother the offices she had been denied to pay her own mother. The obsequies lasted for three weeks by order of the King: daily services, nightly vigils, tapers burning on the altar night and day.

The baby prince did not fulfil Chapuys's cheerful announcement when he wrote home that Edward was dead. He was a big child and handsome, very fair, for his mother had been a pale fair woman, without the reddish tinge to his hair that both his half-sisters inherited. An active, merry child, he delighted when his minstrels played, and when he could stand would dance and frolic to the music in a manner that captivated those who looked after him.

He was fond of both his sisters, both of whom adored him, of Elizabeth, four years older, who shared the same amusements, and of Mary, old enough to be his mother, who never came even to visit him without bringing him a present, a gold brooch with a figure of St John the Baptist, a coat fit for a prince of crimson satin embroidered with gold and pansies of pearls, a gay cap she had embroidered herself, a book bound in gold. Elizabeth, a thrifty child, gave him on his birthday the same present each year, a cambric shirt she sewed herself.

And he was the apple of his father's eye. He could not bear to be long parted from his son and would take him to his hunting-lodge, or spend the day caressing and playing with him, or hold him up for his people to see what a strong, goodly prince they had, whereupon they would clap their hands and cheer themselves hoarse. He was known as England's Treasure, and until he was four years old his health gave no cause for concern, a strong, healthy child who took even teething in his stride.

These were unhappy years for his sister Mary as she saw the splendour, wealth, authority and power of the old faith gripped by the crown. The lead had been stripped from the roofs of the smaller monasteries and those they had housed turned loose on an inhospitable world. Now it was the turn of the large foundations.

She saw on her father's big thumb the finest jewel in Europe, which had been filched from England's mother Church where it had lain for four centuries when a French king gave it as an offering to St Thomas. It took twenty carts to carry away the treasure on the shrine alone in Canterbury Cathedral. Throughout the land religious houses were broken up, dismantled and dese-crated. It was probably for giving charity to some of their dis-possessed who came to her door that Mary incurred her father's anger, and for a time her own household was broken up. She wrote Cromwell, fearing the worst of the matter had been made to the King and promising not to offend in this way again.

Was she the only one who noticed how suddenly and strangely silent London had become without the chiming, ringing, clanging and pealing of cascades of bells? It was the monasteries which had provided hospitals for the sick poor, the blind and the in-sane, and London had been full of them. Now the population was swollen disproportionately with an influx of vagabonds, master-less men and the needy ill.

But it was not only the nameless who burdened her thoughts, it was what was happening to those dear to her that dragged at her heart. Her father had begun to bulk portentously, he suffered from what was called in contemporary accounts 'the King's sore leg', a varicose ulcer in his thigh. No longer could he hunt as in the old days, pursuing the chase with his hounds, but shot from stand or butt. And as he aged the more suspicious he became.

In his eyes, his and Mary's kin, because of their birthright of Plantagenet blood, were claimants. Round them obnoxious renegades would be likeliest to gather, all true to the old religion, would-be usurpers of his beloved son should he, King Henry VIII of England, not be there to uphold his God-appointed right to the throne. And the fact had to be faced, he would not always be there.

The Countess of Salisbury, bound to Mary by memories that went as far back as she could remember, was held prisoner in the Tower, with her eldest son Montague, a younger son, Geoffrey Pole, and her nephew Exeter.

Threatened with torture, Geoffrey Pole betrayed both his brother and their cousin, although the little he could betray did not amount to treason except in the ready ears of his examiners. He tried to smother himself with a cushion, but they gave him the life he could not take, and his freedom to go his own way all his terror-stricken days, like the last leaf on a tree twitching even when the air was still.

The examiners, Cromwell was one, had to admit that Lady Salisbury dealt with them as though she were a strong and constant man instead of an old woman. The evidence against her was said to be arms found in her coffer, the pansies her enemies read for Pole, the marigolds for the Lady Mary, the tree growing from them with a purple shield the coat of Christ—all symbolizing as plain as could be that Reginald Pole was to marry my Lady Mary and between them the old religion would again shoot up and flourish in England.

Montague was attainted and executed, he who had ridden at Mary's right hand when she, as chief mourner, followed at dawn Queen Jane's hearse from Hampton Court through countryside dank with November mist. His cousin Exeter was executed with him, leaving behind him in the Tower his wife, who so shortly before had borne England's prince at his christening, and their young son Edward Courtenay who was to grow to manhood enclosed by those grim walls. Montague also left his son, who was never seen again.

Without property, servant or even a warm cloak, their grandmother waited in the Tower until her hour too struck. She sent Mary a last message and a special blessing when they took her up the slope of Tower Hill. But she, the lion-hearted, refused to lay down her royal head at Henry Tudor's behest, and was butchered.

Some winters ago a friend had written to Reginald Pole, passing the years with his books amidst the beauty of Italy, that it was the general opinion in England the Princess Mary would marry him because of the love she had borne him from infancy. But the Italian who penned that letter was unaware that Princess Mary's preferences had nothing to do with her marriage. Her hand was played by others who shuffled bridegrooms into her pack when it suited them, or drew out an earmarked king or jack for another scrutiny.

She was told it was her father's pleasure she should receive at once as suitor Duke Philip of Bavaria. Her blood must have run cold when she heard the name, not because he was the hero who had defended Vienna against the Turks, not only because he headed the League against her cousin Charles, but because he was a Protestant. Instantly she replied she had no wish to offend the King's Majesty but neither wished nor desired ever to enter that kind of religion, rather would she continue still a maid all her life.

But she had learnt her lesson in a hard school and wrote to Cromwell after the messenger was gone that she submitted herself entirely to her father's will. It was Cromwell himself who brought to wait upon her the only one of her suitors ever to woo her in person. He was heard to comment that he had never seen mass until he came to England.

Philip the Fighter, who was not even an eldest son, saluted her with a kiss, which was a declaration of marriage, and gave her a cross of diamonds as a love-token. He was thirteen years older than she, and as she could speak no German and he no English, they conversed in Latin or through an interpreter. Probably he was her only wooer who regretted his courtship came to nothing, for he was to return to England more than once to press his suit. After his first visit, Mary was so ill her doctors feared for her life; they asked for Doctor Butts to come to her, as he had been with her in such cases in times past.

She knew when Philip the Fighter first paid court to her that her father's marriage to his kinswoman, Anne of Cleves, was on the cards. It had dawned on both the French king and the Emperor that their mutual warfare was draining their resources and benefiting only England. Locked in hostilities with each other, neither had been able to take advantage of Henry's vulnerability when his northern counties rose during the Pilgrimage of Grace. The new Pope, Paul III, had therefore lent his good offices to negotiate a ten years' truce between the two enemies, and the long-cherished project of a joint attack on England was reviewed, the Pope as his contribution taking upon himself to encourage the Scots to invade their neighbour at the appropriate moment. For the first time in his life Mary's father found himself isolated.

To correct this dangerous imbalance Cromwell advocated an alliance between England and the strong Protestant princes in Germany who were as much a thorn in Charles's side as the Scots were to Henry. But his sovereign was lukewarm because of his dislike for the uncompromising Lutheranism of his proposed allies.

It is important to remember that he hated Lutheranism, and upheld the doctrine of transubstantiation, celibacy of the clergy and the traditional liturgy of the Church to the end. Like his subjects he was orthodox to the core. His principal Protestant leaning was that towards the Bible, which was to him 'that most precious jewel, the Word of God', a copy of which he commanded to be placed in every church from which the priest should read to his people in their own tongue every Sunday.

Only when Charles began to accumulate guns and ammunition in the Antwerp area, preparatory to invasion of England, was Henry prevailed upon to form a precautionary alliance with the German princes and Denmark. Only then was he prepared to listen to Cromwell's suggestion that he should marry Anne of Cleves, whose beauty of face and body excelled even the loveliest as the golden sun excelled the silver moon. Her brother's family claim to the Duchy of Guelders was the very barb of the thorn in Charles's side, his lands most favourably placed for invasion of Charles's dominions should the need arise.

Mary, with Elizabeth at her side, was at Greenwich to greet their new stepmother, who had been storm-stayed at Calais by boisterous December winds. Their father, unable to restrain his impatience to see his bride, who would take days on winter roads with her train to reach London, had already caught his first glimpse of her. His reply was ominous when it was reported to him that his six-year-old daughter ardently desired to see his new queen. 'Tell her,' he replied, 'that she had a mother so different from this woman that she ought not to wish to see her.'

Her age alone might have given his advisers pause, for she was thirty-four. But there could be no drawing back now she was in his realm with the elaborate preparations already made for her welcome and the wedding which was to take place almost at once. Not to go forward would cause too great a ruffle in the world, and drive her brother into the arms of the Emperor and French king. But someone would have to pay for this. His head was not too much to ask for making his sovereign a laughing-stock before the whole world. From first to last this was Cromwell's doing.

The King averred from the first he would never have a child by her, and she found sharing his bed as distasteful as he found it with her. For a handsome pension with manors and estates, she agreed to resign the title of queen and to the annulment of their marriage, signing the necessary deeds and documents with alacrity and affably returning her wedding-ring before it had been six months on her finger.

Mary had much in common with her father's fourth bride; both were direct without a trace of subtlety, both found the daily round of a quiet court life not restricted but pleasurable. So that Henry's elder daughter enjoyed visiting his one-time wife, at one of her manors forfeited by Cromwell, and being entertained by her in still another rich new dress of extraordinary fashion from her trousseau. Anne of Cleves could even greet her recent husband's new bride with acclaim, so glad was she to see another by his side.

Not so Mary. Her father's marriage to his fifth bride was an unproclaimed affair which took place in the same month as the annulment of his fourth and on the same day that Thomas Cromwell, too rich and ruthless to have friends, came to his un-lamented end.

The daughter of Katherine of Aragon could not bring herself to pay the reverence she had paid Jane Seymour and Anne of Cleves to this girl, not yet twenty and so diminutive she might have been a child, with her red hair and pert, uptilted nose. Niece of the Duke of Norfolk and therefore cousin of Anne Boleyn, Katherine Howard was the member of a family inimical to the King's elder daughter, although by heredity and predisposition Norfolk's allegiance leant towards the old faith. But neither heredity nor predisposition carried any sway with England's premier nobleman where his sovereign was concerned: wherever and whenever that massive figure shifted his weight, there would be found Thomas Howard taking up his stance.

At once two of Mary's favourite maids were removed to reach her who was queen now, and although Mary learnt to adapt herself to the new order at court there was not the same place for her there that there had been in the past. It was Elizabeth, Katherine Howard's small cousin, who held the favoured position.

This was their father's Indian summer. He was forty-nine when he took his fifth wife, a panorama of a man, the landscape of his face unfurrowed, the bluff of his brow unlined, the promontory of his nose only beginning to coarsen. And for these idyllic months of early marriage he was able to hold his winter at bay. Something of the old agility returned to that gargantuan form. It was as though in his young wife he recovered his lost youth, and she who brought about this miracle was like a goddess.

The blow was all the more cruel when it did fall little more than a year after the wedding day. His sovereign refused to believe when he read what Cranmer could not bring himself to tell him by word of mouth. He had chosen the rose as her symbol, and called her his rose without a thorn. His Council had to bring forth proof after proof not only of looseness before their marriage but of looseness during it when she accompanied him on his long-promised progress to his northern counties. His young wife had made a cuckold of him.

He was never to be the same again. Time at last caught up with him, vanquishing all the magniloquence of youth, and the greyness of age took root.

Mary was hurriedly escorted from Syon to join her brother's establishment. The suppressed house where nuns had once prayed was needed to lodge the woman who had been Queen of England and her armed guard, the woman who, but for the grace of God, might have borne a son during the short time she shared the King's bed. She and her lovers were put to death for committing the worst crime they could have committed, that of confounding the succession.

Mary was with her brother as he recovered from his first serious illness, a quartan fever (today it would be called malaria) which he took while his father was on his northern progress. He was four years old now, big for his age and a handsome boy as even grudging foreign ambassadors had to admit. It took him some months to throw off the ague, but when he did begin to mend he did it in a hurry.

Apt to learn, he could express himself clearly in English,

Greek and Latin before he knew his alphabet, and he soon outgrew his hornbook with its coloured letters. His illness interrupted his lessons from his first tutor, Dr Cox.

It was a far cry from the days of his sister Mary who had been
taught under the rigid tutorage laid down by the Spaniard Vives.
Dr Cox devised the game of a military engagement as an assault
on ignorance to divert his small scholar and keep him interested.
Edward conquered Cato and Aesop with zest and took Latin
exercises and Bible readings in his stride. But he baulked at
learning by heart Solomon's tiresome proverbs and was lack-
lustre when told Captain Will must be overthrown before any
progress could be made. Cox might belong to the advanced
school which believed learning was adventure and discovery, and
recourse to punishment a sign of defeat: 'Whatsoever the mind
doth learn unwillingly, with fear, the same it doth quickly forget.'
But he was old-fashioned enough to know that discipline is a form
of love, and he loved his pupil. It took the sudden sharp sting of
a buffet to overthrow a startled Captain Will.

An Italian first guided the Prince's hand to form his letters, a
Fleming taught him the lute, a Frenchman his mother tongue,
but it was his English tutors who influenced him, above all Cheke
who took the place of Dr Cox. Compared to the young brilliant
Cheke even the enlightened sensible Cox was a trifle humdrum.
Cheke was said to have laid the very foundations of the new
learning in Cambridge, where young minds dared to break up
the ground and leave outworn unfallowed fields of thought and
usage to the old. All his tutors loved their young pupil, and he
held each in affection, but it was Cheke he loved most of all,
Cheke who meant most to him. The tall gowned figure of his
mentor was always behind him throughout the passing years as
others came and went amidst the shifting scenes.

And with the new learning went of course the new religion:
Cox, Cheke, Ascham were all Reformers, but they did not think
of their Protestant faith as new. They did not set out to abolish
an old Church to establish a new one in its stead. To them reform
meant re-form, to make better by removing, or become better
by abandoning imperfections, innovations and faults.

Edward was a sweet-natured, affectionate child. He had his
sister Mary's generosity, and her thought of making gifts appropriate, a gilt chalice for her and a basket of the new rare arti-
chokes, for Elizabeth a necklace and a pair of embroidered

stockings. He enjoyed the companionship of his chamberlain's small daughter, Jane Dormer, the same age as himself, and called her 'my Jane'. They would look at his books together and dance when the musicians played, and when he won at cards he would say: 'Now, Jane, your king is gone, I shall be enough for you.'

He was six years old when he was brought to meet his new stepmother. Both his sisters had been present to hear the twice-widowed bride plight her troth to her third husband. This wedding was no hole-and-corner affair like those of the Howard cousins, but took place at Hampton Court with all due observances, although without the pageantry that marked that to Anne of Cleves. But this was no political union to impress the world; it was the marriage of a sick king in need of a helpmeet.

Katherine Parr was thirty-one when she became Henry VIII's sixth wife. She looked very small that day as she stood beside her bridegroom. He was fifty-two, and his sands of time were running out, but magnificence still clung to him. It was his personality not the monstrous body one saw on his wedding day, amicable and benign on so pleasant an occasion.

He never shut the door against her as he had against some of his former wives. She was not afraid of him as young Katherine Howard had been when, goaded with pain, he raged and blamed. Her presence was always soothing, and he would sit with his thrombosed sore leg on her lap while he disputed with his doctors.

She was a tender stepmother to all three of his children, who loved, looked up to and patterned themselves on this gifted woman with her serene brow and hazel eyes, her delicate features clear-cut as those on a miniature. The ten-year truce between France and Spain had not run more than half its span when they were once more at war, with England now allied to the morose Emperor. When Henry, despite his doctor's warnings, insisted on crossing the Channel to lead his army in person against his old rival Francis, his children lived together with their stepmother, for the most part at Hampton Court. It was a period for all three of blessed family life.

For Edward she supplied the place of the mother he never knew, and he loved her dearly. He had thrown off the effects of the quartan fever, but its very severity made his doctors uneasily wonder if after all he had inherited his father's constitution, an uneasiness that was conveyed to their sovereign.

Henry's corpulence was such that it was unlikely he would have any further children with his latest wife, but the succession after Edward of these unlikely offspring was naturally enough firmly nailed into an Act when the marriage took place, an Act that also covered, in those days of uncertain life, the dreaded eventuality of the heir's death before he could leave issue. In that case his father decreed the crown was to pass to his daughter Mary; failing Mary and her heirs, to his daughter Elizabeth. That both his daughters were now accepted in the direct line of succession made a vast difference to their prestige and circumstances in the eyes of England and the world, particularly in the case of Mary. Roman Catholics both in England and abroad looked upon Elizabeth as a bastard born to the King of England's concubine when his legitimate wife was still alive.

The younger daughter was nearly ten when her father married for the sixth time, and the three and a half years before his death marked a pleasant interlude in her life, as it did for her brother and sister, because of the sweetness of her new stepmother. Unlike Mary, Elizabeth had much of her father in her, and sometimes their contact had the action of metal against metal. No one now knows why, but he was so angry with her shortly after his last marriage that he refused to see her and forbade her to write to him for a whole year, passing over to France without a sign that he knew of her existence. But her stepmother plied her pen so adroitly on young Elizabeth's behalf that, when her father sent his hearty blessings to all his children, his little daughter knew she was forgiven and was eloquent with gratitude to her stepmother for having brought about the reconciliation.

Unlike her elder sister, she gave promise of being tall and she had the white skin of all Henry's children. There was something very pleasing about this spirited child, with her hair more red than golden and eyes that had some of Anne Boleyn's beauty.

She was to surprise her teachers with the facility with which she learnt. Hers was the thrusting mind of the male that reached back into history and out into the realms of geography, architecture, mathematics and astronomy. Without the same need for application as Mary, she carried her acquirements, her skill with languages, with both panache and grace.

And, unlike her elder sister who was always ailing, Elizabeth was strong. Letters to Mary throughout the years from her sister and brother time and again allude to her ill health. 'In the same manner as I put on my best garments very seldom,' Edward assured her, 'yet these I like better than the others, even so I write to you very seldom yet I love you most. Moreover, I am glad that you have got well, for I have heard that you had been sick.' 'Good sister,' elaborated Elizabeth, 'as to hear of your sickness is unpleasant to me, so it is nothing fearful, for that I understand it is your old guest, that is wont oft to visit you, whose coming, though it be oft, yet is never welcome; but notwithstanding, it is comfortable, for that *Jacula Praevisa minus feriunt.*'

Handwriting in a Tudor schoolroom was taught as an art, the Roman hand like printing used for ordinary correspondence, and the decorative style more like drawing which took years to perfect. Edward was more anxious to transmit his thoughts to paper than to hold himself back embellishing his handwriting as he went along. Mary's Italian hand was bold, square, uncompromising, epitomizing a sentence she often wrote, 'I will be plain with you.' Elizabeth was the only one of the three who perfected the decorative style. As her elegant fingers drew her steeples of letters and adorning convolutions the thoughts which they formed and circled were to weave with the same intricacy through parenthesis and high-flown simile, until not only the reader but the pleased writer was put to it to know what was meant.

As Mary moved about court, as she bent over her careful accounts, as she sat with her ladies working on the embroidery of an enormous chair for her father, as she stood sponsor to a lord's son or for still another cottager's child, it was noticed that she was enveloped in a melancholy so profound it was reported to Francis. As a prospective father-in-law, he had inquiries instituted to discover if this melancholy could be the symptom of a disease that made her incapable of child-bearing.

The girl who was born in the same month as her kinsman, Prince Edward, joined their stepmother's household, and the name, the Lady Jane Grey, began to appear in Mary's accounts as the recipient of gifts from her affectionate cousin. To pass from the harshness of a hectoring worldly mother, who never forgave her and her two sisters for not being sons, into the care of the Queen, with her love of things of the mind, was to Jane like passing into paradise.

She had had a tutor, a Cambridge man, since she was four and could read Coverdale's Bible by the time she was six. More advanced in her studies than Edward, the distance between her and his younger sister was less than Elizabeth's four-year seniority merited, but she had neither her cousin's exuberance nor excitement. Hers was a self-contained character, holding close against assault from any quarter what she held dear; and what she held dear, with a will that did not know what compromise meant, were certain principles and fixed opinions. Her parents' chaplain foresaw of her: 'Whatever she has begun, she will complete—unless she be diverted by some calamity.'

She was Henry's grand-niece, the grand-daughter of his favourite sister Mary. This small, neat, composed girl, her Tudor skin so fine and fair it was sprinkled with freckles, was mentioned in the direct line of succession through her mother in his will if, and God of course would forbid so cruel an outcome, his own three children all died without issue.

There was another child, the infant Queen of Scots, born at her father's death, who was grand-daughter of his elder sister Margaret, but he had not included her in the succession, for she was to marry Edward. The marriage and peace treaties between England and Scotland had been agreed on both sides in 1543 and ratified by the Estates of Scotland.

Henry had completed the union of Wales with England and was now King of Ireland. Scotland alone prevented his title to Emperor of Great Britain, but now his army had beaten Scotland to her knees, her king was dead and his baby daughter espoused to his son. Certainly the Scots, a rude, rough nation, saw to it before they signed that there was no loophole for annexation, but Henry showed what he thought of that by seizing, barely before the ink was dry on the treaties, a rich fleet of Scots merchant ships.

The Scots retaliated by crowning their infant queen. This ceremony infuriated her great-uncle, who was further incensed when it was followed by her subjects declaring the English treaties null and void and renewing their ancient alliance with France.

There was only one answer Henry could give to such barefaced defiance. He sent Edward's uncle, Edward Seymour, into Scotland to take by force the girl he was determined should be his daughter-in-law. Seymour was to inflict all the misery he could, lay waste the country, seize Edinburgh and put to fire and sword man, woman and child. And as he went he was to declare Henry VIII King of England chief governor of the queen and protector of the realm of Scotland.

Seymour, whose own views were that such tactics would exasperate rather than quell, was overridden by his impatient sovereign, and carried out his instructions to the letter as a good commander should, except that he did not return with the infant queen. The Scots hurried her with her French mother before the harrying invaders from one stronghold to another in their barbarous country.

Henry had had the glory of entering Boulogne at the head of his troops, and the treaty he had just signed with France was favourable to him in every respect. He, king of half a small island, was recognized as an equal in Europe by Francis and Charles. Scotland was the one sore that refused to heal. Preparations were now being made for Seymour to invade the northern country yet again. It was not enough for him to be known as the Scourge of the Scots. This time he must not fail to bring back the infant queen. His sovereign could not last for ever.

He had made his will and discussed it with his Council. He had always preferred to surround himself with men of differing opinions, and throughout had kept the factions balanced as he thought fit: Norfolk, Gardiner and their followers who thought change in religion had gone far enough; Cranmer, Seymour, Dudley zealous to go further. Preponderance one way or another was dangerous, and he was too astute to commit himself to either party, instead he had played one against the other. But he realized the light of the new day, his son's day, would fall on the men whose faces were turned towards it; he also realized they were less likely to undo what he had done. The regency council he had nominated contained both schools, but was weighted towards the new.

Cranmer of course. He who was the boy's godfather. Henry had been the strength behind Cranmer in the past, the imprint of his forcible mind was surely stamped upon the wax of the churchman's now. Paget had been a good servant, and was sound. Dudley—the fact that he came from a tainted stable minded him to be careful of his step.

One of Henry's first actions when he came to the throne had been, acting on advice, to send to the block Dudley's father and his fellow councillor. It had enhanced his golden popularity even more, the dispatch of the two tax-gatherers who had helped his careful father to amass his millions. Henry had taken a much shorter time to spend his father's fortune than it had taken his parent to build it. Instead of a fortune he was leaving his son a debased coinage and a deadweight of debts.

He had handed to Edward Seymour the fair copy of his will at the end of December after it had been witnessed. As his son's uncle he could be trusted to serve him well, but not his younger brother Thomas, who was also Edward's uncle. If he had been a ship he would have been all sail. Nor Gardiner, although his friends went on their knees, and pleaded for him to be made one of their number.

If Cranmer was a churchman before he was a politician, Stephen Gardiner, Bishop of Winchester, was lawyer before he was churchman. Henry alone knew how to handle the contentious man known as 'Wily Winchester', 'Stephen Stockfish', 'Doctor Doubleface', and Henry would not be there when the regency council took office. Sixteen commissioners was what he willed, no one man to have supreme authority, he alone, their sovereign, was fit for that. He had provided for every exigency that might befall, and removed any claimant who could threaten his son's right to his father's throne.

Suddenly the balance was destroyed. Norfolk and his mountebank son Surrey found themselves in the Tower, the father made to suffer for the son, who had quartered his coat-of-arms with the royal arms and asked who had more right to be Protector when the King died than his father.

The royal prerogative was challenged. The Norfolks with their blue blood could well cause trouble during Edward's minority when his father was no longer there to keep them in their place. Henry had shown in the past his unanswerable method of dealing with possible pretenders, and he was taking no chances where his son was concerned.

Silent crowds watched the poet Surrey go to his death, he who had been called the most foolish, proud boy in England, who had threatened the inheritance of their rightful little prince, England's Treasure, His Majesty's most noble jewel, whose reign was to inaugurate a golden age. His father's execution was stayed only because the king who ordered it was dead before it could be carried out.

When Henry VIII died on 28th January 1547 he was in his fifty-sixth year, and had reigned for thirty-seven. He left behind him three children, each born of a different mother, each one of whom was to reign after him, none to leave issue.

Of his two daughters, one at his death was approaching thirty-one, the other in her fourteenth year, both with the Tudor ambition, one inbred with aristocracy, the other thrusting and zestful. And his only son, nine-year-old Edward, the stamp of nobility upon his brow, who stood as his father had stood at his age with his legs apart, distributing his weight equally. But whereas his father had been sturdy he was slender.

Book Two
Edward VI
January 1547–July 1553

'Speak well of archers, for your father shot a bow.'
Proverb

Chapter Six

It is unlikely that Edward was aware anything was afoot, certainly every care was taken not to disturb the atmosphere around him. For one thing his uncle and his companion arrived at Hatfield in the middle of the night. No one else knew the King had died after midnight except those in his palace of Whitehall where he now lay, chilling as the small hours crept towards the new day he would never see.

The child who did not yet know he was king saw his uncle in the morning. Edward Seymour, Earl of Hertford, was everything a manly boy could look up to and revere, one who carried his victories as a soldier lightly on his handsome shoulders, generous, warm-hearted and approachable, so that the common people shouted for him as he passed and ran to kneel before him.

As the uncle looked at his nephew that morning, he must have thought that his beauty and the grace of his carriage made him a fit prince to inaugurate what was to be a golden reign. Seymour was so sure the power he was seeking was not for himself. It was to put right what was wrong in the land, to bring in an age when justice ruled and the rich did not oppress the poor, an age not of disputation about religion but the blossoming of the faith of the Reformers, when the gentleness of spring would follow the winter of severity.

And still he did not tell him. Instead he and his companion, two of the sixteen executors nominated by their late master to carry out the provisions of his will, travelled with him to Enfield where he would have the comfort of his sister Elizabeth's company. Edward was very fond of Elizabeth. It is impossible to say which sister was his favourite, he loved both for different reasons. The formality of royalty was to separate him from them, particularly from Mary because those round him were antagonistic to the religion she represented, but he never outgrew his natural affection for them. He had so few to whom he belonged.

It was the following day that, in the panelled presence chamber surrounded by his suite and Elizabeth by her attendants, he granted the audience humbly desired by his uncle and travelling companion. It was not a large room lit on that January day by the fire on the great hearth, the capering flames dancing on the motto engraved over the chimney-piece, 'Service alone is virtue: the rest is a cheat'.

He saw, and Elizabeth watched the two men kneel before him, heard them tell him he was now King of England. But it was the realization that their father was dead which had a catastrophic effect on both children: it was as though the walls of the fortress in which they dwelt secure were suddenly breached. Both vulnerable, they clung weeping to each other.

Before Edward was taken from Enfield the following morning, he was aware he was now the King's Majesty. It was conveyed by the awe of those around him and the attitude of the strong man beside him who was his uncle. To the boy Edward Tudor and the man Edward Seymour kingship was not a divine sanction to do what the wearer of the crown willed, it was the privilege of him who was called to the throne by the grace of God to do God's work.

This awareness was strengthened the nearer they drew to the Tower, the stronghold of London, where custom decreed in these debatable times a king should lodge while preparations were made for his coronation. The crowds surged in the narrow streets to await his approach, agog for what they would see.

He did not disappoint them. Few could remember in these short-lived days the accession of his father, but this was no king in the prime of his manhood entering his own. To them there was something heavenly about the fair boy smilingly answering their acclamations and removing his cap to them. It was his eyes they noticed, never had they seen such starry eyes. 'God save King Edward!' they shouted as the Tower guns volleyed their salute. God would save him because God had sent him to be their king.

The young monarch made ready response to every demand. At three o'clock in the morning after he arrived in the Tower, he agreed under his canopy of State that his uncle should be pro-claimed Lord Protector of the realm and Governor of his person since, as he afterwards remembered, all the gentlemen and lords did so agree because he was the King's uncle on his mother's side.

But not all had agreed, and within two months, when a new

patent for the Protectorate was drawn up in the King's name by the Protector himself, it was signed by seven only of his co-executors, who were no longer Edward's guardians appointed by his father but Edward's own nominees appointed for him by his uncle.

The day after his father's funeral, Edward exercised the royal prerogative by investing sixteen peers. The first was much the most elaborate when he elevated his uncle, now Lord Protector, to be Duke of Somerset. And the Duke of Somerset stood beside him as he untiringly girded the new lords with their swords and placed their coronets on their heads.

He fitted the mantle over the shoulders of John Dudley, Viscount Lisle, whom he had made Earl of Warwick. The man's dark gaze held his with a kind of burning intensity: he was not to be one of the seven signatories of the Protector's new patent. And he noted the man who knelt before him as Thomas Seymour and rose Baron Seymour of Sudeley, not only because he was his uncle but because Thomas Seymour saw to it even a king would notice him whom no woman could overlook and no man underrate.

In streets, whose conduits gushed with red wine, hung with tapestry and cloth of gold, fluttering with flags and streamers, he reined in his horse to listen to children singing his praises in sweet jingle, heard orations from Faith, Justice and Truth ('I, ancient Truth that long time was suppressed'), and watched the spectacles, pageants and scenes enacted for his entertainment. Only when the Mayor of London presented him with a purse containing a thousand crowns was he at a loss, for he was unable to hold it. He wondered why they had given it to him, under the impression kings bestowed largesse, did not receive it, and was told by his uncle it was the custom of the city.

But of all the marvels he saw that day the one that delighted him most was when, in St Paul's churchyard, a tumbler shot like an arrow, his arms spread as though they were wings, down a rope from the steeple of the church to the ground. A foreigner he was, from a place called Aragon in Spain, who came and kissed his foot before he swarmed up the rope again. It was long before the King's Majesty, all his train behind him, could be induced to move on.

His people watched his slender silver figure progress from the Tower to the Palace of Westminster, the jewels on his white velvet cap glancing in the frost-bright light, making a halo round his angel head. They saw him in the State barge borne by the tide from Westminster to Whitehall on his way to his coronation clad in crimson velvet embroidered with gold and furred with ermine.

Because of his tender years the ceremonial was cut from twelve hours to seven. The banquet after it lasted for four, with each course brought in to the sound of trumpets and preceded by two nobles on horseback. The anointed king sat between his godfather Cranmer, who as Archbishop of Canterbury had crowned him, and the Protector. His other godfather he never saw again, for the Duke of Norfolk was kept in the Tower throughout his reign.

No women were present at the coronation or the banquet. The Protector, with much on his mind, may have baulked at the precedence to be determined between so many females in the line of succession and two royal widows of the deceased king. More probably it was purposeful rather than inopportune.

Jealous of the affection Edward held for his stepmother and fearful of her influence over him, he was to ensure that any meetings between them were rare, so private as to appear stolen, and it was the Protector himself who doled out separate visits from each sister with a niggard hand.

The prescribed approach to her young brother was that of votary to deity. Five times she had to kneel to him before she sat down so far from the head of the table that the canopy of State did not hang over her. When she entered his private apartments, she was not permitted to converse beside him on a chair: instead bench and cushions were provided for her.

This excessive deference, in the case of his sisters to prevent intimacy, was imposed on all, as though to endue the boy king with a sense of the authority he possessed only in name.

The man who had made himself Lord Protector looked upon himself no longer as the servant of the King but as the chosen servant of God, the sword-bearer of His justice, appointed by Him to rule and be a shepherd to His people, a man who used the royal 'We', addressed the King of France as brother, and refused to take to heart the French ambassador's sharp rebuke to remember who and what he was.

Francis I survived his old rival Henry VIII little more than a couple of months, and it was when the French embassade arrived in England to announce the death of their king and the accession of Henri II that Edward became conscious of this shift in his uncle's attitude towards himself, a shift all the more meaningful to a boy who had been both consecrated and crowned.

It was essential for the representatives of each country to create a good impression on the other for the sake of their new alliance, the French because of the sensitive subject of Calais and Boulogne, and the English because they were well aware the new ruler of France had been the leader of the party most strongly opposed to England during Henry's reign. Negotiations in the past for Mary's marriage to Henri had proved as abortive as all the others, and he was now married to an Italian, Catherine de Medici, who after nine years of childless marriage had provided the French royal nursery not only with a sickly Dauphin but three more pallid sons and two daughters.

Edward and the Protector received the embassade headed by de Vieilleville, who announced what was no longer news, the death of their king. Before the boy could reply, he heard his uncle beside him declare in rapid French that His Majesty had lost both a father and a brother, and did not yet know their language well enough to declare his friendship for their new king. Edward could take no part in the rest of the proceedings as they were not conducted in Latin but in French with guests who could speak no English.

He might preside the following day, in the chair of State surrounded by his ministers, when both parties settled down to negotiate the new alliance, but it was the domineering Protector who not only opened the meeting but carried it on in a duel of French with de Vieilleville. Edward was painfully aware of the Frenchman's contempt for the Englishman's boastful taunts when de Vieilleville cut in with a personal thrust that brought an angry flush to his uncle's face and ill-concealed satisfaction to his fellow Councillors.

With his uncle Somerset Edward was made to feel more like the Protector's nephew than His Majesty. Very different was the Protector's younger brother, Thomas Seymour. There was always a certain excitement round him, a stir of pleasant events, who treated him not only as though he were king but as though they were of the same age. Edward could wish he saw more of him.

The man he had created Baron of Sudeley and preferred to the exalted office of Lord Admiral could have wished so too, and he was not one to be foiled. Ever one to shoot his arrow high, he had already applied to the Council to marry the fourteen-year-old

Princess Elizabeth, sister of the King, and made an essay towards her elder sister. One Seymour in their midst taking upon himself the full panoply of royalty was enough for the Council, while the Protector himself considered such a claim presumptuous from someone raised already to such heights only because he happened to be not the King's uncle but the Protector's brother.

Thomas Seymour did not believe in trusting to his equals; they not only had something to lose but could prove rivals—not that any could out-rival him, except his elder brother who had taken upon himself the Protectorate instead of sharing it, as he should have done, with him. No, his policy was to make use of the lower class who had everything to gain furthering the aims of their superiors, and what he needed in this case was a go-between, someone who could have speech with his young Majesty when no one was near, who could tell the Lord Admiral when His Grace was wont to rise in the morning and go to bed at night.

Nobles escorted him to and from his bedchamber, each with his own hereditary charge of towel, ewer, posset-cup. Others waited in his chamber, one to remove his shoes, another his hose, another ready with his nightshirt and nightcap. The great bed on its dais on which his father had lain had already been prepared, surrounded by halberdiers, by a select army of yeomen, grooms and pages, under the direction of a gentleman-usher, and searched lest anything dangerous to its royal occupant had been interposed between the sheets, mattresses or rich velvet hangings.

The new gentleman-usher installed in his privy chamber was a personable man called Fowler who, aware of his position, would never presume, and who went about his duties with alacrity. Edward knew he was the recommendation of his younger uncle, and when the man passed through an ante-room assiduous on his duties, or helped him to change his clothes during the day when he came in hot from tennis, he was wont to ask him how his uncle Seymour did. And always the well-primed Fowler had an affectionate message from the Admiral to deliver to his nephew.

On one such occasion the servant remarked, after a judicious pause as though the idea had suddenly struck him: 'And it please your Grace, I marvel my Lord Admiral marrieth not.'

His uncle's celibacy had probably never entered his nine-year-old nephew's thoughts, and he made no reply. Certainly the younger Seymour had been the most brilliant match at Henry VIII's court after his sovereign himself. He had wooed the twice-widowed Katherine Parr with ardour, but had retired from the lists whenever his liege had entered them. Katherine was in love with Thomas Seymour when she married the monarch, and the indiscretion of her former suitor towards herself had caused her great unease while she was the consort of so suspicious a husband.

'Could Your Grace be contented he would marry?' prodded the indefatigable Fowler.

Edward accepted as natural that his sanction should be asked before his courtiers undertook marriage.

'Yea, very well,' he said now, always pleased to agree with those he liked.

'Whom would Your Grace he should marry?' asked Fowler, coming to the kernel.

'My Lady of Cleves,' was Edward's first suggestion. A minute later he had second thoughts. 'Nay, nay,' he repudiated, 'know you what? I would he married my sister Mary, to change her opinions.'

Mary was beginning to be a charge on her small brother's conscience. Last year he had written to their stepmother urging her to prevail upon his elder sister to give up foreign dances and merriments which did not become a Christian princess. His tutors did not approve of dancing, gaming and cards, and they probably exaggerated Mary's participation in all three. Her love of dancing was not so much the Tudor love of gaiety as release for the naturally reserved. When she was younger she had played for high stakes, probably in the dubious hope of replenishing her precarious finances, but no one in court circles frowned on gaming, and it was taken so much as a matter of course that Mary had given her sister money for cards when she was a little girl.

Edward's remark that he would like his uncle to marry her to change her opinions meant of course to change her religion. He was the first sovereign of England to be crowned with the glorious title Defender of the Faith, and the Faith of which he was the Defender was the true Faith which came straight from the Source of Christ, not the false faith propagated by the Bishop of Rome to whom his elder sister adhered. He loved her, but the older he grew the more fixed became his abhorrence of her religion.

Thomas Seymour laughed when told by Fowler of the King's suggestions regarding his prospective bride. Despite the fact that his brother kept His Grace so close (Fowler said he was not half a quarter of an hour alone), he managed to engineer a private interview, when his young nephew was asked if he would be content if he married the Queen Dowager.

Edward was only too happy to aid two people of whom he was fond. There were long walks through unfamiliar parts of one of his palaces, through galleries and small ante-rooms where no one waited, to the apartments of his stepmother. On such occasions the Lord Admiral usually happened to be present.

Katherine was the classic example of a learned, high-principled woman subjugated by her love for an attractive rascal. She prayed her precipitate suitor for seemly time to allow the dust to settle on the grave of her liege lord, quailed at the thought of his intimidating elder brother's wrath, yet before March was out, before she had been widowed for a third time less than two months, she not only exchanged rings but was secretly married to her fourth husband.

Edward was to remember some years later the anger of the Lord Protector when he learnt the identity of his brother's secret bride. The boy wrote to his stepmother promising that if any grief should befall them he would be a sufficient succour. Fowler relayed messages to the young king about how hardly the couple were being treated, his younger uncle, very much the injured party, not allowed to keep the jewels which King Henry had given his wife on their marriage—yea, even her very wedding-ring was retained.

The hard-working Protector was too occupied with the multifarious affairs of the country to concentrate upon the feelings of the small, slight nephew in whose place he ruled. It was a mistake his younger brother did not make. 'My uncle of Somerset dealeth very hardly with me,' Edward confided to Jane Grey's father in an uncharacteristic confidence, 'and keepeth me strait that I cannot have money at my will. But my Lord Admiral both sends me money, and gives me money.'

The nation's exchequer had never been lower, and the Protector wished his nephew to participate in his plans for economy, far-reaching plans which, Edward was intelligent enough to know, did not include his land-hungry elder uncle.

Surely the most joyful office of a king was to do good to those who loved him, to reward those who served him. It was to bestow he needed money and he, the King of England, had an empty purse.

Henry VII, the first of the Tudors and Henry VIII's father, holding the red rose of Lancaster. Painting by an unknown artist.

ELIZABETHA · VXOR
HENRICI · VII ·

Elizabeth, Henry V[...]
Queen and mother of He[...]
VIII, holding the white r[...]
of York. Painting by
unknown artist.

[...]e Lady Mary after Queen.

Mary, probably twenty,
the year she was reconciled[...]
her father.

Edward painted in his th[...]
year (1540) by Hans Holb[...]
the Younger as a Christr[...]
present for Henry VIII.

PARVVLE PATRISSA, PATRIÆ VIRTVTIS ET HÆRES
ESTO, NIHIL MAIVS MAXIMVS ORBIS HABET.
GNATVM VIX POSSVNT COELVM ET NATVRA DEDISSE,
HVIVS QVEM PATRIS, VICTVS HONORET HONOS.
ÆQVATO TANTVM, TANTI TV FACTA PARENTIS,
VOTA HOMINVM, VIX QVO PROGREDIANTVR, HABENT
VINCITO, VICISTI. QVOT REGES PRISCVS ADORAT
ORBIS, NEC TE QVI VINCERE POSSIT, ERIT.

O little boy, so like your father grow,
    That you true heir of all his grace we know;
The great round world, nature and heaven too
    Can give no more; and now, in honouring you
Honour is overcome; and all men's prayer
    Can reach no further for your father's heir
Than that you equal him. Kings, once of old revered,
    You have o'ercome; no victor now be feared.

Family picture painted *c.* 1545 by an unknown artist. Henry VIII has Edward on his right side and Jane Seymour, Edward's mother, on his left. Her likeness is believed to have been taken from the wax effigy carried at her funeral. Mary is seen entering on right of picture, Elizabeth on left.

LEFT **Mary** at twenty-eight by an unknown artist. The year 1544 was a happy one for Mary when she was living with her stepmother Katherine Parr.

CENTRE **Edward** painted when he was nine (1546), by an unknown artist, shortly before his accession.

RIGHT **Elizabeth** painted at thirteen at the same period as Edward at nine and almost certainly by the same unknown artist.

Elizabeth I
as depicted on a silver sixpenny coin.

Edward VI
gold coronation medal

Mary I
silver-gilt medal by Jacopo da Trezzo, 1555

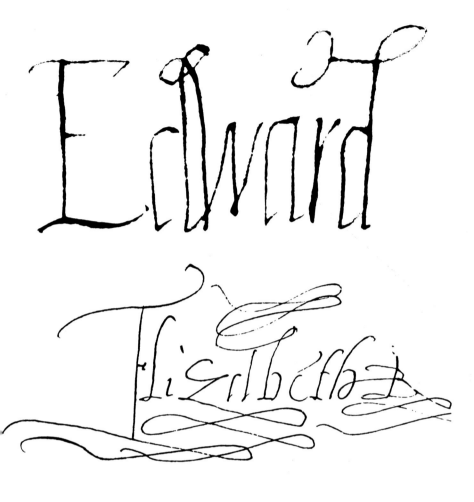

TOP Signature of Edward; CENTRE Signature of Elizabeth; BOTTOM Part of Document supposed written by Mary.

Elizabeth painted probably in the early 1580s when in her late forties.

Through the insidious Fowler it was borne in upon him that the Lord Admiral would supply any sum, large or small, he wished. And Fowler was the carrier of the benefactions from uncle to nephew, the bearer of the letters which it was his business to solicit from his young master as proof he received only what he demanded.

Access to the King became easier for the Lord Admiral in late summer when his brother led the largest army ever to cross the Border to force the Scots to hand over their queen. He was about to carry out in his own name Henry VIII's tactics which he as a general deemed unwise two short years ago, and he was deaf to advice.

Seymour took full advantage of his new-found entry into his nephew's presence. No opportunity was allowed to slip by without some insinuation against his brother to undermine the King's confidence in his Governor. My Lord Protector's invasion of Scotland was madly undertaken, it was money wasted in vain, he would never return without loss of a great number of men—or of himself.

'I desire you to write a thing to the Lords of the Council for me,' he began shortly after his brother had left for Scotland

They were alone but for the boy's tutor, Master Cheke, whose long gown hid his thinness and made him appear even taller than he was and who remained so stationary in the background that as far as the Lord Admiral was concerned he might as well not have been there at all.

The peremptoriness of his tone at once challenged the child's instinctive royalty.

'What?' he demanded shortly.

His uncle's immediate change of tune came too late. Edward was not ingratiated by the assurance that it was for no ill thing, it was for the Queen's Majesty. Probably the piece of paper he wanted him to sign was a request for the jewels which the Protector, under the influence of his hectoring wife, refused to return, but Edward did not give him time to elaborate.

'If it is good,' he said coldly, 'the Lords will allow it. If it is ill, I will not write it.'

'The Lords will take it in better part if you wrote it,' persisted his uncle.

'Let me alone,' said his nephew.

After the slight pause that fell when the courtier took his leave,

Cheke said with approving emphasis from the background: 'Ye were best not to write.'

Never again did Edward feel the same with this splendid uncle and his open-hearted camaraderie; some warmth had gone from their relationship. Now the boy was wary. With few intimates, there was a certain withdrawal in his attitude to others. He was after all the son of the man who had said that three might keep counsel if two be away. His opinion of his two Seymour uncles was tacitly expressed when he was heard to refer to his step-mother's brother as 'mine honest uncle'.

He still shared the sports and pastimes of the boys, known as the King's children before Henry VIII died, elder sons and cadets of the men around his father. All were older than he. Robert Dudley, the handsomest of Warwick's stripling sons, was the same age as Elizabeth. Edward had something of his father's exuberance, and entered games and studies with the pride to excel by his own efforts, accepting defeat when he was out-paced and outshone. But the difference between him and his companions was they had walked in the coronation procession to the Abbey each bearing a part of the regalia for the schoolboy who was now king.

This apartness might make for loneliness, but those with whom he was intimate, so few he could count them on his one hand, meant a great deal to him. The spirited Barnaby Fitzpatrick might be four years older, but in a friendship that never cooled it was the conscientious young king who acted as his mentor and not the other way about, giving him advice, arranging even for the harum-scarum Irishman's servants to be paid, so that Barnaby was to sign himself some years later 'the meanest and most obliged of all your sevants'.

Henry Sidney could be classed as another intimate; eight years older, he was never one of his schoolfellows. He was the gifted, handsome son of the chamberlain whose little grand-daughter Jane Dormer had charmed the King's son and, when Edward himself became king, Henry Sidney was his cup-bearer.

The Lord Admiral was unaware there was anything amiss between him and his nephew and counselled Edward in their next interview to be like other kings and take upon himself to rule. Then he could dispense of his own as he thought fit. He pointed out what a very beggarly king he was who had nothing to play with, nor give to his servants. His nephew was too bashful in his own affairs—why did he not bear rule like other rulers?

'I am well enough,' came the reply stubborn with pride. 'I need not.'

He was asked for whom he would like money. They leapt into the boy's mind—beloved Cheke, Belmaine who taught him French, a bookbinder, the upright Master Latimer who preached the true Word from the sacred Book, the Lord Privy Seal's trumpeter who played when Edward skirmished in the garden at Hampton Court, dear cheerful Barnaby Fitzpatrick, the tumblers he had watched from a window in Greenwich Palace bouncing like balls, leaping and somersaulting for his delight. So motley a procession, jostling one another in his memory, all united by the same claim, he was their king. And his uncle not only accommodated him but provided further bounty for still another list of benefactions.

When the amounts he had relayed to his sovereign nephew through Fowler ran into three figures, the Admiral presented his account in kind. It was quite simple, all Edward had to do was use his royal prerogative and choose his own Governor. To achieve that he had merely to write a few lines to his Councillors asking them to transfer the Protectorate from his elder to his younger uncle.

Cornered, Edward faced the man he no longer liked or trusted. The memory of his tutor saved him. If Master Cheke agreed he should, he promised to write what his uncle wished.

As the Admiral was busy bribing his fellow Councillors, who demanded more than an easily pleased nephew, he had no doubt this underling would also prove amenable. He wrote out on a piece of paper what he wanted the tutor to make his pupil sign, 'My Lords, I pray you favour mine uncle's suit.' All the tutor had to do after that was to take it to the Council and the Lord Admiral would see to the rest. But the underling refused to do even that little. Opposition always made Seymour violent, and he assaulted the man with a battery of abuse.

His younger uncle's prophecy regarding my Lord Protector's essay into Scotland showed little sign of coming true, for the English virtually annihilated the Scots army. The battle of Pinkie Cleugh, when the 10th September 1547 was marked on calendars across the Border as Black Saturday, was celebrated by the English. Edward knew the tally off by heart: 11,000 Scots slain,

1,000 of them lairds, many prisoners taken, amongst them the Earl of Huntly, Chancellor of Scotland, for the loss of 51 English horsemen, almost all gentlemen, and one footman.

No invading army could subsist on a poor, barren country such as Scotland, and when the month's supplies the English had brought with them ran out the Lord Protector marched home, leaving behind him a trail of reeking landscape. He returned in such a blaze of glory it was overlooked that he had failed to bring with him the infant Queen of Scots.

Prayers had been said in English churches that Easter petitioning God to accomplish a marriage between King Edward and the Queen of Scots for the happy union of their realms. There were those, and the Lord Admiral was one, who hoped to benefit themselves by marrying the Lady Jane Grey to the King, but Edward himself did not contemplate her. It was his Scots cousin he desired, not his English one. He was a king's son and he looked for a king's daughter as his bride. Jane Grey was but the grand-daughter of his father's younger sister and her mother would take precedence before her. Mary Stewart was the grand-daughter of his father's elder sister who had married the Scots king.

It was marked when the young king bade goodbye to the Earl of Huntly, permitted to return to Scotland to effect the marriage, how eagerly he asked about little Mary Stewart, begging him to bring her back as his bride. 'The marriage may be weel enough,' the dour Scot replied to Somerset's question, 'but I haud not with the wooing of it.'

'The Scots and English being made one by amity, having the sea for a wall, mutual love for a garrison, and God for a defence should make so well agreeing a monarchy that neither in peace need they be ashamed, nor in war afraid of any worldly power.' The splendid sounding words of the Duke of Somerset's new proclamation rolled across the northern country that spring, with their tail lash that if his terms freely offered were not accepted he would chastise them again by fire and sword.

He did not lead the assault across the Border to carry out his threat in person. Because of his brother's intrigues, because of the sporadic unrest when the rearguard of the old religion withstood the inopportunity of the new, because of the dispossessed tenants with their flocks of hungry children clattering into London for redress against landlords who were turning their ploughlands into grass for sheep, he did not choose to leave the country for still another incursion into Scotland. Another went in his stead to show the power of England to a country too poor to plunder.

Mary was writing to the Lord Protector, a correspondence that as it accumulated became more and more controversial between two whose contacts in the past had been equable. Her father's will was the subject which entangled their relationship.

It had suited the Protector's purpose to suppress what he did not wish revealed, so he had no one to blame but himself that no denials on his part could uproot the widespread, erroneous belief that Henry VIII had forbidden in his will any change in religion during his son's minority.

Mary was painfully conscious of the sweeping changes made in her brother's name by his first Parliament. She heard of rude apprentices and flouting serving-men who called the sacrament of the altar the sacrament of the halter, and the holy bread Round Robin and Jack in the Box, knew that Stephen Gardiner, Bishop of Winchester, found himself in the Tower because he had preached before the boy king at Easter that the mass was the foundation of religion.

She was thirty-two now, a small woman whose beauty of complexion still gave her a deceptive look of youth, belied by the spareness of her face, the height of her angular brow. A foreign ambassador found her gaze keen and searching; it was neither, it was the gaze of a short-sighted woman straining to see what was before her.

After Whitsun, in the residence where she had newly arrived to re-establish her household, her half-sister Elizabeth was writing to their stepmother. Her breath came and went quickly, as it always did when she was disturbed. That it should have come to such a leave-taking from one to whom she owed so much, and one who was now in doubtful health, big and sickly with child.

With the permission of the Council, she, the King's sister, had remained in the Queen Dowager's care. These households of the great, moving from country manor to town mansion, furnished room for smaller self-contained units. Elizabeth when she joined her stepmother found her cousin Jane Grey there, with her attendants and tutor, to be schooled in the manners of the court. Elizabeth had her ladies, her tutor, her precious Kat now married to John Ashley, a distant cousin of her young mistress on the Boleyn side.

The girl must have learnt of her mother's terrible fate, but there are only two recorded instances of her having uttered her name. The knowledge of the death she had died must have lain at the bottom of her mind with the weight of stone. Throughout her long life she never let an opportunity pass without doing a benevolence whenever she could to any connection, however humble, of her mother's.

'Although,' she wrote, 'I could not be plentiful in giving thanks for the manifold kindnesses received at your Highness's hands at my departure.'

Wherever the Queen Dowager made her residence lacked neither charm nor even gaiety, and the enlightenment of the new learning. The tutors of Jane and Elizabeth were all Cambridge men, whose teaching was yoked to religion and the intellectual. The younger Jane's mind closed round what she was taught, Elizabeth's broadened and accommodated.

'Truly I was replete with sorrow to depart from your Highness,' she continued.

When the Queen Dowager married the Lord Admiral, Elizabeth, with grandiloquent thanks, had declined Mary's suggestion that her sister should join her household. It had been pleasurable to know that acceptance of such an offer on her part would have cast a slight on their stepmother.

'. . . And albeit I answered little,' her face flushed as she remembered, 'when you said you would warn me of all evils that you should hear of me.'

The twenty years between the rollicking new master and his wife's young charge had not stopped him romping with her as though they were of an age, but not like brother and sister. No brother would have parted her bed curtains in the morning, he still in undress, and made a dive at her. That was the excitement of it, the difference in their ages, and the knowledge he was not her brother.

Her stepmother, whose room was below hers, began to accompany her husband on these matutinal visits. Together they would tickle Elizabeth as she lay in bed. Once, in the garden, her stepmother had held her so that she could not run away while the Lord Admiral cut her gown into a hundred pieces. She was wearing a black gown that day.

It was when the Queen Dowager surprised her husband kissing her stepdaughter that the decision was reached, without dispute or question. The girl must leave.

'For if your Grace had not a good opinion of me, you would not have offered friendship to me that way, that all men judge the contrary. But what may I more say, thank God for providing such friends for me?'

It was finished at last, the letter that had to be written. The girl who penned it was not fifteen. Throughout that bourgeoning summer she was ill with blinding headaches, so that Kat did not go far from her. It was purveyed to every court in Europe through assiduous ambassadors that the Princess Elizabeth suffered from amenorrhoea—like her sister Mary.

And it was during that summer, in August 1548, when the English army was still in Scotland, that the six-year-old Queen of Scots was smuggled out of her country and convoyed safely across the sea.

Instead of bride to Edward King of England she was now trysted to the infant Dauphin of France.

Chapter Seven

The news was brought to Edward in the autumn of that year that his stepmother had died giving birth to a daughter. Even the tenuous connection he had had with her since his accession had been broken, for she had after her marriage inhabited her husband's town house at Chelsea and Sudeley Castle in Gloucestershire rather than rooms in one or other of the royal palaces to which as widow of the late monarch she had been entitled until her clandestine fourth marriage. But the death of the woman to whom he had written before he was nine that it was impossible for him to love her more must have affected the eleven-year-old boy now crowned king.

He discovered a new kingdom that winter where he could sit by himself not only writing but creating—his black and gold velvet desk with its silver-gilt inkpot, sand-boxes and seals, in which he could keep his very own treasures: some coins, a scent-burner Cheke had given him, the quadrant his father had left him, a set of astronomical instruments. He had always been fascinated by the starry firmament of God's heavens by which men guided their ships.

This was no translation of another man's English into French as he had done in the past. The subject, a treatise in French against the Pope's supremacy, may have been suggested by the tutor, but no Cheke looked over his shoulder as his unguided hand filled twenty-four pages with words which came at his bidding: 'Jesus wore a crown of thorns . . . but the pope has a triple crown . . . Jesus washed the feet of his disciples, but the pope has his feet blessed by kings . . . Jesus paid tribute but the pope receives all and pays nothing. . . Jesus healed the sick, but the pope rejoices in bloodshed. Christ bore his cross, but the pope is carried. Christ is a lamb, but the pope is a wolf . . . Christ ascended into heaven, but the pope will be cast into hell.'

He began his treatise at the end of December and finished it in March. From that day his active pen was seldom still. They followed one after the other, dissertations, essays, discourses on the Reformation of Abuses, 'these sores' with their carefully annotated medicines and plasters, commentaries on good laws and statutes, which should be made plainer and shorter that they could be better understood. There were papers on what the young author called 'devices', such as the reforming of the service of the Order of the Garter by removing St George in entirety as a superstition, an innovation that left speechless the Lords of his Council, all adherents in varying degrees of intensity of the new religion.

He dedicated his treatise against the Pope's supremacy to his uncle, 'Lord Protector of his person and defender of the realm', whose wife about the same time let the King see a small volume dedicated to herself which was not only translated but illuminated by a young kinsman of Edward.

It is not known what Edward thought as he turned over the tiny pages, rich with borderings and coloured initials, of 'Paleario's Treatise of the Benefit of the Death of Christ', whether he was critical of or piqued by the work of a fellow author, or if he wondered about the writer, a young man whose nursery and schoolroom had been the grim walls of the Tower since his father, the Marquis of Exeter, of the Pole family, had been executed there and his grandmother mown down because of their Plantagenet blood, a young man who in his narrow existence had never learnt to master a horse or handle the long bow. It is unlikely that Edward realized his kinsman was detained in prison because it was in the interests of those enjoying his inheritance to keep him there.

On the title-page he read the words written in gold: 'To the right virtuous lady and gracious princess Anne, duchess of Somerset, Edward Courtenay, the sorrowful captive, wisheth all honour and felicity.' Perhaps the word princess caught his bright gaze because he wrote firmly to her on the title page the monitory sentence: 'Faith is dead if it be without workes, Your loving nevew Edward.' And on the last page of all the recommendation: 'Live to die, and die to live again. Your nevew Edward.'

Parliament reassembled after the Twelve Days of Christmas and London was full as lords and commoners rode to Whitehall. The Book of Common Prayer was made law by the Act of Uniformity which replaced mass by the Supper of the Lord. It became known as King Edward's Liturgy, and the King was described as the most noble ruler of his ship, even our most comfortable

Noah. Shorn of symbol, the service was to be said aloud in plain English. And the Commons, restless with Somerset's autocracy, asked that His Majesty should be better ordered and not kept so close.

The subject of their consideration was fast asleep as usual on a night in the middle of January when he was awakened by the sudden warning barking of his pet dog outside the inner door of his bedroom. The next minute the whole palace was startled by the report of a pistol shot. Before it could echo, the dog's furious barking abruptly ceased.

The speeding of footsteps down long passages, shouts afar off and raised voices nearing—Edward and his chamber servants heard them all, as the gentlemen of his Privy Chamber hastened into his room.

It was his Uncle Seymour who had shot his little dog dead, his Uncle Seymour who had a master key to let himself into the private garden and so reach his bedroom without having to pass through the palace, who had come with two servants in the howe-dumb-dead of the night to kidnap him and, finding the door unexpectedly bolted on the other side, had silenced his faithful dog by shooting it. All he could say when he was discovered, smoking pistol in hand, was, 'I wished to know whether His Majesty was safely guarded.'

It was pieced together for the King bit by bit in the days to come, as count after count was laid against the Lord Admiral, now in the Tower, all of which he defiantly repudiated. The Master of the Mint had been clapped in too, who had betrayed his trust by producing counterfeit coin to pay the troops Seymour had raised and hoped to use after he had kidnapped the King and murdered not only his brother the Lord Protector but all others who stood in his way.

His Council, and in particular his uncle Somerset, believed the King was very fond of his younger uncle and that there might be some difficulty to receive his assent for the signing of the death warrant. He was unaware, for he only thought of his nephew as an adjunct to himself not as a personality in his own right, that the boy's affection for his attractive brother had dried into distrust. He did not take into consideration the shock the eleven-year-old king must have received when he learnt the explanation of the uproar on the other side of his bedroom door, when he knew who it was who had shot his faithful dog, a royal boy in whose consciousness lay half-buried memories of the ominous deaths of other royal boys, minors as he was a minor.

Depositions were taken from everyone, even from the King himself, of earlier contacts and conversations each had had with the imprisoned Lord Admiral. His Majesty's truthfulness must have chilled the Protector when he saw it transcribed. To the insinuating remark of his younger brother about himself, 'Your uncle is old, and I trust he will not live long', had come the revealing response from their nephew, 'It were better he were dead'.

One of the thirty-five counts against the Lord Admiral was his presumptuous and illegal courtship of the Princess Elizabeth whom he hoped to marry, murder his lawful sovereign and usurp the crown as husband of his sovereign's sister.

If the Council could prove that the Lord Admiral had proposed to the Princess Elizabeth, which they had forbidden him to do, the penalty was death. If they could prove that the Princess had accepted his proposal, she too was guilty of treason, for neither she nor her sister Mary could marry without their consent. But the commissioner sent to interrogate Elizabeth could extract nothing from her, although he could see from her face she was guilty. He assured the Protector the Princess had a good wit and nothing was gotten of her but by great policy.

Unfortunately for Elizabeth a great deal was gotten from her cofferer, whose accounts were found to be in a disgraceful condition, and from Mrs Ashley, her governess or mistress, when they were held in the Tower for questioning.

If the Princess admitted that Mrs Ashley or her cofferer had urged her to accept the Lord Admiral, then the Council could place the blame squarely on their doorstep, but Elizabeth refused to admit any such thing even when, aghast, she read their signed confessions.

Her treasure of a Kat was a born babbler, and she had told the cofferer the reason why the Princess had been forced to leave her stepmother's charge. There it was, tumbled on the pages for all to see.

Kat had always wanted the Lord Admiral for a husband for her. 'Your old husband now is free again,' she told the girl after the Dowager Queen's death, 'you may have him if ye will.' 'Nay,' Elizabeth replied. 'Ywiss!' exclaimed Kat, 'you will not deny if my Lord Protector and the Council were pleased therewith.' When Elizabeth drew the card representing the Lord Admiral, she would laugh and blush, and Mistress Ashley would crow with triumph.

Every conversation her cofferer, when he came to London, had had with the Lord Admiral was there for her enemies to read: how the Lord Admiral prevailed on him to urge his young mistress to speed the grant of lands to which she was entitled under her father's will; how the Lord Admiral wanted them in the west, near his own; how the Lord Admiral was warned the Council would never agree to the grant if he married her before it was through.

But despite the damaging confessions, they were unable to incriminate the Princess, who wrote indignantly to the Protector regarding the shameful slanders that were going abroad against her honour and honesty, both of which she esteemed above all else, that she was in the Tower and with child to my Lord Admiral. She prayed that he might let her come to court to see the King's Majesty that she might show herself there as she was.

Her prayer was not answered. The Council considered Mrs Ashley, still in the Tower, a totally unsuitable person to be mistress to the King's sister and sent the commissioner's wife to take her place. The Princess wept all that night, and loured all the next day. After informing the commissioner if she had not Mistress Ashley for her mistress she wanted none, she took it ill when he told her she needed a mistress every single hour and would be better with two.

It was noticed she began to droop as the trial drew to its close, and she heard that the prisoner's houses were to be dispersed. The commissioner's wife reported that Her Grace could now not bear to hear the prisoner miscalled and spoke up for him as she had not been wont to do.

Keenly she was watched when told of his unrepentant death, and is reported to have said, 'This day died a man of much wit and very little judgment', an epitaph so fitting it reveals much preparation in its composition.

She was ill throughout that summer, and Mistress Ashley was allowed to return to her in August. The following month her cofferer once more joined her household, but from then onwards his young mistress examined his accounts herself and no new page was turned until she had signed the last one.

She lived most circumspectly at Hatfield, her favourite manor, built of rose-flushed bricks, spending her days in study with the famous Ascham, reading the New Testament in Greek, and passages from Sophocles chosen by her tutor to strengthen her mind against misfortune. She translated passages from one foreign language into another, and spent three hours daily poring over her favourite study, history.

Ascham could not speak too highly of his pupil, it was not only the grasp and reach of her strong mind which impressed him but the becoming modesty of her manners, the simplicity of her dress, her smooth unadorned hair.

She wrote often to her brother, explaining that any irregularity in her correspondence was not prompted by her slothful hand but because of her aching head, and took care when writing to him in Latin to inscribe herself, 'I, whom from your tender infancy, have ever been your fondest sister.'

The year 1549 was not a propitious one for any of Henry's three children. After the dust of his younger uncle's execution had settled, a period of isolation set round Edward. His beloved Cheke had been removed from him, and was now back in Cambridge, because the Council had discovered he had accepted fifteen pounds from the Lord Admiral. And Mary, like Elizabeth, was ill throughout the summer months, irked by the arduous letters she had to write to the Council, who had drawn her attention to the law to which she was not conforming that mass was now forbidden and must be replaced by the new service.

Mary's replies were not shortened by one word no matter how ill she felt. After bidding her chaplain sing more solemnly than ever three masses instead of two, she baldly assured her correspondents she had offended no law, unless a recent law of their own making for the altering of matters in religion, which her conscience told her was not worthy to have the name of law but was an offence to God.

Not only Mary repudiated the new service. The men of Devonshire and Cornwall refused to receive it, saying it was like a Christmas game. They clapped their hands for joy when they told the priest they would have none of the new fashions and he gladly put on his cope and vestments and said mass in Latin. They demanded the religion of their fathers and the extinction of Protestantism by fire and sword, and suggested that the Lord Cardinal Pole, who was of the King's blood, should be sent for from Rome and promoted to be one of the King's Council.

Not only had the Protector a religious rebellion on his hands but civil war. He sent too few troops to quell the rebellion so that reinforcements had to be called for; and he issued a proclamation in London against the robber gentry, which meant nothing to them or their victims in Norfolk or Suffolk. The peasants took the law and the countryside into their own hands, tore down the paling and hedges the landlords had erected to enclose common ground and killed the sheep and deer grazing where they had lived before they were evicted.

Nothing was hidden from the young king. One of the landowners, come to appeal for help against his tenants before the King's Grace and the Lord Protector, never forgot the boy's grief and perplexity, or his distress when he learnt that his uncle was contemplating another invasion of Scotland before the year was out.

The bridge over the Thames at Staines was destroyed for fear of an attack on London. His fellow Councillors overruled the Protector and the reinforcements sent were German and Italian musketeers. Never before in the history of England had their rulers used alien troops against their own flesh and blood. In their fury the outnumbered, half-armed villagers hurled themselves against trained and equipped mercenaries. This was not war, it was massacre.

A second assault on Norwich was led by the Earl of Warwick. Many of his men had already been defeated, and there was little heart for attack. Instead they urged retreat until the arrival of reinforcements, but their commander was too much of a soldier to abandon his post—death was better than dishonour, the rebellion would be put down or he would lose his life. According to the ancient custom in times of great peril, he and his fellow knights kissed each other's blades, thus swearing fealty to one another.

They won back Norwich, and the battles that followed, killing three and a half thousand in their cavalry charges. In the blaze of that summer bodies swung from gibbets on village greens and gallows-trees as a warning of what happened to rebels, and the Earl of Warwick, smouldering like an ember at the Council table, was the hero of the day, not the Duke of Somerset, who issued a general pardon.

The Council blamed the Princess Mary as the instigator of and menace behind it all, whose face was set against them, the rulers of the country, every one a landowner. No matter how the rebels against the new service and the peasants against their masters swore loyalty to the King, everyone knew they were countrymen clinging to the old faith and a left-off way of living in their rude villages and remote, unenlightened towns. The King's elder sister was the conduit by which the rats of Rome would creep into their stronghold unless every step were taken to block her.

Cheke was back with Edward; he had won his return by writing the official reply to the demands of the rebels. But nothing in this dread year was as it had been. The King was at Hampton Court at the beginning of October. There was nothing untoward about that: the gay, brilliant interior had always delighted his father who had embellished the palace of a primate of the Church into a country residence fit for an athletic king, whose various queens had delighted in its gardens.

But there was something untoward about this visit—the people around him for instance, his preoccupied uncle, his godfather, the Archbishop of Canterbury, Sir William Paget and Sir William Petre and one or two other members of the Council, Mr Cecil, his uncle's industrious secretary, a small man with a domed head—whose concerted presence began to achieve an uneasy significance.

It was his uncle, now sleeping in the room next to his, who broke the terrifying news that there was a conspiracy against him, the King. The conspirators were certain Lords of the Council whose aim was not only to depose the Lord Protector and Defender of his royal person, but to murder him since they knew that only over his dead body could they hope to seize the King.

The palace suddenly filled as five hundred armed men in the Seymour livery arrived to guard both nephew and uncle, and Edward wrote a letter dictated by his uncle to two of the commanders who had led his troops in the late troubles to rescue them from the conspirators with all the forces they could muster.

There was something claustrophobic about the next twenty-four hours, when the smallest happening within became magnified as they waited for the answer that never came from without. Sir William Petre was sent from Hampton Court to parley with the conspirators. He did not return, instead he joined the conspirators.

Edward was wakened by his uncle, telling him they must be gone. The moat round Hampton Court had been filled, but it was a palace, not a fortress, and they must make for the stronghold of Windsor under cover of darkness before their enemies could arrive to take them. The child was not only dressed but armed, with the jewelled dagger his father had given him.

Flanked by his uncle and godfather with Paget and Mr Cecil, King Edward left the palace. Trumpeters heralding his approach, the tiny procession was lit with flaring torches and surrounded by yeomen of the Guard as it came out under the archway of the Clock Tower.

The green without was thronged not with soldiers, come from all over England to his rescue, but with a jostling crowd armed only with curiosity.

Once over the stone bridge the party stopped, and Edward looked at his uncle for his signal. Ever prompt, the boy stepped forward to address the jostling crowd.

'Good people,' his youthful voice rang out through the dark, 'I pray you be good to us—and to our uncle.'

The good people cheered vociferously. His uncle was now beside him, had taken his hand, his uncle—that tower of strength on which the world could rely.

'I shall not fall alone,' the boy heard the familiar, full-throated voice declare. 'If I am destroyed, the kingdom will be destroyed. Kingdom, commonwealth—all will be destroyed together.' The nephew felt himself thrust forward that there could be no mistake his uncle was pointing at him. 'It is not I that they shoot at—this is the mark that they shoot at.'

Sparks flew from their restless horses' hoofs as they mounted, reining in not to cause hurt when they moved through the crowd. A picture has come down to us from a spectator of the young king, white-faced through the dark, waving his dagger and shouting to his people, 'Will you help me against those who would kill me?' They roared back at him, 'God save Your Grace! We will die for you!'

Together the boy and man galloped through the night and did not draw rein until the bulk of Windsor Castle loomed through the darkness to which their eyes had grown accustomed The great entrance hall, the chill of stone upon it, swallowed their voices. They were joined by Paget and Cranmer, who was determined above all else to remain beside his godson, and some hundreds of armed men, the noise of whose arrival slammed through the castle. Edward, unable in this nightmare to know who was friend and who foe, asked, 'What do you here at such an hour?' 'Sir,' his godfather attempted to assure him, 'suffice it that we are here.'

No preparations had been made for the unexpected guests and the castle was unprovided with the most ordinary necessities. It yawned with corridors where the bulge of stone was uncovered by arras. 'Methinks I am in prison—here are no galleries and no gardens to walk in,' Edward said to Paget on the second day of their sojourn. It was then the councillor noticed he had caught cold.

Paget was the Protector's best friend. Backed by Cranmer he persuaded Somerset to allow them to mediate between him and the Lords in London, who had already given assurances that, though criticism had been made of him as Lord Protector, attack on his person was out of the question.

Somerset knew the day was lost: the two commanders of the King's troops had declared themselves for the Lords, who put their promise in writing that he would be deprived of neither honour nor property if he would submit to the formality of arrest. On their faith and honour they promised him safety: all they desired was the reconstruction of the Protectorate.

Edward was in good spirits when he received the Lords at Windsor three days later. He showed no trace of cold and welcomed them all with a merry countenance and a loud voice. He presided over the meeting, when he was told of the Lord Protector's faults, ambitions and vainglory, how he had entered into rash wars, and been negligent of defences, enriched himself at His Grace's expense, ever followed his own opinion, nipped those who did not agree with him, and did all by his own authority —all of which his nephew can have had little difficulty in believing.

The Protector begged only for his life, which was granted him by gracious order of the King, and pleaded guilty to all the charges laid against him. When he rose from his knees after making full submission he had lost the Protectorate, marshalship, all his movables, vast lands and two hundred manors.

The shock of what he had been through and the loss of the familiar depressed and unsettled Edward. Care was taken to distract him with outdoor sports and pastimes. England's bravest fighting man and best lance was there to encourage him to arm and tilt, manage horses, draw the bow, run at the ring and com-

89

pete in tourneys. Unlike his uncle Somerset, the Earl of Warwick had always time to shoot at the butts with him. This tall, dark, vital man, vibrant as a bow of yew, resistant to stretch and compression, did not converse with Edward as an uncle with his nephew but as though the boy were a man.

The Council had not rid themselves of one Lord Protector to allow another to take his place, and none was so stout in this belief as the Earl of Warwick, slipping into fourth place of the oligarchy. Unlike Somerset he listened to advice and the precise and imperious French were approached about a treaty which the able Paget advocated. England would have to agree to evacuate Boulogne, that costly feather in every Englishman's cap, leaving all its fortifications, for the tune of four hundred thousand pounds, and could not press her age-long claim for pension since France was obviously not going to pay it. That would leave only Calais, but the disease of war would be cured and across the Channel Henri II would be England's good friend instead of dangerous enemy. As the negotiations began to ripen Edward received from the Emperor Charles the gift fit for a king of two superb Spanish horses.

On his return from Cambridge Cheke encouraged his pupil to summarize such events as debates in Council, dispatch of ambassadors, honours conferred, and 'other remarks as he thought good'. Notes were written down for him to copy into the thick red volume with its gold clasps which he called his journal. The initial entry, like a prologue, is a précis of the first nine years of his own life compressed for him into half a dozen short sentences. 'The yere of our Lord 1537 was a prince born to king harry th' eight,' Edward began enjoyably in his own up and down writing on the virgin page.

The voice of a tutor can be heard in the factual entries written in the third person, but in these written in the first it is an eager boy who pens other remarks he thought good. 'I lost the challenge of shooting but won at rovers.' Chagrin cannot be concealed when he writes of another contest, 'And my band touched often, which was counted as nothing, and took nothing, which seemed strange, and so was of my side last.' His love of rich stuffs, shared by both his sisters, and his eye for colour, are revealed in his descriptions of ceremonial, but foreign and military affairs take precedence over all else.

The precarious financial situation of the country was also a preoccupation with its careful ruler. The government were in the position ·of all heavily involved debtors, in this case to foreign bankers, having to pay for more accommodation at ruinous rates of interest. The King was being secretly briefed by the Clerk of the Council, and the prolific notes in his journal on the subject give the impression he was keeping watch on his Council. His earnestness was not overlooked by some who foresaw the nemesis bound to overtake his advisers when their young master attained the steadiness of age and handled such affairs himself. Northumberland was ever one to cast in his hand deep.

Edward was no longer told of and expected to subscribe to decisions after they had been taken: he would sit on occasion at the Council table himself listening to the pitch and toss of debate, able when all turned to him to pronounce his opinion with clarity, learning to divide the subject into heads as he had already learnt when writing his treatises, wise enough to leave the final pronouncement to the Lords. So that the Venetian ambassador noted that no other sovereign was so much beloved by his counsellors or country as was King Edward of England, nor was any who gave greater promise.

Perhaps there was not the same zealous attendance at sermons that there was in the good Duke's day, but the Earl of Warwick was winning for himself a great name as a reformer, giving posts to foreign and other uncompromising Protestant divines, and encouraging their access to the King. The boy's religious fervour sometimes outran even his most zealous mentors as when, going through the service of consecration with Hooper before he was made a bishop, his gaze fell on the wording of the oath, 'So help me God, all saints and the holy evangelists.' 'What wickedness is here, Hooper?' he exclaimed excitably and, crossing out the offending passage, wrote clearly above, 'So help me God, through Jesus Christ.'

Only Cheke realized the pressures that were being exerted by the people, the preachers, the politicians, on his pupil, who rose with aplomb to every demand, and the tutor tried to prevail on some of the divines to approach the King through him. But the Earl of Warwick's suggestion that His Majesty should sign all the principal resolutions passed by the Council entailed his presence at most of their meetings. Very soon it was not thought necessary for the members of the Council even to append their signatures. No longer was the royal prerogative a token but a reality.

The one-time Protector was allowed to leave the Tower in February, not four months after he had entered it, when he gave a bond for his good behaviour, which he meticulously kept. Master Cecil, who had been taken there with his master, was permitted to leave it before him, and soon became the Earl of Warwick's assiduous secretary, attending on the King before a Council meeting to acquaint him with the business of the day, and assured by the Princess Elizabeth that she knew he did not forget her. The secretary was a distant kinsman of her cofferer.

Nothing could have been more cordial than the King's reception of the Duke of Somerset when nephew and uncle warmly embraced. He dined with His Majesty, was invited to become once more one of the court circle and resumed his duties as a Privy Councillor.

Never before had so powerful a personage had so gentle an unseating. He had asked for his life, now he had not only life but liberty and the restoration of property which had not already been granted elsewhere. But although little difference could be seen in the familiar noble figure, he was like the fabled eagle blinded because it had flown too near the sun, who walked as one accustoming himself to another sphere.

The Duke's reconciliation with the Earl was sealed in June when Warwick's eldest son was married to the eldest of Somerset's six daughters. The King graced the wedding with his presence, and the glad day was given over to feasting and dancing, and the spectacle of tourney. After supper he rode back to Westminster through the dusk of a summer's night.

The five sons in Warwick's quiver were again out in strength the following day when Robert was married to Amy Robsart, daughter of Sir John Robsart. It was not so important a wedding as yesterday's. Robert might be the handsomest of the Dudley brood all glittering with good looks but he was the third son, not the heir. Nevertheless the wedding of a son of the Earl of Warwick was important enough to warrant the King's presence, who watched instead of the chivalric combat of yesterday a carnival of sports and pastimes, culminating in the gentlemen guests hanging a live goose from a pole and fighting each other for the prize of its head. It was a lusty age, when every nobleman kept his own bear-garden.

The progress Edward made in autumn was a short one, but wherever he stopped became the focal point for whole families of the great to pay reverence to their young sovereign. Their importance was measured by the length of their retinue, and much the longest was that which followed the Marquis and Marchioness of Dorset, so soon to become the Duke and Duchess of Suffolk, to be received by the King at Oxford.

It was the month of October when he and his cousin Jane, their eldest daughter, attained their thirteenth year. The boy's Tudor fairness had that dazzling quality which attracts attention; her hair was sandy, not quite red. He was growing apace, his long straight legs giving promise that he would be tall like his mother and father, without his father's bigness. She was small but prettily formed, which made for grace; she gave an impression of stillness, only her eyes lively under their arched brows and her pretty mouth mobile, revealing little white teeth.

She had returned to her parents after the Queen Dowager's death, at whose funeral she had been the chief mourner, but it was not long before she again rejoined the household of the Lord Admiral, who had pledged her father, for the promise of two thousand pounds, he would marry her to the King's Majesty— once he had unclasped the King from his brother's hold.

If to find herself in the Queen's household had been paradise to little Jane Grey, to return to her parents, after the Lord Admiral's arrest, no nearer a king's bride than she had ever been, was hell. Children were not brought up tenderly in her day, but neither of her sisters received such severe treatment from their parents as did Jane. Of course neither of her sisters looked upon their gambling pursuits, their sporting proclivities and other amusements as indulgences and dissipations. Neither Katherine not Mary sided as Jane did with the Dorsets' chaplain, who took his patrons to task for the extravagance of their dress and for allowing their tenants to celebrate Christmas with the pagan rites of the old religion.

Mary had always been very fond of her small second cousin Jane, and when the delighted Dorsets were invited to spend Christmas with her she gave the girl a pearl and ruby necklace. She probably did not hear of the reception another gift of hers received when the reluctant recipient eyed the shining dress of tinsel cloth of gold and velvet with parchment lace and demanded what she should do with it. 'Marry, wear it, to be sure,' her old nurse told her briskly. 'Nay,' the difficult Jane rejoined, 'that were a shame to follow my Lady Mary against God's word, and leave my Lady Elizabeth which followeth God's word.' But it certainly was repeated to Mary what her young cousin said when she passed through her chapel where the Host stood on the altar as it always had stood, although forbidden by the law of the land. 'How can He be there who made us all, and the baker made him?' Jane wanted to know.

Mary's prescience warned her that the fall of the Protector and the rise of the dark star Warwick boded no good for her or her fellow religionists. Summoned to Windsor, she delayed as long as she could, pleading ill health, knowing full well she would be questioned by her brother and his Council regarding the strange rumours he had heard about her mass. But in December she was forced to obey the command.

To her brother she paid the deference of His Majesty's humble, obedient and unworthy sister. She offered her soul to God, and her body to His Majesty's service. When she said she would rather His Majesty took away her life than the old religion, in which she desired to live and die, he replied stiffly he desired no such sacrifice. His Lords repeated to him her hope that His Grace would not be wroth with her, his poor suppliant, till he was of an age to judge for himself, and the voice of the elder sister was heard again when she told him before them, 'Riper age and experience will teach Your Majesty much more yet.' 'You also may have somewhat to learn,' he replied sharply, 'none are too old for that.'

In her man's voice, both before her brother and facing them alone, Mary bludgeoned the Lords with the truth. She reminded them they had said no masses for her father's soul as he had commanded in his will, that she was the daughter of the King who had made them out of nothing, snapped back that her father's will had made her subject to them only in the matter of her marriage, revealed her contempt by declaring she knew them to be all of one sort, that their deeds were always ill towards her, that they wanted her death, and hardened His Majesty against her.

'How now, my lady?' she heard herself interrupted loudly by the Earl of Warwick. 'It seemeth that Your Grace is trying to show us in a hateful light to the King our master without any cause whatsoever.'

His colour was high, but his long narrow face, the eyes watchful under their peaked brows, had a shorn look, for he did not wear his beard flowing as did other men. It and his moustache were neatly clipped to reveal his red mouth with its protruding underlip.

Two of her chaplains were in the Tower when she was summoned to London in March. She entered the city at the head of a long retinue of peers, knights and gentlemen at arms. She and each of her followers wore the badge of their faith, a black rosary and cross. The faithful tramped miles through the fields to welcome her, and Catholic townsmen followed the procession from Fleet Street and along the Strand. Once they were home and could speak freely behind locked doors, they told of what they had witnessed and felt that day, of the armoured horsemen they had seen in the clouds and the three suns all at the one time in the sky, and of how the earth had shaken under their feet from one end of the city to the other.

To lead into London followers proclaiming they were adherents of a prohibited religion was not only ill-advised but senseless, for it achieved nothing except a consolidation of the Lords against her, and was a cruel offence to her young brother.

To Protestants the terrible plague that had swept off close on a thousand souls in London alone by the end of January was clearly divine punishment because His laws were not being carried out by the rulers of the land. There had been dire forms of the sweating sickness in the past but none surely of such horror as this type called New Acquaintance and Know-Thy-Master. Now spring was here, it showed little signs of abating, nor would it until this evil in their midst was extirpated and God's Holy Word was obeyed.

Yet she won the hard-fought honours of that visit and was allowed to leave of her own free will by a surprisingly submissive Council.

A day or two after her departure, a Council of bishops and peers prayed for the King's presence. Instead of the orderly Master Cecil it was one of the Lords himself who waited upon him, and some of the man's agitation was communicated to the boy who entered the Council Chamber in haste and perturbation, as though his realm were about to be sacked.

His disquiet was not calmed when he heard his Council, on their knees, imploring him to a man to allow the Lady Mary her mass—for the time being. The startled boy demanded the reason of so sudden a change of front, and a very hot letter from the Emperor, which the Council had received during Mary's visit, was read out to him declaring war on England if his cousin the Princess were not suffered to use her mass. And England was not ready for war until she had France bound to her as an ally, when it would not be in the Emperor's interest to wage it.

In the battle that followed Edward found himself deserted, a lonely champion whose reinforcements were all invisible, facing a united front. The Lords themselves took little part. Warwick had seen to that by consulting the clergy first before the burden of decision was thrust on the boy king, but they supplied a rearguard of numbers.

Edward heard the man who had consecrated him as Christ's Vicar to see God truly worshipped declare that there were good kings in the Old Testament who suffered ill alterations and yet were good kings. His royal godson reminded the Archbishop of Canterbury of the evil Abraham had done when he lay with Agar, and when David took Uriah's wife—did Scripture set out that we should do as they? He tried to rally his listeners to fear God with him rather than set God's will aside to please an emperor. The danger to trade was mentioned, England's best customers were lands unfortunately included in the Emperor's realms, and was countered by what had happened to their forefathers when they broke their covenant. He who had preserved David would preserve him. Unconsciously he was echoing his sister Mary's words when he said he would rather lose his life and all he had than agree to what was wrong. It was pointed out his life was not his own, that all he had was the charge of the realm, at which he broke down, crying, 'I will shed my tears for both.' Not all his godfather's reassurances could comfort him as he realized he was being overruled. 'Be content, be content,' he sobbed, and told them what he had once told his Uncle Seymour, 'Let me alone.'

His sister Elizabeth was what their half-sister Mary was not, a learner. Already she knew not to repeat her own mistakes and was learning from those she saw others make. No one could have carried herself more modestly than she when allowed once more to visit her brother. A king's daughter attracted attention because she was a king's daughter, but the young Elizabeth stood out because she was so different from the others of her sex who formed the court circle. Where their costumes were rich and elaborate as fashion dictated, hers were simple; where they sparkled and shone with jewels, she went unadorned; where their hair was curled and double-curled, hers was glossy. As she moved quietly to and from private audiences with her brother, no one thought to remember the wild tales which had disgraced her name so short a time ago.

And Edward was happy for her to be with him, he called her his sweetest, dearest sister, and his sweet sister Temperance. Perhaps his only uneasiness after her departure was regarding her ardour for Protestantism. Certainly she had no leanings to the old false faith and her godly zeal was much praised, but she had taken no steps when earlier he had tried to enlist her help to convert Mary. He did not realize that even at seventeen Elizabeth knew not to involve herself in the impossible.

His sister Mary's victory was short-lived. The Lords, no longer intimidated by the Emperor's threats since the French alliance was strengthened by treaties, could move in against her, and for two years her household had no mass. The harried Mary had to send away her chaplains for their own sakes. She herself had mass but behind locked doors and in fear and trembling. Only three of her most devoted servants knew of it, knew which in their midst was a priest in disguise who could give to their mistress what she could not live without.

Joyous festivals and celebrations that summer, in which neither of his sisters took part, sealed the friendship with the French and the betrothal of the King of England with the King of France's eldest daughter Isabel. Nothing, even an almost empty exchequer, was allowed to dim the splendour of the English entertainment of the embassade from across the Channel. The guests were loaded with magnificent gifts and ate from plates of gold which had recently enriched mitres, relics, missals and primers.

The Duke of Somerset was one of the Earl of Warwick's supporters when he was created Duke of Northumberland. Yet he had not been consulted about any of the honours conferred that day, although as one of the Council he should have been. Still another straw to show in which direction the wind rising against him was veering.

He watched his one-time secretary kneel Master Cecil and rise Sir Robert, and one after the other each of the new duke's faction ennobled by his nephew the King. The Marquis of Dorset was now created Duke of Suffolk. He and his wife had exculpated themselves of any hand in the Lord Admiral's treason by supplying the Privy Council with most useful evidence against their prisoner.

To Edward this investiture was not as others when he raised the known and unknown. It was the day before his fourteenth birthday and he who was born to give had the joy of knighting two of those he loved the most when he made his tutor Sir John Cheke and his friend Sir Henry Sidney, both of whom as Gentlemen of his Privy Chamber were close to him. Henry's star was high, for he was trysted to lovely Mary Dudley, daughter of the new duke. Her father wore his garnered honours with the distinction of one who has merited them.

So valiant a Protestant as he was held in high repute by the clergy and visiting divines, one of whom declared he was always with the King and like a father to him, adding, 'He governs all.' The imperial ambassador noticed he was dismissed when the King received the signal from the Duke, on whom he kept his gaze. But Northumberland had much for His Majesty's ear when clergy, divines, ambassadors, functionaries and attendants were not present. He began therefore to cultivate the habit of visiting the boy in his bedroom at night, and to Edward there was a certain thrill about these talks with this dark man in the silent short hours of the morning. His Majesty would startle and discompose the Lords at the next Council meeting with his knowledge of questions on hand which had certainly not been inspired by Master Cecil's careful notes.

His midnight visitor distilled into his hearer's mind, drop by drop, information regarding the Duke of Somerset. His uncle was beginning to voice singular policies with which none of the Lords could possibly agree—just as though he were Lord Protector again. He had advocated that Gardiner, the Bishop of Winchester, should be freed and restored to his diocese—His Majesty would remember the sermon he had preached before him on St Peter's Day when he said that the mass, that abomination, was the foundation of religion; and there could be no doubt that the one-time Lord Protector was planning to reinstate the popish religion, for now he was pleading toleration for the Lady Mary.

Days before Edward's uncle felt for the second time within two years the touch on his shoulder, the plot which lodged him once more in the Tower was recorded with breathless urgency in his nephew's diary, how the Earl of Warwick and divers others were to be called to a banquet and there have their heads cut off, how the apprentices of London were to be incited to rise up and the great seal taken, how the Duke of Somerset willed that the alliance with France be broken and he, the King, marry his third daughter, the Lady Jane Seymour.

There was so much in his own experience to colour what he heard about his uncle, and no friend of the Duke of Somerset dared show himself at court, but there is evidence that the nephew did not accept everything he was told. In his journal he noted that Somerset confessed to having planned the assassinations; when he wrote to his friend Barnaby Fitzpatrick he used the expression 'which he seemed to have confessed'. No word of this confession appears in the closely written records of the trial. And we know, although we do not know their contents, that he refused to sign at this time certain documents placed before him.

Of that scene enacted behind closed doors, the imperial and French ambassadors passed judgment on the little they heard. The Spanish ambassador declared firmly, 'His Majesty is supposed to grieve for his uncle's arrest, but that I do not believe. His mind is poisoned against him.' But the Frenchman was of the opinion he had pleaded for Somerset's life.

To be opposed by the very boy to whom he had given the authority of decision was for Northumberland like the master being outmatched by his pupil. His reaction was all the more violent because it cloaked, even from himself, his helplessness. Edward heard him rage and storm as he had heard his uncle Somerset rage and storm.

He was depressed as the year drove to its end and his uncle waited in the Tower for his execution. It had not been a good year for England. In April he had had to show himself to his people to damp down flaring rumour that he had succumbed to Know-Thy-Master, and in August his Council had proclaimed the shilling was now worth sixpence and the groat twopence, so that it was said men lost their friends by the sweat and their money by the proclamation. A bad harvest for the second year running added to the misery of rising prices and the issuing of coin two-thirds of which was base metal.

Every effort was made to divert His Majesty. When he moved to Greenwich to keep the Twelve Days of Christmas the festivities to entertain him had never been more brilliant or varied. He wrote of them in his journal the day after, on 7th January, finishing with the words, 'Then a banquet of 120 dishes. This was the end of Christmas.'

Chapter Eight

Edward was with the imperial ambassador on the morning of 22nd January 1552 in the Palace of Westminster when they heard passing outside a great concourse of people. The sounds they made were curious, they did not march like soldiers but seemed to stumble like cattle, and in the suddenly stilled room shuddering sobs could be heard broken by cries for judgment to fall from above. To the King's wondering question, the ambassador replied that it was the crowds returning from the execution of the Duke of Somerset on Tower Hill that morning. The silence was long before His Majesty said, 'I would not have believed that he would have been a traitor.'

Edward lived very fully; as well as his studies, ceremonial, affairs of State, he was hardy enough to undertake the most strenuous exercises with the tirelessness of youth. Except for a quartan fever when he was four, he had enjoyed perfect health until April of this year. Then he fell ill of what his doctors diagnosed as measles and smallpox, though he was left unpocked. He could not have survived such a combination, and was probably suffering from a very bad attack of measles, which prepared the ground for the assault of something more deadly.

The imperial ambassador, who saw him at the end of the month, reported that he was completely recovered and in high spirits. Edward himself wrote lightly to his friend Barnaby Fitzpatrick saying he had been ill of 'the smallpox, which hath letteth us to write hitherto, but now we have shaken that quite away'. It was some weeks later that the imperial ambassador noticed His Majesty had some difficulty in reading letters from the Emperor, as though his eyes were troubling him.

Although his recovery seemed complete, his portraits begin to portray him still handsome but fragile, his head a little to one side, which gives him a wistful look. He was now in his fifteenth year, approaching that age fatal to so many male contemporaries of his race, when both his father's elder brother Arthur and his own half-brother, the illegitimate Duke of Richmond, had succumbed to consumption.

He spent most of the spring that year at his pleasant palace of Greenwich set in green pasture-lands, only the river a-stir with barge, boat and ship, branching with masts and billowing with sails amongst which the winds tugged and drummed. Never had he been more lively or gay, looking forward to his first really important progress, the first of many he would take in the years to come, as his predecessors had done before him, travelling deep into England, his England, to see his own people and be seen by them.

They stood in green parkland, the great houses where he rested at night, their gardens sweet with herbs and fragrant with flowers. His cavalcade came upon villages, drowsing in the heat of summer, hidden between folds of hills, and filed through narrow entrances of handsome towns with houses as fair as those in London, painted and repaired so that he would see them at their best. Beyond their environs all was wild, untamed, unbroken. The sun could penetrate only in glimmers and shafts the forests where he hunted, spotting the undergrowth like a toad's back, a twilight to which the huntsman grew accustomed and could detect with both eye and ear its watchful denizens.

He came and went amongst the people, their boy sovereign, and they were to remember him always. Frail as a shell on the seashore through which you could see the light, his Portsmouth citizens thought he looked. At Reading they noticed how gently he returned the mace to their mayor. At Southampton Bishop Bale, his father's friend, heard Edward greet him from a window, leaning out to congratulate him on his recovery from illness, telling him he must not do too much, as though he were the old man's father. And a little girl at Wilton standing all by herself saw the most beautiful sight she was ever to see, the young king, who had outstripped his followers, gallop past her. Only the two of them alone in Felstone Lane.

As the progress advanced it was noticed he was exhausting himself, but like his father he would not admit to tiredness. And like his father he made a detailed inspection of the fortifications at Portsmouth, to find them out of date despite their massiveness. Before he left he devised how they should be strengthened.

Nature itself had provided it with enough water to bear the greatest ship in Christendom.

Not long after his return Edward received a man after his own heart, Girolano Cardano, a famous Italian astronomer, from whom he accepted his learned books. The boy king was unaware that as well as scientist, mathematician and man of letters, Cardano was a celebrated physician who had recently cured the Bishop of St Andrews of what had been wrongly diagnosed as cancer. Before he returned to Italy, he was summoned to London by Edward's Councillors, alarmed at the change in the boy's appearance, to give them his professional opinion on His Majesty's condition and to cast his horoscope.

After the customary punctiliousness of even a private audience, Edward embarked at once on the subject that enthralled him by inquiring, 'What is there in these rare books of yours on "The Variety of Things"?'

The author replied that in the first chapter he had shown what had long been sought for in vain—the course of comets.

'What is it?' he was asked eagerly.

The boy was somewhat below middle height, pale-faced, with grey eyes, a grave aspect, decorous and handsome. Of a bad habit of body rather than a sufferer from fixed disorders, he had a somewhat projecting shoulder-blade, but this did not amount to deformity.

'The concourse of the light of the planets,' the scientist replied.

'But seeing the planets are moved with several motions, how comes it that the comet neither dissolves nor scatters with their motion?' Edward wanted to know.

Cardano made notes at the time, amplified some years later, of the several audiences granted to him, at the last of which His Majesty appeared very tired. He felt this boy of so much wit and promise was nearing a comprehension of the sum of things. He saw the mark in his face of death that was to come too soon. Otherwise he was comely, because of his age and of his parents, who had both been handsome. Hindsight and the doctor's interview with the King's Councillors perhaps coloured his summing-up: 'It would have been better, I think, for this boy not to have been born, or if he had been born, not to have survived—for he had graces.'

The Councillors struck him as corrupt, bad, bullying and unscrupulous men, and Northumberland as the most corrupt and the hardest. They might all speak Latin and Italian fluently, but they seemed to twist the words in their mouths which made it difficult for him, in his nervousness, to make them out. Not satisfied with his inconclusive diagnosis, they demanded a horoscope which had to be shaped by Cardano to act as a safe conduct for himself out of this alien country. He had therefore to read the omens of a great calamity into 'His Majesty would always suffer delicate health although he might possibly live to be fifty-five years.' It was not the hundred gold crowns he received from the King he was to remember but a boy of wondrous promise.

As the King's condition deteriorated, his chief minister made up to Mary to lull any suspicions she might have of his intentions, but his fear of Elizabeth's position was greater, although she was not heir-presumptive. If either came to the throne, he would lose his political omnipotence, without which life was not worth the living. The Roman Catholics would have much to redress, but the Protestants rallying behind the Protestant Elizabeth would be even more formidable. What he failed to take into consideration was the temper of the populace.

His people heard their beloved King was abed again after Yule. He had overheated himself after a strenuous game of tennis—that proved how well he was—and had drunk too copious a drink of water too quickly. What were they thinking of, allowing him to do that? He was at Westminster now, and the Princess Mary passed through London on her way to visit him, so he must be himself again. Only she left a day or two after her arrival, and the Candlemas festivities they were to share did not take place.

February was Mary's birthday month, and the woman who rode along Fleet Street was thirty-seven years of age. This visit to her brother was quite different from any other, for she found herself accompanied through London by the wives of those who held the highest position in His Majesty's realm while at the gates of the Palace of Westminster their husbands were gathered to greet her, headed by the Duke of Northumberland himself.

For three days she waited before His Majesty was well enough to see her. Well enough! He lay in the great bed, the little brother who had always been so glad to see her when he had been small, propped up with pillows and bolsters, the only strong thing about him the hard cough that racked his body. The Spanish ambassador, who accompanied her, noticed his right shoulder was much higher than his left. There could be no intimacy between brother and sister for the short time she sat in his room, heavy with the smell of unguents and resins, because his doctors were present throughout and the patient had difficulty in breathing.

They said his doctors were never away from his bedside, but he saw some of his Councillors every day—he, not they, insisted on that. They said they were going to bring forward his majority by two years, which would make him rule by himself at the hind end of this year when he reached sixteen in October, instead of waiting until he was eighteen. That betokened nothing ill, he was wise enough to rule on his own, their God-given king. What an awakening there would be for some who could be named when he unmasked their greed, enriching themselves at his expense. The Black One must be the richest man in England, and the King, their beloved king, one of the poorest. It was enough to make good King Hal rise in his grave so it was.

They said it had begun already, the unmasking, when he was strong enough to preside at a Council meeting. No one knew what had gone on behind those closed doors, but the King's high voice had been heard crying out at them, 'You pluck my feathers as if I were a tame falcon—the day will come when I will pluck yours!' The Councillors had come forth reeling, holding on to each other for support.

You were lucky to find yourself in the pillory, bloodier sentences were carried out than that every day to stop the mouthing of what everyone was saying, that the King was dead. But he did not ride to Westminster to open Parliament, when he would have given the lie to rumour. Instead Parliament went to him at Whitehall. They said he wore a train of crimson velvet ten yards long and sat on his chair of state in the Great Hall hour after hour signing Acts. He must be better, his old self again, to be able to do that. And he knighted the Lord Mayor of London.

They have taken away our crosses, lights and bells, and what have they put in their place? Where have all the chalices and jewels and plate gone now they have made the altar into a table plain as a board? And the church lands and mansions and prebends that were to be sold to succour the poor? The poor have no almshouses now, or hospices, or spitals for the sick, the blind and insane, no seat at monastery or nunnery gates, for there are no monasteries or nunneries any longer, or a brother or sister to put a filled bowl into their hands without the asking.

But the King, our king, bless his golden heart, has given his own Palace of Bridewell to the homeless, seen that St Thomas's was rebuilt for the sick and re-endowed Grey Friars for the poor. The Lord Mayor came away not only with their charters but security for their maintenance. All before the King left London in the State barge with the guns firing their salute and the flags capering in the April breeze on his way to Greenwich, where he would get better. That was all he needed, country air. They said he was strong again, walking every day in the gardens between good Master Cheke and his friend Sir Henry Sidney.

In April, before he left London, Mary received from her brother a handsome table-cut diamond, a gift that carried its own portent in the eyes of her advisers. Omens, portents, suspicions, forebodings, were raised round her while the thorn blossomed and cherry and apple tree flourished in the valley which flashed with water as she waited in the manor of Beaulieu and made fruitless efforts to visit her brother.

In the sunken garden at Hatfield, where flowers bloomed with a brightness they showed nowhere else, the twenty-year-old Elizabeth walked and waited. This was her favourite establishment, where she had spent much of her youth, and the little brother who had shared with her so many of its sunlit hours had gifted it to her on that memorable visit to him only two short years ago. Like her sister, she now made every effort to see him, and like Mary her every attempt was foiled, nor were any of her letters allowed to reach him.

A school of dolphins was sighted in the Thames, and a whale at Gravesend. Two gentlemen were drowned on their way to the bear-baiting, and a dog was seen on Ludgate Hill with a piece of a dead child in its mouth. As such extraordinary and dire happenings took place, which could surely only presage the death of princes, there was a fortuitous shifting of the ambassadorial scene, familiar figures disappearing in the draughtiness of departure and new arrivals to fill their places.

The Venetian ambassador had bowed himself out before the King left London at a farewell audience. He thought His Majesty still very handsome, but it was obvious he was about to die—in heresy too, which the foreigner deplored, for that was not His Majesty's fault. With the right upbringing he might have been saved.

A new French ambassador was now in residence, Antoine de Noailles, of noble birth, valiant soldier turned diplomat. His

Majesty's betrothal to the eldest daughter of the French king gave him a cachet and entrée his fellow envoys were denied, particularly the newly arrived imperial ambassador, Simon Renaud. Each man represented his master, which meant what was good for one was bad for the other, and the fall of the cards at the English court decreed that the French king trumped his imperial majesty. But Simon Renaud could wait; subtle, astute, vigilant, he had none of the bold gamester instincts of de Noailles. The heir presumptive, when and if the King died, was the Princess Mary, cousin to his master. He reported when he saw His Majesty for the first time in April at Greenwich that he was wasting away, and one of the royal doctors confided to him that if their patient did not get much better within a month he could not live throughout the summer.

His doctors indeed held out no hope despite Edward's gallant rallies, which sent Northumberland's hopes soaring and which appeared to those who loved him like the answers to their prayers. Edward himself was no longer buoyed up by the optimism that so often protects the consumptive. He could now read his own death-warrant in his own terrible symptoms.

Before April was out, he was no longer able to walk in the gardens and had to spend his time indoors, his doctors with their revolting prescriptions always in attendance, his tutor and Henry Sidney his closest companions, his thoughts feeding on what was more to him than life itself: his inheritance, which was a gift from God, his realm.

Could he, who was God's Vice-Regent and Christ's Vicar, consecrated to see God truly worshipped and idolatry destroyed within his own dominions, the Supreme Head of the Church, elected of God and commanded only of Him, leave his trust to a half-sister who would lead it back into the darkness of the Bishop of Rome's fold?

Even although she was his sister whom he loved, he could not do it, even although his father had placed her first in the succession in his will. Nor Elizabeth, whom he had placed second, for as his chief minister pointed out the Lady Mary could not be put by unless the Lady Elizabeth were put by also. She might be a Protestant, but the same thing would happen when she married that would happen when her elder sister married: the foreign prince, of course a Catholic, would abolish all the realm's ancient rights and immunities until he extinguished the very name of

England. Thus either sister would wreck the Reformation which their father had begun and which he with God's grace had brought to so goodly fruition.

'Have at the crown, by your leave!' courtiers said behind their hands when they heard the King had given his consent to the marriage of his cousin the Lady Jane Grey to Guildford, the Duke of Northumberland's only unmarried son. The Duke gave out that the King would grace the bridal, but His Majesty's presence was the one thing lacking on this splendid royal occasion to which neither the French nor the Spanish ambassador was invited.

Edward made several drafts of 'My device for the succession', dividing it into carefully numbered heads as was his wont. 'For lack of issue of my body. . .' they each began. The first draft stipulated that the crown should come to the heirs male of Frances, Duchess of Suffolk, provided they were born before his death, which entailed that it should pass to the heirs male of her eldest daughter, and after her to to her sisters' heirs male. The second draft decreed that the crown should pass to the Lady Jane herself, the Reformation would be safe in her hands, and her heirs male. The final draft laid down that neither Mary nor Elizabeth could succeed as both were illegitimate. All were written in his own hand, whole lines scored out and words amended by him as he discussed each with his chief minister.

The boy's sufferings had now reached such a pitch they were wellnigh intolerable. He could only lie on his back and was tormented by bed sores, so weak he could not keep down the food his doctors were forcing on him and was given spirits in the mistaken hope they would restore him. He was often delirious. Sometimes the delirium cleared, as when he saw the big body of the Duchess of Suffolk standing in his room and heard her relinquish her claim to the crown to her eldest daughter Jane, when he looked into his tutor's compassionate face bending over him and whispered, 'I am glad to die', when he felt for Henry Sidney at his side and would not let him leave him.

He longed to be quit of this miserable and wretched life, if God would but grant His faithful servant strength first to secure the succession. He may not have been aware that his own doctors, familiar as bedposts, had been replaced by two strangers, one Northumberland's own doctor, the other a professor of medicine from Oxford, or that they too faded and a female ministered to him in their place. She had asserted with such certainty she could cure His Majesty as long as she was left in sole charge that his desperate chief minister placed the King of England in her hands. She called the medicine she administered 'restringents', and the first dose effected an immediate rally.

He was strong enough the very next day to sign the grant of Christ's Hospital with a promise of four thousand marks a year. Two days later he was ready to admit to his presence the Lord Chief Justice, the Solicitor-General, the Chancellor of the Exchequer and the Attorney-General who had been summoned to his bedside, round which were gathered the ubiquitous Northumberland and some of his fellow Councillors.

Supported by his attendants, coughing and gasping for breath, His Majesty informed the kneeling judges he wished the succession to be altered, instructed that his will, now drawn up and signed by himself, be read out, and commanded them to make a deed of settlement based on its articles.

To his high displeasure, despite the final clause of the will they had just heard that any person going about to undo the device or interfere with its arrangements would be guilty of high treason, a distinct murmur of protest reached him from the lawyers. It was crystallized by the Lord Chief Justice, who pointed out that His Majesty's device was against the will of succession, which being an unrepealed Act of Parliament still stood.

The thin face turned towards them was set and became inimical. They marvelled that anyone so weak could be impelled by such intensity.

'We will hear no objections,' he warned them. 'We command you to draw the letters patent forthwith.'

The Lord Chief Justice inquired if he and his fellow judges might be allowed to study the document. They backed from the presence when permission was granted.

Before they returned the following day, Edward heard from the Duke of Northumberland that they refused to draw up the deed. As the judges approached the dais they saw at the bedside waiting for them His Majesty's chief minister buttressed by Privy Councillors, their faces implacable with disapproval. But it was His Majesty himself who made them tremble. Edward was unaware that at that moment he was terrifyingly like his father, who brooked opposition from no quarter.

'Where are the letters patent?' he demanded fiercely. 'Why have they not been drawn?'

He brushed aside the Lord Chief Justice's wavering reply that to do the same would be to put the Lords and themselves in danger of high treason and would achieve nothing with an angry, 'Why have you refused to obey my order?'

'To refuse were treason,' the Duke of Northumberland shouted at them.

The Lord Chief Justice burst into tears. 'I have served Your Majesty and Your Majesty's most noble father these nineteen years,' he said, struggling with his sobs, 'and loath would I to be disobey Your Grace's commandments. I have seventeen children,' he added with some irrelevance. 'I am a weak old man without comfort.'

Stonily Edward ignored his plea.

'If these writings were made,' the judge said painstakingly, 'they would be no use after Your Majesty's decease, while the statute of succession remaineth in full force, because it could only be abrogated by the same authority whereof it was established, that of Parliament.'

'We intend to have a Parliament shortly,' countered the King.

'If that be Your Majesty's intention,' the Lord Chief Justice put in eagerly, 'this matter may be deferred to the Parliament, and all perils and dangers saved.'

Edward felt as if his blood vessels were about to burst.

'I will have it done now,' he said inexorably, 'and afterwards ratified by Parliament. On your allegiance—make quick dispatch!' His gaze fell on the Chancellor of the Exchequer. 'And what will you do?' he demanded.

'I will obey Your Majesty,' the man promised.

'And what say you, Sir John Baker,' his sovereign inquired of the Solicitor-General, 'for you have said never a word this day?'

'I will obey Your Majesty's command,' he replied.

'Away with you, then,' His Majesty dismissed them, 'and make speed.'

The document was brought to him to sign with 'the King's proper hand, above, beneath, and on every side'. After him the judges subscribed and the Privy Councillors, the eldest sons of peers, the Officers of the Household, the Secretaries of State, the Knights of the Privy Chamber and the sheriffs, until more than a hundred signatures were marshalled on the parchment. The circumspect Cecil, who had resigned his office as Secretary and hidden his money and papers, pleaded sickness but was ordered sharply by the King to add his name. The fair-minded Cheke demurred. Never, he said, would he distrust God so far in the preservation of His true religion as to disinherit orphans, but as a Councillor he was bound to sign and his name appears—perhaps under pressure, perhaps because he had not the heart to distress his royal pupil. But the most important signature of all was lacking, that of the highest Church dignitary in the land, the Archbishop of Canterbury, Thomas Cranmer.

The Council told the King he refused to subscribe, saying he was forsworn to my Lady Mary by King Henry's will. They did not tell him that his godfather had asked to see him alone, which Northumberland for one would never have allowed. He interrupted him harshly when he appeared before the King, but his godson said gently to him, 'Be not more repugnant to my will than the rest of the Council.' 'You alone must not stand out,' he told the man who loved him more than he loved anyone in the world, and Thomas Cranmer signed that his godson could die in peace.

For ten days he had not eaten. Now the false stimulus the female charlatan's 'restringents' had so spectacularly achieved as spectacularly collapsed and her nostrums, which probably included arsenic, began to exact their hideous toll. The patient's legs and arms swelled, his fair skin darkened, his nails came off and he lost his silvery fair hair, while his fingers and toes became gangrenous. He was still conscious, but could speak little, and smiled instead of thanking those who tended him.

On 6th July 1553 the most violent thunderstorm in the memory of man swept across Europe. In England the air was insufferably close with that stillness that foretells disaster, and at noon darkness fell like the clap of doom.

Henry Sidney was with him, a gentleman of the bedchamber, his favourite servant and his doctors. Northumberland, when he saw the end was near, had dismissed the quack and reinstalled the court physicians. Edward lay so still that Dr Owen, who had been present at his birth, thought he had died, but he began talking to himself. In an access of love Sidney took him in his arms.

He turned his head and gazed at Sidney, then looked round the room.

'Are you so nigh?' he asked. 'I thought you had been farther off.'

'We heard you speak to yourself,' Dr Owen told him, 'but what you said we know not.' The boy smiled and said, 'I was praying to God.'

He appeared to sink into unconsciousness and some leaden hours passed. Then they heard him whisper, 'I am faint', and supported him on either side. He said clearly, 'Lord, have mercy upon me—take my spirit', and died in their arms.

At last the storm burst over London, thunder reverberated like vengeance, lightning forked, rain fell in torrents, trees were torn up by the roots, houses and bridges swept away in the floods, and a church spire crashed to the ground.

Already Simon Renaud, the Spanish ambassador, had written to Mary, addressing her as 'Your Highness'.

Book Three

Mary I
July 1553–November 1558

'And thus much for archery, whose tale if it be disordered, you must bear withall, for she is a woman, and her mind is passionate.'

Quoted in *The Book of Archery*, 1840, George Agar Hansard

Chapter Nine

The solitary horseman pounded through the glimmering July night to where Mary rested at Hoddesdon in Hertfordshire on her way to London in response to the Duke of Northumberland's bidding—her brother was on his deathbed and desired to see her. In the few minutes in which she listened to the message he brought her life changed.

The King had died that day. If she continued on her journey her destination would be the Tower as prisoner of the man who held London and who intended to have his daughter-in-law Jane Grey crowned in her stead.

Mary did not lose time before she was in the saddle again, accompanied by only two of her women and six gentlemen of her household. They swung north now and chose the longer route, because there was not the same risk of being intercepted by horsemen from London. Also it led to Farnmouth, where she could take ship for the Netherlands—should the worst come to the worst. Always in moments of crisis, her first instinct was to turn to her cousin the Emperor Charles. She had delayed long enough before she left on her hazardous night journey to dispatch word to the new imperial ambassador that she was making for Kenninghall, in Norfolk, a manor of her dower lands.

But as she rode, straight as an arrow shoots, she did not think of the worst coming to the worst. Through all the trepidations, alarms and dangers of the days that followed, with the knowledge that Northumberland's son Robert Dudley and 300 horsemen were scouring the countryside to fetch in the Lady Mary, when she celebrated mass at daybreak with her host, who risked his all to shelter her, when she passed through enemy country riding pillion behind one of her gentlemen who was dressed in servant's livery, her heart was high, and she was manful.

She arrived at Kenninghall on the second day after she had left Hoddesdon, and there she wrote to the Council. She assumed that she had succeeded and that they recognized her as queen, although she found it strange she had not been informed of her brother's death two days after the event. At the time she wrote very few people even in London knew that the King was dead, for it suited Northumberland's purpose to keep it secret as long as possible. Carefully she continued, 'We shall and may conceive great trust, with much assurance in your loyalty and service, and therefore for the time interpret and take things not to the worst, that ye will, like noblemen, work the best', and concluded by calling upon their allegiance.

Sir Harry Jerringham and Sir Henry Bedingfield brought their tenantry to her standard, but she was advised to leave Norfolk; it was too open and Kenninghall could not withstand assault. She recrossed the river into Suffolk and made for the royal castle of Framlingham, which rose with its three moats on a bare green eminence from the trees that wooded the district. The men of Suffolk mustered to her cause; they were coming in from every quarter, the nobility and clusters of the common folk.

News filtered through from London. Bills had appeared at crossroads and market-places and stuck on church doors, pronouncing that both the King's sisters were bastards and the elder a papist into the bargain. At every street corner the heralds proclaimed the small cousin, upon whom she had heaped gifts in the past, Queen Jane, but there was no tossing of caps in the air. Only the archers of the guard had disturbed the frozen silence by shouting 'God save the Queen'.

Carts were rumbling through London's streets filled with weapons, heading for Cambridge, that evil town, the seed-bed of the new heretical teaching, its every citizen her enemy. It was to be the base from where Northumberland would mount his attack. Already he was on the march; he had left London by Shoreditch, on his way to take her.

The most ominous sign was the six ships which hove to at Farnmouth, baulking any escape. They were laden with ordnance. Framlingham Castle had no cannon; the only weapons which Mary's ever-increasing army had were what each man carried. Lord George Howard came over to her, to be followed by that stout Protestant Lord Grey. Howard had fallen out with Northumberland's eldest son on the way, and Grey had come to blows with Northumberland himself. The crews of the six ships made known they were Queen Mary's true subjects and would throw their captains into the sea unless they declared themselves likewise.

A placard was posted on Queenhithe church; someone had seen it with his own eyes, saying Mary had been declared Queen of England and Ireland in every town and city with the exception of London. Framlingham Castle now had the great guns from the six ships to defend it, and 500 men picked as her personal bodyguard to defend her from all her enemies.

On the evening of 18th July a band of men rode from London, headed by Lord Paget and the Earl of Arundel, to tell her that the Lords of the Council, those who had not already slipped away to join her, with two heralds and three trumpeters, had proclaimed her Queen of England at the Cross in Cheap and St Paul's. Her people were delirious with joy. They were banqueting in the streets and drinking to her health by the light of bonfires.

This was the day the Lord had made, she could rejoice and be glad in it. Her mother had written to her all those years ago, 'When they have done the uttermost they can, then I am sure of the amendment.' Now was the amendment. Chapuys had told her she must submit to her father to save her life that she might be preserved to do a good work. This was the good work she had been preserved to do. Without a shot fired, without the slaughter of a single soldier, she had entered her inheritance as queen to restore England to the true faith of Christ.

She ordered the crucifix to be set up in the parish church at Framlingham, and wrote to the Pope entreating him to send her cousin Cardinal Pole to her. Together they would return their country to his fold.

Elizabeth sent her congratulations on the collapse of the Queen's enemies, and Mary sent word for Elizabeth to travel to Wanstead at the beginning of August that they could enter London side by side. The younger sister had received the same summons to London from their brother's chief minister as had the elder, but had remained where she was at Hatfield. Either she was too wary to deliver herself into the Duke of Northumberland's power when hearsay was reporting that the King was already dead, or she was counselled by William Cecil to bide where she was.

The meeting between the sisters could not have been warmer; liberation from the peril that had threatened both made their greeting heartfelt and spontaneous. Mary, whose danger had been so much more imminent and who was the more demonstrative, held Elizabeth's hand all the time they spoke together.

London, swept and decked, was waiting for its queen as her procession entered at Aldgate. Tapestries made fine the house walls they covered, and aldermen made bright streets lined with the city's craftsmen, and expectant with charity children in their red dresses and blue caps agog to make their oration.

They knew she was the Queen because her gown of violet velvet was so rich, stiff with gold and encrusted with pearls. They heard her thank the Lord Mayor for his greeting, saying she remembered the city to have been always good to her. They wept for joy at that, and vowed it always would be.

The imperial ambassador was there to watch the cousin of his royal master enter her capital in triumph. She was responding to the love of her welcome with smiles that lit and sweetened her careworn small face, and he thought she looked more than middling fair. But it was her sister who held his hard gaze.

It could be told at a glance that she was good King Hal's daughter from the glint of her hair and her bearing. The Venetian ambassador noted the display of her beautiful hands to attract attention to herself. On this young woman, Protestant or no Protestant, was pinned all the French ambassador's hope. He whose profession it was to trace his rival's secrets knew that Renaud had visited the Queen before she came to London, and already the talk of a Spanish marriage was in the air. No Frenchman could view with equanimity the English glove on the Spanish hand.

She might be half her sister's age, but his first glance told Simon Renaud that here was someone who would have to be reckoned with. 'The Princess Elizabeth,' he said, 'is greatly to be feared; she has a spirit full of incantation,' and within a month the Pope Julius III was to write that the heretic and schismatic sister of the Queen was in the heart and mouth of everyone.

Her ardent people watched their queen pass along Leadenhall and through the Minories to the Tower, while bells pealed and clashed, trumpets blew and cannon fired like great thunder.

In the gateway of the Tower, Mary paused, for three men knelt there. As wonderingly she looked down at them, she was moved to tears. Those great walls which were her bastion had incarcerated them, and the young man who looked a mere lad had of the three been its denizen longest. For fifteen years of his twenty-seven his horizon had been bounded by turret, tower and portcullis. In this narrow world where his father had been executed, Edward Courtenay, the last sprig of the Plantagenet White Rose, had grown to manhood dowered with the beauty of his royal race.

It was years since Mary had seen the second kneeling man, the aged Duke of Norfolk, whose attitude towards her in the past had fluctuated with her fortunes. Now she was his queen, he could shelter beneath the cloak of her regality for the few years granted to him.

And the third was Stephen Gardiner, Bishop of Winchester before his enemies and hers had stripped him of his See, imprisoned him without trial, deprived him of books, pen, ink and paper.

She held out her arms to them in an embracing gesture. 'You are my prisoners!' she exclaimed. Then gently she raised each one, and kissed him.

No one knew when the pitiable body of the boy, on whose every breath a kingdom had hung, was borne from Greenwich in its sealed coffin up the river to Whitehall. His funeral did not take place until a month after his death when his sister entered London as queen. She would have had him buried by the rites of the Roman Catholic Church, but the Emperor's ambassadors, realizing what an effect such an action would have on London's predominant Protestants, advised her, most holy as the wish undoubtedly was, not to persevere in it. While the King was interred with Protestant rites in Westminster Abbey, the Queen and her ladies attended Requiem Mass in the chapel of the Tower, and prayers for his soul at her command were repeated every day throughout her reign at the high altar before which he was buried.

The people whose hearts had sung for joy that he was their king watched the last journey, from the Palace of Whitehall to Westminster Abbey, of the boy known as England's Treasure. As the funeral car passed, covered with cloth of gold, their weeping, cries and sobs drowned the sound of muffled drum and horsehoof. Thomas Cranmer officiated at the burial service and the interment took place, to the scandal of foreign ambassadors, without candle or taper for him at whose christening all the torches had been lighted.

Mary believed that Protestantism in her realm was not firmly rooted and that reconciliation could be effected with those wanderers who did not return to the path of the true faith. What she was totally unprepared for was the attitude of her Protestant people towards her religion, for the violent struggles that took place even before her coronation between Protestant and Catholic for the possession of pulpits, for the cries of 'Papist! Papist! Tear him down!' when one of her chaplains preached at St Paul's Cross, for the riots that took place when mass was said. The day her first Parliament rose, a dead dog with a shaven crown and a rope round its neck was hurled through the windows of her presence chamber. It was the Protestants' brutal answer to Her Majesty's clemency: no compromise, no accommodation. 'Hold fast! Keep together!' was to be their rallying cry.

She began her reign with the irremediable disadvantage of having as her Councillors the very men who had so recently sworn allegiance to the usurper they had set up in her place. To punish all the leaders of the rebellion, as the practical Renaud pointed out, would leave her with no Council at all. The men who had rallied to her cause had to be rewarded for their loyalty, as well as Mary's faithful servants throughout her lean years, so that her inflated Council was unwieldy for size. It was divided roughly into two camps, Protestants who bore no loyalty even to one another but each to his own interests, and Roman Catholics who saw with increasing bitterness men reap the spoils of office who had been traitors to the crown they now professed to serve.

Mary had at her side one wise in the affairs of the world, a skilled lawyer, churchman and experienced diplomatist whom she made her Lord Chancellor, Stephen Gardiner. A woman who needed a firm hand on her helm, it was her unwisdom that she did not turn to him, a man who knew the temper of her people, but to Simon Renaud, because the Englishman advocated what she did not want to hear and the Spaniard what she did.

It was taken for granted she would marry. She herself did not contemplate that she could possibly rule alone, nor did her Council or her people. Only one man advised her to remain single, and leave her future in God's hands, and that was her cousin Cardinal Pole. For that reason the Pope did not grant her earnest plea to send him to her lest he influenced her adversely. Pole knew at thirty-seven years of age her chance of bearing heirs to the crown was highly improbable, and if the practically impossible did happen it could imperil her life. He also knew that the bridegroom proposed for her was the Emperor's son, Philip of Spain. Her impeccable cousin might have been exiled from his native land for over twenty years, but he was still an Englishman, and both Emperor and Pope were aware they would receive no help from him to place his country in the hands of a foreigner.

Gardiner told the woman he crowned that her people would never abide a foreigner over them, they expected her to choose the most suitable bridegroom that Providence could possibly provide, young Courtenay whom she had created Earl of Devon, English born and bred of the blood royal.

When Mary said, looking down at her coronation ring which she always wore, that her realm was her first husband and no consideration would make her violate the faith she had pledged to her people, her mind was already made up to marry Philip of Spain.

At her coronation Elizabeth had been closest to her. She led her by the hand in these early days, and never dined in public without her. But a Catholic court was no place for the Queen's Protestant sister, and when the Queen withdrew her approbation Elizabeth asked for books or teachers to correct the errors in which she had been bred. Mary saw to it she had both. She did notice Elizabeth trembled and paled when asked about her beliefs, but, reassured at what she heard, Mary gave her a diamond and ruby brooch and a rosary of white coral, which Elizabeth did not wear. Renaud was more sceptical; he would have been even if he had not heard that on her way to her first mass the Princess had been overtaken by such sudden pain she asked one of the Queen's ladies to rub her stomach for her.

In his opinion the safest place for the Queen's sister was the Tower, but even although Her Majesty knew that was also the Emperor's opinion, her sister remained free to exert her baleful potentiality of French patronage and Protestant popularity. Even those already housed within the citadel were not lying there under the shadow of doom. The woman who had worn her crown (Renaud always referred to her as Jane of Suffolk), was comfortably lodged and able to walk in the gardens by special permission of her queen, and the five sons of Northumberland exercised themselves on the leads.

For treason so heinous that her crown was placed on another's head, armies raised against her and her assassination planned, only eleven were brought to book, and of these three dispatched on the block that they would trouble her no more. There was even difficulty in procuring her signature for the arch-traitor's death when she heard that Northumberland had recanted. He

promised Bishop Gardiner to do penance all the days of his life—
were it but granted to him, even in a mousehole. It was only after
the imperial ambassador obtained a private audience with her that
she signed the death-warrant.

The longer she remained at her sister's court, the more aware
Elizabeth became that she had overstayed her welcome. She asked
for leave to spend Christmas at Hatfield.

The sisters' parting was warm with relief on both sides. Mary
agreed to Elizabeth's passionate entreaty not to believe what she
might hear of her without giving her a chance to speak for herself, and Elizabeth left with the gift of a beautiful sable hood from
her sister.

The 500 gentlemen, who in her white-and-green livery had
escorted her to Wanstead, rode by her to Ashbridge. It was the
beginning of December and their bridles jingled like bells in the
frosty air. An hour or two after their departure Mary was told the
Princess had sent back messengers asking for a litter, and would
Her Grace return with them copes, chasubles and other accom-
paniments of Catholic ritual?

Mary was no longer deceived. It was now as much an obsession
with her that Elizabeth should not come to the throne as it had
been with Edward that she herself must not succeed him. She
would have altered the succession if she could, but had to leave
to God to bring about what she was unable to achieve. She told
Renaud, what she wanted to believe herself, that Elizabeth was
no half-sister of hers and so had no right to the throne. She made
herself see in Elizabeth's face, instead of the features of their
father, those of Anne Boleyn's musician, one of the five men
found guilty of being her paramour.

With the irritant of her sister's presence removed, with the
knowledge that envoys were on their way from Spain to conclude
the marriage treaty, Christmastide was gay for Mary. She moved
like a butterfly escaped at last from its cocoon, stretching and
fluttering her cramped wings in the sunshine of her own court at
this season of gifts and goodwill and cheer, with music to her
heart's content, able to indulge in her passion for rich stuffs and
costly ornamentation that was the birthright of Henry VIII's
children.

The Emperor's envoys were greeted with salvoes of guns when
they arrived in London, but they received no welcome from its
silent, sullen citizens, who pretended not to look at them, and

their servants were pelted with snowballs by irreverent school-boys. They left with such speed not a fortnight later that they had no time to take leave of the Queen.

Like fires set by the one hand, three insurrections broke out in three different parts of England, their tinder the Queen's projected marriage which, if it were allowed, would mean the over-running of the country by outlandish men. Already rumour was spreading like wildfire, men swore at least a hundred hated Spaniards had been seen disembarking at Dover, each in full armour—they must have reached Rochester by now.

Lady Jane's father kindled the rising in the mid-counties, its object the restoration of his Protestant daughter on the throne of the unpopular Catholic queen. But Lady Jane's name did not catch fire like two brands on brushwood—Princess Elizabeth's and young Courtenay's. Princess Elizabeth must take her sister's place and marry the man her people had wanted Queen Mary to marry, to give England princes of their own blood to rule over them.

Two of the revolts, in the mid-counties and the west, were easily stamped out, but not the third. The men of Kent had always been unruly, and they advanced on London itself. Triumphant with numbers, their leader, Sir Thomas Wyatt, dictated their terms from Blackheath: that the Queen and her Council be surrendered to their custody.

Mary rode to the Guildhall when she heard that the picked men of the Trained Bands, sent out to intercept the traitors, had defected to them with all their artillery. 'A Wyatt! A Wyatt!' they cried as they turned to charge against the royalist troops reinforcing their rear.

The Queen told her citizens that she did not know how a mother loved a child, for she had never had a child, but she assured them as their lady and mistress she as earnestly and tenderly loved them. She promised to abstain from marriage as long as she lived if the union did not seem advisable to all the nobility and commons in the high court of Parliament. She told her good subjects to pluck up their hearts, and when she asked if they would defend her against these rebels, they answered with one voice they would.

In the small hours of the night when a man's courage is at its lowest ebb, her Lords came to her, with Pembroke and Clinton, the captains of her army. They gathered round the great bed in which she lay, shadowed by its curtains. Wyatt had left Deptford Strand and was making for Southwark. They had a boat waiting for her at Whitehall stairs; she must flee—while there was still time.

Crossroads, when one false step might lead to abyss, always threw Mary into an agony of indecision. She sent for the imperial ambassador and asked what she should do. Renaud did not advise so much as state. If she must needs go, let her go to the Tower, but once she left London Elizabeth would be queen and true religion would be down.

She spoke to the two captains and said she would stay if they promised to be true to her. They promised joyfully, and on their knees, like men at prayer, begged her to remain because God would give her the victory—Pembroke swore he would not look on her face again until the rebels were crushed.

She forbade that the guns of the Tower should be fired upon Southwark, for that would undo and kill many poor men and householders. Dr Watson officiated in the chapel of Whitehall with armour beneath his vestments. A deserter from the rebels brought the news that Wyatt had crossed Kingston Bridge and would be at Hyde Park Corner within two hours. 'All is lost! Away! Away! A barge, a barge!' the cry went up. 'But where is Lord Pembroke?' she asked in reply, and when told he was in the forefront of the battle she said: 'Well then, fall to prayer, and I warrant we shall hear better news anon.' Again it came, her unfailing touchstone, 'God will not deceive me, in whom my chief trust is.'

Learning it was bruited she was going to the Tower, she sent a message to the Lord Mayor that she would remain where she was to see the uttermost. Panic and terror tore through the palace, 'such running and shrieking of gentlewomen, such clapping and slamming-to of doors and windows, as was appalling to hear'. The uttermost came within hours when she saw Wyatt brought a prisoner past the window where she sat and watched.

In a London made hideous with corpses dangling at every street corner, the Queen came to the Temple-bar at the city's boundary to sign the death-warrants of Guildford Dudley and his wife Jane of Suffolk. Mary knew there was no alternative, Jane's father and uncles had been the instigators of the revolt in the mid-counties, and as long as the competitor for her throne, no matter how dormant herself, was allowed to exist there would be uprisings in her favour. But, despite the rigorous Simon Renaud, and the bullying Lords of her Council, she grasped at one straw remaining to her. The offices of their heretical beliefs were denied to prisoners. Mary sent her own confessor to the Tower to befriend her cousin and respited the execution in the prayerful hope that she would choose life and the old faith rather than death and the doom of the heretic.

Jane told the chaplain her time was too short for controversy, but in the little they had together the Roman Catholic suffered to think this girl's beliefs cut her off from eternal salvation, while the girl was bewildered to discover that a papist whose piety was truer than that of many a corrupt Protestant she could name was barred for ever from the paradise she was about to enter.

He prayed that he might accompany her to the scaffold that was now inevitable, and she consented. There is something infinitely touching in the question she turned to ask him at the end, 'Shall I say the *Misère*?'

But there was one still at large whom her Lord Chancellor had warned the Queen throughout was the chief danger to her, and that was her sister. Mary wrote recalling her to London with all convenient speed when 'the unnatural rebellion against God and us' broke out. Elizabeth replied she could not move as illness made her utterly unable to travel. The Council were highly suspicious—they had heard she was going to leave Hatfield and pass into Berkshire, thus stretching as far a distance from her and London as she could. It was then Gardiner took the step he admitted was unusual but, as he said, the times were unusual, and everyone knew de Noailles was in the conspiracies up to the hilt; besides, he had recently married one of Elizabeth's maids of honour.

The Frenchman's courier was intercepted on his way back to France; as the Englishman fingered through the dispatches he came across a copy of Elizabeth's letter to the Queen.

Three Councillors with a strong escort left London to bring the Princess from Hatfield, but Mary saw that one of the three was the girl's great-uncle, and that two of her physicians preceded them with her own litter for the invalid. By the time they reached London by easy stages Wyatt was a prisoner and had incriminated both the Princess and Courtenay in the plot. Courtenay was sent to the Tower on the day Jane Grey was executed and Elizabeth left Hatfield on her journey south. Wyatt's rebellion very nearly succeeded; for he reached Ludgate, which it was believed Courtenay was to open to him, but de Noailles contemptuously counted out one who was useful neither as friend nor foe by saying he was so timorous that he would suffer himself to be taken before he would act.

It is out of the question to believe that Elizabeth would consider uniting herself either in marriage or conspiracy with a creature light as a shuttlecock, nor was she likely to be active in any plot whose failure would automatically cancel her claim to the succession and carry with it the sentence of almost certain death. But it was probable that she was aware of Wyatt's intentions and waited to see what fruit they would bear.

There was no doubt that she was ill with what the doctors diagnosed as 'watery humours', recurrent swellings of her body which today would be called nephritis, and she was prostrate with anxiety. But the physicians could not say she was too weak to travel, and her uncle knew the longer the delay before she set out the worse impression it would create.

There was little to comfort her at Whitehall when all but a few of her servants were parted from her and she found herself lodged in a part of the palace where no one could reach her unless they passed through the guard. She was under the same roof as her sister, yet for all her importunity no nearer her.

She was not prepared for the message brought her by two Lords of the Council, and was aghast. They had come to accompany her forthwith to the Tower. This was the Chancellor's doing, she could not believe her sister knew of it; if she did, surely she would grant her audience before such a step was taken. All she asked of them was to allow her to see the Queen. When they intimated that was impossible, she besought them to let her at least write to Her Grace before she left. One said no, but the other, affected by her distress, yielded.

She sat down and wrote to Mary, the sister who had been fonder of her in the past than Elizabeth had been of her, penning in her beautiful hand all that was in her agitated heart. It was a long letter—as long as it takes a tide to ebb. When she turned over the page her writing became larger and less even, but when she came to the signature each letter was delineated as faultlessly as a masterpiece.

By the time it was finished, folded and addressed she had missed the tide, but the day's grace availed her nothing. Mary refused to read her letter when it was brought to her, and angrily turned on the Lords for not carrying out their instructions.

At ten the next morning the hooded barge slipped down the river. It was Palm Sunday and a day grey with rain. Terror suffocated Elizabeth when she realized she had been landed at Traitors' Gate, under which her mother had passed never to return. With the water lapping over her shoes, she sat down on a wet stone and refused to go farther. 'You had best come in, Madam,' urged the Lieutenant of the Tower, at a loss, 'for here you sit unwholesomely.' 'Better sit here than in a worse place,' she returned, at which one of the gentlemen who had accompanied her broke down and sobbed aloud.

She stood up then and demanded why he was giving way when he should be supporting her. Her truth, she said, was such she thanked God her friends had no cause to weep for her, and she passed through the gateway and into the Bell Tower.

Her Chancellor could tell Mary that as long as the Princess Elizabeth lived there was no hope of her kingdom being tranquillized, but the Princess Elizabeth still lived. The imperial ambassador might stipulate that the trials and executions of Courtenay and Lady Elizabeth should take place before the arrival of His Highness, but there was neither trial nor execution, although his words unerringly found Mary at her most vulnerable. Tears sprang to her eyes when she said she would rather never have been born than that any harm should happen to His Highness. It cannot have been reassuring for the prospective bridegroom to have it impressed upon him to bring his own physicians and cooks.

He was eleven years younger than she. A widower with a son, he had no wish to marry one whom, when he mentioned her among his friends, he referred to as his aunt. But he was the obedient son of a father upon whom he had modelled himself since he had been small. He was well aware that the alliance with England, so close to the Netherlands, would give Spain an inestimable advantage over the most intractable country of his father's far-flung empire. He was as well aware of the importance of schismatic England's returning to the incorruptible unity of the Roman Catholic Church.

The marriage treaty, drawn up by touchy Englishmen, left him only with disadvantages, but he had taken the precaution, in the first Sunday of the New Year, 1554, to swear by Our Lord, by St Mary and by the sign of the Cross, before witnesses, that although he had authorized his commissioners to act for him, he had done so only that this marriage with the said queen might take place, but by no means to bind himself or his heirs to keep the marriage articles.

He received detailed instructions from his father on how he and his suite must deport themselves to give no offence to the unaccountable English once they arrived in their country. Meanwhile his son should send some ring or jewel of value which his bride-to-be would be eagerly expecting.

Philip took his father's instructions to heart and was to carry them out to the letter, but he could not bring himself to make any personal contact with the woman destined to be his wife, even when he received a message, conveyed through the imperial ambassador accredited to the English court, that the Queen would like to write to him with her own hand but it was not for a lady to begin. It was the Emperor who sent her a ring well worth looking at which she could show to those around her. And in the end it was the lady who did write first, making a woman's excuse that the Spanish ambassador was sending off a courier, a formal enough letter in French announcing the consent of the English Parliament to their marriage.

The Lords, divided as they were on each and every question, could not agree what was to be done about the Queen's younger sister. She might not have given anything away to them, her questioners, but neither had she cleared herself. She could not be kept indefinitely in the Tower, particularly with the Queen's marriage taking place in Winchester and London already beginning to empty of its personages, nor as certainly could she be set at liberty. Mary therefore sent Sir Henry Bedingfield with a strong guard of a hundred men to convey her to the distant hunting-box of Woodstock, near Oxford, solitary in its great park of sentry beech trees.

Both Mary and Elizabeth, as daughters of Henry VIII, had a parentage that singled them out from all others, but whereas Mary was like the moon whose light is the reflection of another's, Elizabeth was of the sun that shone with its own brightness. Her personality was such that as well as attracting attention she responded as dramatically.

Her journey to the fastness of Woodstock was a triumphant

progress, news of which as it reached Mary, the imperial ambassador and Gardiner called forth their angry reaction. First of all the citizens, as they saw her barge slide upstream to Richmond, crowded to the banks to give her a cheer. Too much good English blood, both noble and common, had already been spilled for a foreigner, and they rejoiced to see the noblest of all pass to what they mistakenly believed was freedom. The merchants at the Steel-yard so far forgot themselves to fire off three salvoes of artillery in salute. When the Princess was on land it was no better. Bedingfield might have the four men at Ashton clapped in the stocks, but by that time the church bells they had rung had proclaimed the joyful news to the district that the Lady Elizabeth was in their midst. He could do nothing about Lord Williams of Tame, expected to provide a night's lodging for his charge and their party, who prepared a magnificent banquet, to which he had invited the neighbouring gentry to do her honour. Whole villages turned out to cry, 'God save your Grace!' and her litter became so burdened with cakes and wafers and flowers that its beautiful occupant had to beg their donors to desist.

Woodstock was not the Tower, where Elizabeth's hopelessness had been such that she had thought of writing to ask Mary that she might be executed by the sword and not the axe—the one privilege granted to her mother. When Bedingfield appeared with his pikemen in blue coats she thought they had come to escort her to the scaffold. But the summer days passed torpid with ennui, laden with the fear that she would be forgotten in this green backwater all the days of her life.

> 'Much suspected, by me
> Nothing proved can be
> Quoth Elizabeth, prisoner,'

she wrote with a diamond on a window-pane, and when she heard a milkmaid singing she thought how much better her lot was than hers, and her days merrier.

Mary also was waiting—for a bridegroom who did not come. The letter he at last sent her, with a gift his father had once given to his mother, a great diamond set in a rose, were by the time they reached her but poor substitutes, for they came when he himself was expected.

The English ships, sent over to escort the Prince from Spain, sailed for Plymouth without orders at the end of June, their captains complaining that whereas they had been promised to serve for one month only they had now served three. The English sailors were rude about the Emperor's ships, which they called mussel-shells.

Mary was only too conscious what a spectacle her plight made for enemies abroad and heretics at home. But when news was brought that the Prince had set sail for Corunna, where a convoy of a hundred tall ships had been lying in harbour for a month, it was like an answer to prayer. At once she prepared to set off for Winchester, where the marriage was to take place.

Antoine de Noailles's younger brother François asked for an audience, which she happily granted before she left. She had always liked him better than his brother, but such was her felicity that it would have embraced even the elder de Noailles. As it happened, Antoine had made François his mouthpiece to crave a favour. Would she, who had re-established in her realm the sacraments of the Catholic Church, grant him the honour of having his newly born son baptized, and choose for him his god-parents?

It seemed so propitious a happening coming at that moment. Forgotten was the knowledge that the mother had been one of Elizabeth's maids of honour, that she, the Queen of England, had not spared words to tell his father exactly what she thought of him. The younger de Noailles was assured that had she not been setting off to Winchester for her marriage that very day, she would have carried the boy to the font herself. As it was she chose the Countess of Surrey for her proxy. She interrupted her own suggestions of first one nobleman and then another for the godparents to ask the questions a woman does ask about the birth of a child. The gratified father exclaimed when he heard that she had spent more patience and time on the subject than he would have asked in four good audiences.

It was not a year since she had been crowned Queen of England that she set out with her bridal retinue for Winchester, a woman of thirty-eight, who had never known what it was to love or be loved by a man, and who had promised the imperial ambassador, on her knees before the Holy Sacrament, that she would love her husband perfectly.

Chapter Ten

She waited for him in the long gallery of the episcopal palace, unable to keep still. Her gown and head-dress were of black velvet, her gown revealing a petticoat of frosted silver, her head-dress lined with gold, her collar and girdle glancing with jewels. It was growing late, and the flare of torch and glow of candle shut out what lay beyond the windows on either side, where the summer dusk was dark with rain. It had rained without ceasing for the past two days, a steady English downpour, described by foreigners as a cruel rain, that fell with the swish of a broom.

He held himself very erect and his gait was stately. They moved towards each other. She kissed her own hand and took his, and he kissed her on the mouth according to the English fashion. Then she led him to the canopy of State and they sat down to talk awhile, she in French, he in Spanish.

His hair and beard were yellow as she knew from his portrait they would be. She had pored over it with her short-sighted eyes, although they told her it should be looked at from a distance like all Titian's paintings. But now she had him beside her she had neither to peer nor to view him from a distance.

His brow was fine, his eyes very blue, his complexion fair. He asked her to teach him the proper English words to say to her Lords when he bade them good night, and she taught him so well that his 'Good night, my Lords, all of you' delighted and surprised them.

Men saw at once that his erect stature was to gain every inch of his height, for he was small, but his face was as princely as his bearing, and his gifts. The Lords were all the richer for his coming, pensions for the noblest, gold chains to the others. Ninety-seven chests, each a yard and a quarter long, filled with bullion, had been unloaded from the Spanish ships accompanying him. With him so amiable the Lords were glad they had added their signatures to the deed the Queen had placed before them, after Wyatt's rebellion, agreeing to her marriage.

They did notice, because they were used to a bold king and his son whose eyes shone when he looked at them, that he never met their gaze under his heavy lids. But his affability was such they were unaware it did not come to him naturally. The benefits accruing from his marriage to the Queen of England, however, were incalculable both in the spiritual and the terrestrial spheres, and any exaction from him was meticulously paid by one who was both resolute and rigid. No trifle was overlooked to make himself agreeable. He could speak no English but told his English attendants in Latin that he had come to live amongst them like an Englishman, and drank some ale for the first time, commending it to his fellow Spaniards as the wine of the country. There were jewels and trinkets for Mary's ladies, and when he asked her to present them to him, he insisted on kissing each one. Already he had learnt that on such occasions it was usual in England to hold his hat, which he said he thought a good custom, instead of keeping it on his head as he would have done in Spain.

Unannounced he came to Mary the following day, through the gardens with but a few gentlemen, to tell her that the Emperor his father had ceded to him Naples, so that the Queen of England would wed not a prince but a king.

Mary's cup of happiness was full. The suspense, fears and setbacks, the long-drawn-out waiting, were of the past, and with her betrothed beside her she began to feel as any maid would feel in cottage or castle on the eve of her wedding to the love of her heart. She had chosen that the ring should not be begemmed but the plain hoop of gold that since olden days any bride in England had slipped over her finger.

They were married by Gardiner, Bishop of Winchester, assisted by five other bishops, each with his own procession. After the magnificence of the marriage service, the splendour of the wedding banquet, the gaiety of the dancing, the bishops, according to the ancient English custom, blessed the marriage bed with its hangings embroidered with the arms and devices of Spain and England—which had greatly disgusted de Noailles when he heard what task the Queen had set the embroiderers.

At the wedding festivities the Englishmen thought with satisfaction that they danced more fleetly than the strangers, while the Spaniards, who had not been allowed to bring their wives with them, considered the English ladies were mostly elderly. Even those who were young, tall and slender were not beautiful to their foreign eyes, although they conceded some were better than the rest. They were not given the opportunity to view the best of all, the Princess Elizabeth.

That autumn her astounded custodian, Sir Henry Bedingfield, informed the Queen that his charge was now performing her devotions according to the Roman rites. He took the opportunity to plead once again to be released from his irksome duty, but once again his petition was refused. When he did receive his discharge the following year he exclaimed that God Almighty knew this was the joyfullest tidings he had ever heard, yet throughout his custodianship of this tantalizing, provoking, changeable ward of his he never failed to refer to her in his painstaking letters to the Council as 'this great lady'.

Mary wrote to her cousin Charles, now her father-in-law, that his son made her happier than she could say as daily she discovered in the King her husband so many virtues and perfections that she constantly prayed God to grant her grace to please him.

The King her husband—the man God had given to her after thirty-eight years to share her bed, to rule and administer for her a difficult country and an intractable Council, a man of her own religion who spoke her mother's tongue to have at her side until death did them part. Their marriage was the consummation, the reward and justification for all she had been made to suffer in the past. It was the cornucopia of fulfilment. Her gratitude to her husband for being what he was filled her with such humility at her own unworthiness that it made her want to kiss his feet.

The bridegroom told one of his friends that when they were alone she 'almost talked love-talk to him'. His friends felt sorry for him. They agreed that the Queen might be a perfect saint but thought she was older than they had been told; hopefully they wondered whether, if she dressed in their fashions, she might not look so old. She appears to have had the effect on them of an albino rabbit, for they noticed she had no eyebrows and that her complexion was white. 'To speak frankly with you,' one of Philip's friends wrote home to another, 'it would take God himself to drink this cup, and the best one can say is that the King realizes fully that the marriage was made for no fleshly consideration, but in order to cure the disorders of this country and preserve the Low Countries.'

To accustom himself to English ways, her husband, within three weeks of their marriage, was transacting business with the

Council. No longer was it necessary for the Queen to spend her days shouting at her Lords—with no result, as Renaud noted. They were not averse to reconciliation with the Holy See, but what was made clear to their sovereign, to Gardiner and now to King Philip, was that her nobles would never part with their abbey lands as long as they could hold a weapon to keep them. She was unable to shame them with her example of restoring all the Church property in the possession of the Crown to its original foundations. They merely warned her that she would not be able to support the splendour of the Crown with such needless disbursement. Her reply that she preferred the peace of her conscience to ten such crowns of England fell on uncomprehending ears.

This year Mary did not suffer from the malaise that affected her each autumn when summer's leaves mouldered on the damp ground. She was 'fatter and of a better colour', and continued to write to her father-in-law such letters about her husband that Charles was heard to comment that his son must have changed. However, he admitted that lovers were scant indifferent judges.

If Charles was one of those born old, then his son was one of those born middle aged. Wisdom is an attribute of the old, which the pedestrian Philip never acquired. Hard at work over details that did not matter, he had none of his father's energy nor his greatness. Other men won Philip's battles for him, for he was an administrator, not a commander, and the glitter of legend and romance never clung to him as it did to his father.

He did not write to his parent of his love or admiration for his wife, for he felt neither. What he told him was that the Council had agreed, since it was for the service of God, that he should take the matter of England's reconciliation with the Holy See into his own hands.

The Pope consented to send Cardinal Pole to England to be his Legate to grant absolution to the apostate realm. But only when the Lords were assured, by the solemn personal promise of either the King or Queen, that the absolution did not depend on relinquishment of their Church lands, did they lift the ban on the exiled Reginald Pole and assent to his return to his native land.

The greatest stumbling-block after all was not His Holiness, or even the Protestant Lords, but Cardinal Pole himself. Neither diplomatist nor time-server, he did not believe the sails of the ship of St Peter should be trimmed to every adverse wind, but steered by God's guidance. And God had no hand in the barter of absolution for the retention of unholy gains. 'You have rejected Christ,' he told the King, but Philip, like the Pope, saw no point in wrecking the ship on an immovable reef: the politic procedure was to go round it. In the end Pole yielded, travelling to Calais by easy stages in a litter, for he was delicate, and sailing for England on the day of his arrival because the wind was fair.

It was November, but spring was in Mary's heart as she rode beside her husband to open her third Parliament in a procession the like of which even Londoners, accustomed to Tudor pageantry, had not seen before. Her cousin was on his way to restore England to the fold of the Holy Father, and she knew now that she was with child.

The thoughts of the man who rode at her side were not so jubilant. He had hoped his studiously amenable disposition towards Mary's Councillors would be rewarded by this Parliament's consent to his coronation. But he knew now that all he could hope for was a Bill appointing him regent should the Queen die in childbirth and the child survive.

It seemed little enough to the man in the beret-cap and black velvet doublet as he watched the Sword of State borne in front of him. Another Sword of State was carried before the woman at his side, each denoting that queen and king were rulers of independent sovereignties. As mere consort of the Queen, not a part of the country's constitution, where would he be in England if queen and child died? Now he had come so far, he must have stakes, other hostages, until he had effected his coronation. And the Queen's half-sister was neither elderly nor sickly.

The Lords and the Commons kept their side of the bargain by passing Bill after Bill restoring the old Acts against heresies, forbidding assemblage of worshippers in secret conventicles, repealing all the religious and ecclesiastical changes made by Henry VIII's parliament from the twentieth year of his reign, and setting out punishments for sedition.

Mary waited amongst her ladies at the top of the palace stairs for the cousin she remembered as a young man, who could write that when her father ploughed him up with the heavy ploughshare of his persecution he found he became more capable of receiving the heavenly seed of faith, hope and charity.

Her husband the King brought him to her. The years can be gentle to the fair-haired. The same oval face she remembered, the same kind, smiling eyes, the same slight figure, a little more bowed perhaps with the stoop of the scholar. This was the cousin who was so much more kin to her than either half-sister or half-brother. With his coming that part of her youth was returning to Mary when the inviolate sacrament was unchallenged upon the altar and the worshipper walked at peace on holy ground. Now when she heard his salutation as Prince of the Church she felt the child quicken and leap in her womb as though in response. 'The day I ascended the throne,' she told him, 'I did not feel such joy.'

In the Great Chamber of the Court at Westminster only Mary stood as absolution was pronounced, for she alone in all that assemblage had been faithful. 'Like a lamp assaulted by adverse winds through a dark and windy night,' the Pope's Legate described her, 'yet kept a light to the hopes of many, and now sheds a bright radiance.' The Lords Spiritual, the Lords Temporal and the Commons knelt in penitence at their schism and disobedience, crying again and yet again, 'Amen!' 'Amen!' When they rose England was once again a Catholic country.

Parliament was dissolved in the middle of January. In February the new Bill restoring the death penalty for heresies, 'much increased of late', was put into action, and a canon, two country parsons and a bishop were burned alive at Smithfield. The bishop was Hooper, with whom Edward had gone through the service of consecration, altering the oath 'So help me God, all saints and the holy evangelists' to 'So help me God, through Jesus Christ'. Ridley and Latimer were to follow, to whose sermons the boy king had loved to listen and whom he was glad to reward for their good words, who had worked out with Ridley how his impassioned appeals for the poor could be answered that God's words led to God's work.

To the palace gate during the night was nailed a notice that could be read in the first light of morning: 'Will you be such fools, oh! noble Englishmen, as to believe that our Queen is pregnant, and of what should she be, but of a monkey or a dog?'

Since she had entered London as queen they had been the hardest things for Mary to bear, the scurrilous bill tethered by a stone, the unsigned leaves of paper scattered far and wide by the newsvendor wind, the placard stuck to the church door.

Early in April, the expected birth month of one already referred to as the young master, Mary with Philip and her household moved to Hampton Court for her lying-in, leaving London with its eager, staring crowds and streets beginning to hum and stifle, for the flat green meads peopled with willow trees at the water-side. Here everything shone, the walls with gold and silver threads, the dazzling blue of ceilings showing through gilded fretwork, a palace magnificent with size.

Awaiting her was a flock of noble and gentlewomen come to assist at her delivery, and a drove of that curious body of women, nurses, rockers, midwives, who gathered like burrs round a royal cradle.

Philip, to ingratiate himself with the English, had ordered two days after the dissolution of Parliament the gates of the Tower to be opened for prisoners implicated in Wyatt's rebellion, and men known to be traitors walked out, stretching themselves in their new-found freedom. Young Courtenay was pardoned, nothing of a definite nature could be brought against him, and he was restored to favour. He asked for and received ready permission to go abroad, with letters for the Emperor, to enlarge his education in a world so big it yawned. He suffered from homesickness, writing to a friend wishing he had remained in England that they might have practised together with their crossbows among the deer. He died from a chill in Venice after little more than a year's exile, unable to receive the sacrament for his swollen tongue and clenched teeth.

Towards the end of April Elizabeth was brought through the wild and wet weather of a late spring to Hampton Court by her custodian Sir Henry Bedingfield. The Queen did not at once send for her, but Elizabeth was told three days after her arrival that the King would see her. She received a message from her sister to wear her richest dress for the occasion, a message that reveals the ambivalence of a woman over-fondly in love.

Nothing is known of what took place at this, their first meeting, between the man who was to become known as Philip II of Spain and the woman Elizabeth I of England. He is said to have re-proached himself in the years to come because he entertained a secret passion for his sister-in-law, and Elizabeth liked to say that her brother-in-law had been in love with her.

Since the birth did not take place in April as expected, the Queen was bound to be lightened at the next change of the moon —or after the full moon in June. But the baby came neither in May nor June. Mary no longer took her daily walks and was said to be suffering excessively. A man was paid two hundred crowns of French gold to regale de Noailles with information culled from one of the best midwives in the town and an old lady who had been with the Queen for more than twenty years. The ambassador faithfully repeated all he heard to his master Henri II.

Her doctor said she ate so little it could not keep the child alive. She might be pale and peaked, but some said she was not pregnant at all, it was a tumour—as often happens with women. She was crouching for hours at a time on cushions on the floor, her knees drawn up to her chin, and she could not have sat thus if she carried a child without smothering it.

Prayers were instituted for the Queen's safe delivery at the beginning of June, and that the infant might be a male child, well formed and witty, and Mary was seen at a window every morning watching the processions going round the court. The Venetian ambassador thought she looked very well. 'In this kingdom,' Renaud wrote at the end of the month, 'the Queen's lying-in is the foundation of everything.' Not only in England, every court in Europe was listening to rumour and waiting for the latest news.

They told her from day to day her pregnancy had been mis-calculated by two months. At the end of July her doctors and women promised she was certainly carrying a child, only the birth would now not take place until August—or even September.

She did not wait for the next change of the moon. Quite sud-denly she left Hampton Court with its swollen population of gentlewomen and old wives and the sumptuous gorgeous cradle in her bedroom with its Latin verse and inlaid English transla-tion. 'Ah, Strelly, Strelly,' she said to one of her ladies in waiting, the only person throughout who had not believed she was with child, 'I see they be all flatterers, and none ever true to me but thou.'

She with Philip and their entourage moved upstream to Oat-lands, usually used by royalty for hunting, perched on its high ground with its tall elms noisy with rooks. She knew now not only that she was not bearing a child but that her husband was about to leave her.

He said he was only going to see his father, the Emperor, and would return in a fortnight's time, but her heart told her as she was carried through London on a litter a fortnight later that she would not feel this anguish if it were for a matter of fourteen days.

The litter was open that her people could see her, for many believed the tales they had heard that she was dead. They gave her a tumultuous welcome, so gladdened were they at the sight of her. They would have liked to see the Princess Elizabeth too, but only heard afterwards that she had shot London Bridge in a shabby barge on her way to Greenwich. Those who saw her said her attendants were so scanty they had been able to count them— four damsels and three gentlemen.

Mary would have liked to go to Dover with her husband, to tease out as long as possible the dwindling time she had left, but she was not well enough to undertake any more journeying, so that he bade her goodbye three days after they had arrived at Greenwich.

A queen has no privacy. All Europe knew she was extraordinarily in love. Now courtiers watched her come with him to the head of the stairs, carrying her smallness with 'a sort of stately sorrow'. Only when her husband kissed each of her ladies in turn did her composure quake because it reminded her of that day filled with so much happiness when she had seen him for the first time.

He took his leave of her, and she turned and moved to a window overlooking the river where, her back to the world, she believed she could weep unseen. As his barge passed below the window, he waved his flat cap to her, and she stood gazing after him, her face blind with tears, long after his bark had disappeared round the bend in the river. For five days he waited for a fair wind to speed him from England, five days he could have been with her.

In the seven months before he left, fifty-four persons were burnt in England for heresy; by the time Mary died little more than three years later the total had risen to three hundred.

That figure is as nothing compared to the religious holocausts on the Continent. It is as nothing compared to the thousands her father sent to the block for political and other reasons, yet Henry was remembered by his people as good King Hal, his daughter by the terrible opprobrium of Bloody Mary. No shudder of horror convulsed London or passed over the country when Henry VIII extirpated Reginald Pole's elder brother and his brother's small heir, when his cousin was executed and his mother slaughtered, because they happened to be of rival Plantagenet blood. But to the English mind there was something peculiarly abhorrent to put to death men and women for their beliefs.

Their giant of a king in his ruby collar and his coat of cloth of gold, buttoned with diamonds and rubies and sapphires, that great father figure more than life size, like the embodiment of England, a transcendent prototype of the common man, personified both the best and the worst of his people. They had welcomed Mary as their queen because she was his daughter and heir, because they had loved her mother, because with her coronation old wrongs were righted. The citizens of London could turn out in their hundreds to greet her because she was alive whom they had feared dead, but there was no identification between them.

Blame for the burnings in Mary's reign cannot be shifted from her, an unvindictive woman, and placed on Philip's narrow shoulders, or at the door of the Roman Catholic bishops such as Gardiner, or over-zealous justices, or her Council or cousin Cardinal Pole, or faceless informers.

Two people and two people alone, one a Dutchman, the other a woman, were put to death because of religion during her brother's reign; we accept that the key to such clemency was set by his enlightened uncle Somerset, with his dislike of bloodshed. But the twelve-year-old Edward thought it a terrible thing for heretics to be burnt, punished perhaps but not sent quickly to the devil in all their error. He burst into tears when Cranmer told him Joan Bocher must die, eschewing all responsibility and sobbing to his godfather, 'I lay the charge therefore upon you, before God.'

At the beginning of Mary's reign every tacit encouragement, including the doors of the Tower left open during her coronation, was given to Protestants to leave the country and rid the Queen and her Councillors of their unwelcome presence, but they remained.

To Mary and her co-religionists Protestantism was as evil as Roman Catholicism was to Protestants. And it must be remembered no attempt was made to distinguish between heresy and sedition. To Roman Catholics one propagated the other. Protestants certainly were more actively seditious than their opponents. A Bill had to be brought in making it illegal to pray for the Queen's death.

'But now,' the voice of Cranmer spoke, 'the omnipotent Governor of all things so turned the wheel of her own spinning against her, that her high buildings of such joys and felicities came all to a Castle comedown, her hopes being confounded, her purposes disappointed, and she now brought to desolation.'

The man who had pronounced the twenty-four year old marriage of Henry VIII to Katherine of Aragon void was taken from Lambeth Palace to the Tower before the coronation of their daughter. He was not of the heroic mould. Neither was Sir William Cecil nor Edward's beloved tutor Sir John Cheke, all three of whom had unwillingly signed the King's Device for altering the succession.

Cecil could not deny his own signature but professed he had signed simply as a witness. Mary thought him a very honest man, and although he did not sit in Parliament he accommodated himself with a discretion that excited neither envy nor attraction.

Mary felt pity for the tutor of whom she knew her brother had been so fond. Cheke could not face the flames and recanted. An outcast from all he had held dear, he left London and went into the country, alive in a world peopled with shades, to die it was said of a broken heart.

Cranmer was nothing if not pliable. He as Archbishop of Canterbury had crowned his patroness Anne Boleyn Queen of England, and within three years as Archbishop of Canterbury had pronounced her marriage to the King invalid and thus bastardized their daughter. It was expected he would explain away his signature on the King's Device by saying he had stood out against signing as had none other. Instead he maintained he had not signed under pressure but from conviction, unfeignedly, and without dissimulation. Mary was not deceived by such boldness, she prophesied he would recant, which he did, again and yet again. She knew he could reap neither sustenance nor strength from his faithless creed.

Her days were cheerless after Philip left her. He wrote her he had had a fair crossing of two and a half hours; after that she had to wait for his letters. She told the Venetian ambassador 'very passionately with tears in her eyes' that for a whole week she had no word from him, and the experienced diplomat watched how she brightened with his well-chosen assurances that the King had not written because he was returning to her so soon. There was not an envoy who did not know that the Queen of England was so intoxicated with love for her absent husband that she would not stick at offending God or man to please him.

Philip's father, who had begun to feel the cold so intensely he said it was in his very bones, resigned his most cherished possession, the Netherlands, to his son, and in the following year his Spanish possessions. It was said in ambassadorial circles, which meant all London knew, that the King had written that much as he wished to gratify the Queen's desire for his return it was not in accord with his dignity to come back and be again no more than her uncrowned consort. But her Lord Chancellor knew neither the country nor the Commons would stand for what was not in her power to grant and what would make void the marriage treaty.

Gardiner had not been well lately. As sometimes happens with the irascible, his shortening days outran his irritability and he made friends with old enemies, showing de Noailles the repairs he was having done to his house, insisting on seeing the Frenchman to the door, saying he wished people to see he was not dead yet. But when he stood up in Parliament he looked much the same as he had always looked, with the tuft of unruly hair, nicknamed 'his grace', standing up as it always stood, and his voice as strong as ever.

Contentious as are those who believe attack is the strongest defence, he informed the jumpy Commons, in the Queen's name, not to be disturbed by false reports regarding the King's authority as there was no truth in them. That night he died.

Only when he was gone did Mary realize what a stout bulwark he had been, for whom there was no substitute. It was the able Gardiner who brought some rectitude into the teetering economy. But if there was no debased coin minted in Mary's reign, the country's poverty prevented the recall of those circulated during her father's time and her brother's minority. It was a poverty shared by its economical queen, who returned several of the great estates, confiscated by the Crown in the past, to their original families, and whose lack of money, de Noailles noticed, was apparent in everything pertaining to herself, even to the dishes put on her table.

Not only was Mary unable to achieve for her husband the crown matrimonial, but she failed to prevail on Elizabeth to marry the bridegroom he chose for her, the Duke of Savoy.

It was essential for Philip's hold on England that Elizabeth be acknowledged successor to her sister and that her bridegroom should be his puppet because the French had in their possession the small Queen of Scots who would soon wed their Dauphin. As Mary Stewart's grandmother had been Henry VIII's elder sister, her claim to the crown of England, in the now foreseeable future of Mary Tudor's death, was unassailable. But no Spaniard could allow England to pass into the control of the French. Regrettable as it was that Elizabeth's mother was not of the proud house of Guise like Mary Stewart's, but a whore whose marriage to Henry VIII when his wife was still living was no marriage at all, Philip had to make the best of what material he had, and His Holiness could be depended upon to remedy any deficiency at the time of the appropriate marriage.

Elizabeth, who knew she owed her reinstatement to her brother-in-law, was with the Queen at Greenwich when he took his departure. There was no longer any playing to the Protestant gallery on the younger sister's part, not only because there was no longer a Protestant gallery to which to play, but because everything would be lost were her sincerity called in question. She shared in Mary's devotions and accompanied her to mass. When questioned on her belief in transubstantiation, for mass was the unbridgeable gap between Catholic and Protestant, she replied:

> 'Christ was the Word that spake it,
> He took the bread and brake it;
> And then His Word did make it,
> That I believe and take it.'

The relationship between the two sisters was now amicable. Mary's reign was plagued with abortive risings and restless plots, but even when seditious material was found amongst her household, Mary assured Elizabeth she did not believe her guilty. A tradesman was punished for saying that that jilt, the Lady Elizabeth, was the real cause of the Wyatt rising.

Mary's changed attitude to Elizabeth was not only in deference to Philip but was coloured by her relief that she, with to Mary welcome obstinacy, refused to consider wedlock. For her sister to be married with royal honours in the pride of her youth and beauty, to bear heirs, would have been insufferable to the older woman who, when she appeared in public after Philip's departure, looked like a corpse, fully ten years older than the great age which forty was then considered.

Therefore the more self-abasing Mary's letters became to her husband as she bent over them in the pricking silence of the night, the more she reiterated that she could not, on her conscience, force her sister to marry against her will, and she found Elizabeth exceedingly averse. Despite her fear of Philip, for she was afraid

143

of him, she was unable to serve him in this matter. 'I shall live in apprehension of your Highness's displeasure, which would be worse to me than death; for I have already begun to taste it too much, to my regret.'

She was beside herself when she learnt that the great King of Sweden was proposing his eldest son as Madam Elizabeth's bridegroom, knowing how detestable such a marriage would be to Philip, who would blame her for not pressing the Duke of Savoy match. Even when danger was past and she calmed down, it was reported to Philip that the Queen was 'still in a terrible taking about it'.

Mary was pleased at Elizabeth's judicious reply to the Swedish ambassador that she could not listen to any proposals of this kind that were not conveyed to her through the Queen's authority, with its rider that if left to her own free will, she would always prefer a maiden life.

Mary requested Sir Thomas Pope to discover what was behind the Lady Elizabeth's constant refusal of suitors—was it an objection to the married state in general? Elizabeth replied to his delicate questioning upon her truth and fidelity, and as God was merciful to her, that, whatever she should do hereafter, she was not at this time otherwise minded than to continue as she was—no, though she were offered the greatest prince in all Europe. The greatest prince in all Europe was Philip of Spain, who had been rumoured, according to the spiteful de Noailles, contemplating asking the Pope to annul his marriage to the Queen of England that he could marry her sister. But such a thought never entered Sir Thomas's mind as he penned his report to his queen that in his opinion her Grace's protestations proceeded from none other than maidenly shame-facedness.

Mary's face had become even thinner, her nights were broken, she confessed the need for Philip's presence was wearing her away; it was said, 'Nothing is thought of, nothing expected, save this blessed return of the King.' Every new act of faithlessness on the part of her subjects, every new injury dealt her by her divided and unstable Council, every gross libel, the hideous picture of herself almost naked suckling Spaniards and entitled 'Maria Ruina Angelica', left her shocked and angry.

Her only moments of peace were when, all jarring discords shut out, she was enclosed in that unshadowed, timeless world of the realities beyond the urgency of prayer. Sixteen Benedictine monks who had not fled took up their offices again in the old abbey at Westminster and she burst into tears at the sight of their black-gowned figures. Greenwich was now her favourite residence, where she liked to watch the barefooted friars move in and out as they used to do. On Holy Thursday she knelt before the old women to wash and dry their feet, crossing them after she had done and kissing each foot, as an eye-witness noticed, as though it were something very precious.

She shared this common ground with her cousin Cardinal Pole, who was proceeding to reform the English clergy with such energy that most of them wished him back in Rome. Spiritually Mary and the Cardinal spoke the same language. Both had unconfused consciences, and the same simplicity of piety. She could lean on him, so much older than she and therefore so much wiser, and her excitability found easement in his quietude. During his long exile the French tried to entangle him against his native country by repeating all the wrongs his house had suffered, but he told them he never forgot he was an Englishman. Now on his return, two generations later, he found the stoniness of his countrymen hard to understand. He who, like Mary, gave gladly, heard himself tell the citizens of London that two Italian cities gave more alms in a month than the whole kingdom of England in a year. He had not only outstepped his generation but outstripped the centuries. To the Bishop of Arras's contention that a good peace could only be made by a good war, he replied war was never good.

The order came from Rome that Thomas Cranmer was condemned to death—the apostate who had continued to fill the See of which the Vatican had deprived him. He who had been the highest ecclesiastical dignitary in England was prepared for his imminent end by harrowing degradation.

He had accepted the papal supremacy, and retracted the doctrine of the Protestant sacrament, admitted he had exceedingly offended against Henry and Katherine by being the cause and author of their separation, which was the seed-plot of the calamities of the realm. Now their daughter waited to hear, what bishop and doctor gathered in Oxford to learn, the triumphant declaration of their faith from this man within flame's breath of eternity.

They brought the news to her. Instead of a crowning vindication of the old faith, she was told that what Thomas Cranmer had repented of was his recantations, which he said had been made for fear of death, and to save his life if need be. To prove his words he held out the hand which had signed them that it might be burnt first.

Mary had always turned to her cousin Charles for advice. She sent a messenger to him to ask his counsel on the disquieting subject of heresy. The fires they were kindling were not extinguishing it, indeed they appeared to be inflaming it. We do not know what Charles replied, but it is unlikely he suggested amelioration when thousands of Lutherans and Anabaptists were being burned, hanged and drowned throughout his dominions.

Philip had more on his hands than to trouble himself about his wife's dubiety and heart-searchings. A truce can be but a breathing-space as the two parties prepare once more for war, and the patched-up Truce of Vaucelles between France and Spain proved one such. It was made more brittle by the machinations of the evil, provocative Pope Paul IV, whose great age was said to be the one blessing among so many mischiefs, but whose hate seemed to lend intensity to his grip on life. To him, a Neapolitan, the French, the Spanish, the English, the Germans, were all barbarians, but he sided with the French because he hated the Spanish more, referring to Mary's husband, King of Naples, as 'Philip, late Charles'. Within months of the signing of the truce the French set out for Italy, and once again it was war between France and Spain.

And still Philip did not return to Mary. Madame de Noailles, when she waited on her to pay her respects, scarcely recognized the unhappy queen. Hard pressed for money, as she had been from the outset of her reign, the Commons looked grudgingly at every loan for which she asked, no matter how necessary, suspicious that what they granted she would feed to her husband for his war in which they were determined not to be drawn. Their misgivings were not unfounded. In Philip's war, whatever England was, Mary could never be neutral. It is known that she 'accommodated her consort' in that one year alone with at least 10,000 crowns. So much sacrifice and suffering for nothing in return was bound to raise a reaction. A story is told of the Queen flying in a fury at Philip's portrait and scratching with her nails his painted face.

He came so soon after the announcement that he had reached Calais that her transport of anticipation melted into that of realization. Side by side they walked through the royal gallery in

Greenwich Palace to their chapel-closet to give thanks for his safe passage. The nineteen months he had been absent flowed behind her unremembered as they disembarked at Tower-wharf and, side by side, were welcomed by the Lord Mayor and aldermen of London. At Windsor, on St George's Day, as she watched him leading the procession of knights he might never have been away.

The Queen was ready to face not only men but also to bend to her will the very elements themselves, to make Philip's war England's war. She felt in some way this would prevent his leaving her ever again. But her Council did not prove malleable. The exchequer was exhausted, and nothing was more costly than war. Granted the French had given them plenty of provocation in capturing and plundering English ships at sea, and the whole world knew they were for ever giving a stir to any plot brewing against the English queen, but they hated the Spaniard as much as they hated the Frenchman. Besides, they knew they might share the heat of the battle with the Spanish but in the hour of victory mighty few pickings would come their way.

The Council was warned by the English ambassador in France of the possibility of invasion after a spy had shown him the plan of a port where the assault was to take place. The port was unnamed, but it looked to the ambassador like Scarborough.

He was right. On Easter Day 1557 a French ship, the *Fleur de Lys*, hove to off Scarborough, to allow a band of Englishmen to disembark, before sailing on to Scotland with French soldiers for their ancient ally and England's hereditary enemy.

The forty-one invaders were all young English malcontents who had taken refuge in France, with effrontery enough for any adventure however hazardous, their eyes so dazzled by the glory that was to be theirs they did not dwell on how it was to be achieved. All were gentlemen and led by the high-born Thomas Stafford, renegade nephew of Cardinal Pole, of royal blood on both sides of his house, who had been made much of by the French king.

They had no difficulty in seizing Scarborough, whose citizens heard the one thing the invaders had prepared, their proclamation. It declared twelve castles were to be handed over to the Spanish king Philip on the day of his coronation; the Queen was half Spanish and as much as she loved the Spaniards so she hated the English; Spaniards were pouching English money and said they would rather live with Turks, Jews and Moors than with the

English—a clear indication they were going to use the English worse. Thomas Stafford had come to save England from the most devilish device of Mary, unrightful and unworthy Queen of England, who had forfeited the crown by her marriage with a stranger.

They were taken prisoner by the local militia without bloodshed, removed to London and executed.

Henri had played Philip's hand for him. In the face of such barefaced incitement, the Council could not but act. In vain the French king protested he had refused utterly to have anything to do with the plot. He had to accept the last thing he wanted to accept—that he was at war not only with Spain but with England, and the balance of power was weighted against him.

At the beginning of June, after only three and a half months, Philip left Mary. He had achieved what he had come to do, what he had sworn in the marriage treaty not to do, engaged her country in his father's French wars. But they were no longer his father's wars, they were his now the Emperor had abdicated and, wrapped in an eiderdown coat even in summer, had retired amongst the friars at Juste to pass his last days in hoped-for peace.

Mary accompanied her husband to Dover that she might be with him as long as possible. At the very end she went on to the shore to be nearer the ship that was bearing him from her.

The improvement in her health whilst he had been with her lasted for a time after his departure. When the subsidy was raised to pay for the war, she sold Crown lands. Five thousand foot soldiers set sail to fight beside Philip's army of Spaniards, Italians and other nations of his empire. English ships were not only on guard in the Channel but appearing where least expected off the French coast, scattering the enemy, even taking a prize, landing Englishmen on French soil to fire a village. When the Scots, allies of France, made an invasion over the Border, Mary thought of heading an army against them.

In August a resounding victory was won for Philip by the Duke of Savoy at the battle of St Quentin, in which the English force took part. London celebrated the triumph with a Te Deum, processions, bonfires and banquetings. God was making it manifest to the world that He was on Philip's side.

But it was a damp, unhealthy autumn, a season that always had a lowering effect on Mary. Philip's letters insisting she should bring about the marriage between Elizabeth and the man who was now the hero of the day were reaching a crescendo of acrimony. He told her she should have the marriage celebrated without asking Parliament for its leave. Her Council was complaining bitterly that the King of Spain refused to declare war on Scotland, although it was because of him they had to suffer their neighbours harassing them at their back door. As the days of the year ran out, she received word from her commanders in Calais that food was short. If they were attacked they would abandon the town to keep the quayside that aid could come from England to the castle.

On 7th January 1558, when the mistletoe and holly had been taken down after the Twelve Days of Christmas, and the Queen was urging gentlemen of every shire to raise men to succour 'the principal member and chief jewel of their realm', Calais fell. The news reached England three days later, and worse was still to come. English ships were unable to relieve Guisnes because of a great gale so disastrously sudden and fierce it was as if it had been raised by sorcery by the Devil himself who had become a Frenchman.

It was a blow from which Mary never recovered. 'When I am dead and opened you shall find Calais lying on my heart', she is reported to have said. She tried to make the unbearable tolerable by scheming how to regain it, and sat at the Council table signing letter after letter. Never must England make peace with France until Calais was restored to her. Her Councillors looked at her lined face, grey as ashes, and hated what they saw because they felt that but for her this outrage would never have happened to them. Yes, they agreed, but what about the King of Spain? He could have saved Calais and had not moved a step: could he, when settlement was finally drawn up between him and France, be counted on to make the restoration of Calais to England a condition?

She waited until she was quite sure before she wrote to Philip in the month that Calais fell that she was with child. He sent over Count Feria, ostensibly to congratulate her on the happy news but less ostensibly to keep him advised. It is unlikely that Philip had any faith in her or her doctors' prognosis, unbelievable that she could become a mother at the advanced age of forty-two. What had not happened nearly three years ago proved that miracles were not going to happen to Mary Tudor.

Count Feria had been in the King's train when he came to

England to be married and was now betrothed to Jane Dormer, Edward's childhood little love, who was one of Mary's devoted maids. The Queen had delayed their wedding in the hope that Philip would return and be able to be present at it with her.

Feria reported to his master that, after the loss of Calais, the Queen's subjects had less respect for her than ever, and fewer than a third of those who used to go to mass now attended. It is not difficult to find the reasons. England would not have been in the war, exposing the country to invasion, but for the Queen who had married a foreigner, and they were sickened by her Church which was burning without abatement the good people of her land.

In May Feria wrote decisively to the King that the Queen was not going to have a child. Since his wife's symptoms did not denote pregnancy, they must indicate a graver diagnosis and there was no time to lose now Mary Queen of Scots had married the Dauphin that spring in a Paris thrilling with joy. The English queen must be made to recognize Elizabeth as her successor.

She was very ill throughout that summer, unable to sleep, so that even at night she had no release from her old enemy melancholy, what her doctors called 'superfluity of black bile'. The death of her cousin Charles in September only deepened her midnight gloom. The peace he yearned for was denied him by the loss of Calais, which he felt so sharply it was said it hastened his death. One by one her few remaining life-lines were being withdrawn. Her cousin Reginald Pole was ill in Lambeth Palace, unable to visit her as she was unable to visit him.

Towards the end of October she had brought to her the will she had made over three years before the hazard of childbirth. She left it as it was, with its bequests to poor scholars at Oxford and Cambridge, endowment for the first hospital for disabled soldiers ever founded, bequests to her re-founded monasteries, the table-cut diamond to Philip which his father had sent her on her betrothal to keep as a memory of her. She had not mentioned Elizabeth by name, the crown was to pass to Mary's successor according to the law, and 'My most Dear Lord and Husband shall have no government, order, and rule within the Realm.'

She added only a codicil revoking the clause in which she had included the hoped-for issue. She who never dissembled, who has been called 'the most honest of Tudor rulers', wrote plainly 'as I then thought myself to be with child'. When she put down her pen, she did not lift it again.

She was unloosening herself from the fusses, strains and demands of every day. When her Council gathered round her weightily enlarging on why she should now nominate her sister as heir, two of their number were able to ride to Hatfield to tell Elizabeth the Queen was very glad she should succeed to the crown. They were instructed to ask her to make two promises, one to maintain the old religion, the other to pay the Queen's debts.

Life as she had known it was receding mercifully from Mary as she was borne towards death on a tide so full it was tranquil. Feria arrived post-haste with a letter from his master. She appeared pleased enough to receive it, but could no longer read what he, unaware he had been forestalled by her Council, had written, pressing her to give Elizabeth in marriage to a Spanish nominee with promise of the succession. The letter, Philip, the court, tugged at her like weeds. She told Feria that if the King made peace without stipulating that Calais was returned to England it would cost her her head.

She was at sea now, far beyond their ken. When she drifted back from unconsciousness, the world had concentrated for her into the loved faces of her women kneeling beside her. She told Jane Dormer she wished she could be at her wedding, she regretted now she had delayed it. Later when she returned and saw they were weeping, she comforted them by saying what good dreams she was having, seeing many little children like angels playing before her, singing pleasant notes.

The long-standing practices of a lifetime sustained her to the end. On 17th November 1558 she heard mass very early in the morning as she was wont to do, and made the responses as she had always made them, passing away with the words still blessing her lips.

Book Four

Elizabeth I
November 1558–March 1603

'An archer is known by his aim, not by his arrows.'

Proverb

Chapter Eleven

She was to remember when she was old the horse hoofs and wheels lurching over winter roads as courtiers hastened from St James's Palace to Hatfield before Mary was dead to secure places at the future queen's court. They clattered through her mind every time during the forty-four years of her reign she was pressed to name her successor. Her angry retorts, to intimidate further questioning on so distasteful a subject, have the echo of the tomb about them. She could by no means endure a shroud to be held to her eyes while she was living. 'Think ye that I could love my own winding-sheet?' She had no desire to be buried alive like her sister, nor that her grave should be dug while she was yet alive. Well she knew the inconstancy of men who turned from the setting sun to worship at the shrine of the rising one.

Feria predicted she would make Cecil her principal secretary. He told King Philip that in his opinion she was a woman of extreme vanity, but acute. He noticed she was very attached to the people, most confident they were all on her side which, to his regret, he had to admit was true. He smarted at her ingratitude when she denied with great spirit she owed her succession to the King of Spain, or his Council, or even the nobles, although she said they had all pledged themselves to remain faithful to her. She owed it to her people and the people alone.

Mary had made her Spanish blood her boast, Elizabeth's pride was that she was 'mere English'.

Feria was not the only ambassador, watching her when she entered London for the first time as queen and during her coronation, who considered her demeanour exceeded the bounds of gravity and decorum. So prompt was her response to the adulation that in the excitement of the moment the acclaimed was at one with the acclaimer. Her thanks to the Lord Mayor for the richly wrought crimson satin purse which held a thousand marks in gold were so moving they raised a marvellous shout of rejoicing. When the child Truth stepped out of one of the pageants to present her with a Bible, she not only received it but kissed it, holding it up in her beautiful hands for all to see and clasping it to her heart, giving 'great thanks' to the City. The Venetian ambassador sourly remarked, at her presentation to the people after her coronation to the accompaniment of trumpets, fifes, drums and organ, with bells making tumultuous the air, it was as if the world were coming to an end.

But he was a foreigner and did not understand their English ways. The world was not coming to an end, this was the birth of a new world. You did not have to wonder which was the Queen, you saw her—there was no mistaking good King Hal's daughter, golden from the crown of her head to the hem of her gown, her jewels clearing a way for her through the flurry of snow. When they cried, 'God save and maintain thee!' she answered with smiles 'God 'a' mercy, good people!' They were her good people as she was their good queen, cheerful as the sun. The Register after recording the names of the Protestant martyrs burnt on 11th November burst into rhyme:

> 'Six days after these were burned to death
> God sent us our Elizabeth!'

On Christmas Day she took her first soundings with regard to religion. After the gospel was read, she swept from her chapel with the whole of her retinue because she knew the officiating bishop had refused to comply with her order that he was not to elevate the Host. Her action caused no outcry, not even a murmur of dissent, but she was not precipitate. Loyalty meant more to her than orthodoxy and it was desirable that the oaths of allegiance at her coronation should be taken by all the nobility.

The difficulty was to find a dignitary who would crown her. Even if the Archbishop of Canterbury, Cardinal Pole, had not died twelve hours after Mary, he would have refused, as the Archbishop of York and bishop after bishop refused, to crown Anne Boleyn's daughter known to be a Protestant, even although 'etc.' appeared tactfully on the first public document of the reign instead of Supreme Head of the Church. In the end the Bishop of Carlisle agreed, but he could not live long with his burdened conscience and died shortly after coronation day.

Elizabeth was not religious as her sister Mary and her brother Edward had been. By schooling and aptitude her mind was open to the new learning, but she was untouched by her brother's burning fervour. Her aim was harmony, not uniformity. Neither fervent Catholic nor stout Protestant, she was able to steer between two extremes and refused to be driven off course by the men she had chosen to fill her great offices of State. Protestantism meant little more to her than the means by which she ascended and kept the throne, and a handy passport into the affairs of other countries. She could sum up her creed towards the end of her life in the few words, 'There is only one Jesus Christ and one faith: the rest is a dispute about trifles.'

Like all autocrats she was a law unto herself. She might say to the Westminster abbots who met her in broad daylight with lit tapers at the opening of her first Parliament, 'Away with these torches! We can see well enough', but candles and tapers continued to burn on her own altar when they were abolished elsewhere, and with her liking for elaborate ceremonial she saw she did not go without it. She never took kindly to the marriages of the Protestant clergy, protesting loud and long about so many wives and children in places where they had no right to be. Her parting words were more like parting shots when delivered at the wife of the Archbishop of Canterbury after she had been entertained in the archiepiscopal palace at incredible cost and herculean effort, 'And you! madam I may not call you; mistress I am ashamed to call you, and so I know not what to call you; but however I thank you.'

Nor would she brook even the most covert criticism of herself from the pulpit, or sentiments which differed from her own. In the exuberance of the new reign she flourished and blossomed into peacock colours and rich stuffs. Edward could scarcely have called her his sweet sister Temperance had he seen her wearing a caul set with pearls and precious stones, and at the same time a gold-spangled hat with a bush of feathers. She took it much amiss when Bishop Aylmer 'seemed to touch on the vanity of decking the body too finely', and interrupted Dr Nowell when in a sermon he began to preach against images in church by shouting at him, 'To your text, Master Dean! To your text! Leave that! We have had enough of that! To your subject!'

It was a single horseman who galloped through the night to acquaint Mary she was now queen, and a single horseman galloped through the early morning mist to confirm to Elizabeth at Hatfield that she was now his sovereign. He was Lord Robert Dudley, whose wedding the boy Edward described in his journal. The new queen made him her Master of the Horse on the spot, a coveted post which gave him a lodging at court.

Born on the same day and in the same hour as Elizabeth, astrologers busy with their horoscopes would have cast their attraction to each other, the fusion and divergence of personalities so closely allied, the fated crossing of their paths. He had known her since they were eight, when they were close enough for him to be her confidant. Both had been imprisoned in the Tower at the same time, he and his brothers after the fall and execution of their father, she under suspected implication in Wyatt's rebellion, where he may have glimpsed her walking on the leads between her guards. When both were free he had sold some property and given her part of the proceeds because he knew she was in debt.

Both were tall and spectacular in appearance, his handsome darkness—an enemy nicknamed him The Gypsy because of his brown skin—a foil to her fairness. A worthy partner to the Queen in the high leaping dances of the day, he, like Thomas Seymour, excelled at all masculine sports. 'A man eminent for his person, deficient in wit and integrity,' ran the laconic contemporary appraisement of him.

Feria noted that Elizabeth was incomparably more feared than her sister, and gave her orders and had her way as absolutely as had her father. She had also her father's instinct for choosing the right men as her councillors. 'This judgment I have of you,' she said to Cecil when she made him her Secretary of State, 'that you will not be corrupted with any manner of gift, and that you will be faithful to the State; and that, without respect to my private will, you will give me that counsel which you think best.'

Both Cecil and his sovereign understood that England must have peace—within as well as without. The ship of state Elizabeth now captained had seldom been less seaworthy, its armoury dismantled, its treasure long since jettisoned, without ballast. 'No war, my Lords!' the Queen commanded at the Council table, and Cecil's maxim read like one of his own minutes, 'A realm gains more in one year's peace than by ten years of war.'

Peace meant friendship with both Philip of Spain and Henri of France. Philip hoped to regain a hold on England because the Spanish Empire's very existence depended on its extended sea communications, and without England these were vulnerable. He strove for a bond stronger than friendship, but it became obvious, despite Elizabeth's delaying tactics, that she was not going to marry her brother-in-law. Within three months he became betrothed to the Princess Isabel, Henri's elder daughter who had been trysted to Edward, an engagement that had to be accepted by England as though it were not the setback it undoubtedly was.

Elizabeth drove the peace negotiations with France she inherited from her predecessor as near a break as she dared before accepting a face-saving formula. The French king was now said to bestride England, with one foot in Calais and the other in Scotland. Henri was also claiming, since Mary Tudor was dead, that his daughter-in-law, Mary Queen of Scots, was Queen of England since the illegitimate Elizabeth had no right to the throne.

The English royal arms engraved on Mary Stewart's seal and plate, embroidered on her tapestry and emblazoned on her carriages were a constant source of irritation and resentment to English ambassadors, while the French querulously demanded with Gallic logic how Elizabeth could style herself Queen of France when their law did not admit the female to rule. But nothing was allowed to mar the first great occasion since she had been crowned when the French embassade arrived in May to receive the Queen of England's ratification of the treaty. All was charm, gallantry and beauty.

It is no figure of speech that Elizabeth's reign was called golden. With courage she at once set herself to restore the currency. She had not only the blood of thrifty merchant Boleyns in her veins, but the blood of her careful grandfather, Henry VII, who had amassed a fortune of millions for her father to squander.

The debased coin of his reign and Edward's was called in, and when Elizabeth went by water to the Tower to visit her mints, she coined pieces of gold with her own hand, pure gold. For the base coin each received its nominal value in new unalloyed money. The government, which meant the Queen, bore the loss, which was very heavy, and only effected by the most rigorous economy, but her people never forgot to whom they owed their waxing prosperity. When she returned from a progress, the citizens of London went to Islington to meet her, hedges were levelled and ditches filled in to clear her way, and so glad and affectionate was their welcome that it was night before she reached St Giles-in-the-Fields.

She had not been crowned Queen of England for three months before Feria was recording gossip regarding her and her Master of the Horse. 'Lord Robert has come so much into favour that he does whatever he likes with affairs and it is even said that Her

Majesty visits him in his chamber day and night.' His wife did not make an appearance at court but remained in the country unvisited by her husband. A sinister report was going the rounds that Dudley intended to rid himself of her—by poison most people thought.

In September the Spanish envoy was told by the Queen on her return from hunting that Lord Robert's wife was dead, or nearly so. She had fallen down a staircase and broken her neck.

The scandal rang from court to court. The English ambassador at Paris wrote to Cecil, 'I know not where to turn me, or what countenance to make.' If the day came that the Queen so foully forgot herself as to marry Dudley, he himself would not wish to live. The tragedy 'so passioneth' the heart of Thomas Randolph, English ambassador in Scotland, that 'no grief ever he felt was like unto it'. Cecil listed six cogent objections against the marriage, number four that Dudley was so violent and mutable in his passions, the Queen could not expect to live happily with him, and number five that he was 'infamed' by the death of his wife.

It could not be denied that the Queen was in love with Dudley, her whole being was infused with desire when he came into her presence. It was even suggested by a tolerant Councillor that marriage with the man she loved would be the readiest way of getting an heir to the throne, but he was in a minority of one. Cecil wrote what the Queen would determine, God only knew. Elizabeth certainly did not. The patent raising him to the peerage was drawn up, but instead of signing it she took a knife and cut it in two. Cecil dispatched a letter to the English ambassador in Paris saying that 'the great matters whereof the world has wont to talk were now asleep', but before it reached him the peerage proposal was alive again. This time Elizabeth said she would not confer the title on those who had been traitors three descents, and Dudley had to be clapped on the cheek to dispel his black dump.

She did not marry him. In the years to come he, laughing and sighing at the same time, confided to the French ambassador that he did not know what to hope or fear, that he was more uncertain than ever whether the Queen wished to marry him or not. He believed she would not marry, but should she alter that decision, he was convinced she would choose none other than himself. She had told him so herself, and he was as much in her favour as he ever was.

It is clear to us now that Elizabeth had a rooted aversion to the married state not only for herself but for others. She spoke with such contempt of the institution of matrimony that the Archbishop of Canterbury had to remonstrate with her. Dudley said he knew her better than any man on earth, and she had told him since she was eight she would never marry. The eight-year-old who had told him that apprehended what manner of death her mother had died.

As Elizabeth of England she was the prize of Europe, and she manipulated her courtships to the top of her bent to suit the politic situation of the moment, involving herself personally with such conviction that even the suitor could not doubt her sincerity or his own desirability. The uniqueness of her position, the publicity and stir with ambassadors and suitors passing to and fro, rival vying with rival, the magnificence of the presents, to be sought after as no one else was sought after, to know that the stakes she was playing for were not Elizabeth's but England's— all not only added zest and lustre but were some recompense for what she was denied in her private life. No matter how dangerously far in the years to come she allowed her flirtations to go, she was always mistress of the situation and knew exactly how much of the tether to allow not only others but herself.

Thrones were the nerve centres of their world, and events such as death or consecration that affected one of these seats of nature were felt in varying degrees by all. In July, a few months after Elizabeth's coronation, Henri II, taking part in a tournament to celebrate the marriage by proxy of his little daughter Isabel to the King of Spain, was wounded by a splintered lance. Within a few short days the heralds were proclaiming, 'Le Roi est mort, vive le Roi.'

The new fifteen-year-old king, Francis II, whom everyone knew was sickly, was a negligible factor to England except that his Queen was Elizabeth's cousin, Mary Stewart, and that her two masterful Guise uncles ruled for her boy husband. A Guise augured no good for England. It was the Duke of Guise, France's greatest soldier, who had taken Calais when the tide was low.

Fifteen months after the death of his father, the heralds were once more proclaiming, 'Le Roi est mort, vive le Roi.' Francis II was replaced on the throne by his ten-year-old brother Charles IX and there loomed from the background the momentous figure of Catherine de Medici holding in her broad hand the puppet-strings of her three minor sons.

The potentialities of Mary Queen of Scots as a widow were infinitely more alarming to the English than when she was the wife of the King of France. Every move she made was bound to upset not only individuals but countries, and thus create tension and crisis. Warning tremors now reached Cecil from wherever she happened to be.

Elizabeth's suitor kings abandoned her to court the younger queen. If Mary Stewart married any of them, and the King of Denmark was boasting he was the strongest prince upon the sea, then, strengthened by his power, she could contest the crown of England. But the alliance the English most dreaded was a Spanish alliance. And it was on a Spanish alliance the heart of the Scots queen, with her Guise ambition, was set, on the most desirable bridegroom in the whole of Christendom, Don Carlos, two years younger than she, the weakly, unattractive son of Philip of Spain's first marriage.

Another death had taken place between that of Henri II and his eldest son, the death of Mary Stewart's mother, Mary of Guise, Regent of Scotland. In June 1560 she died in Edinburgh Castle where she had taken refuge from the Scots Protestants led by Mary Stewart's half-brother, Lord James Stewart. Protestants were known as Reformers in England, Huguenots in France and Lords of the Congregation in Scotland.

As long as Scotland gave footing to French troops she was a danger to England, but to aid the rebel Lords was a violation of the treaty Elizabeth had signed with the French. The Lords of the Congregation might in their own eyes be God's Elect, but that did not save them from being worsted again and again by the papist French troops of a papist regent. It became obvious they could not dislodge the French already in their country without assistance from England before reinforcements Henri II was preparing to send reached the harassed Regent. Cecil saw to it that they received assistance, and his queen blandly assured the Regent's French ambassador, when he demanded an explanation of her broken faith, that she held her honour too dear to say one thing and do another. Grimly he returned to tell his mistress, 'There is more dissimulation in her than honesty and goodwill; she is the best hand at the game living.'

The Lords of the Congregation were not going to allow the grass to grow under their feet after so auspicious an event as the Regent's death, in which they clearly saw the hand of God.

Within two months they had summoned, without the consent of their sovereign in France, a parliament which abolished the Pope's jurisdiction and established Protestantism as Scotland's religion.

London watched a splendid embassade from the north of three earls and their followers, numbering seventy horse, ride through their city to thank Queen Elizabeth for her assistance. A commission of a single man was dispatched to France for royal confirmation to their Acts, which included the recognition of Elizabeth's right to the throne of England and provision for the immediate withdrawal of French troops from Scotland. No one was more affronted than Elizabeth when her Scots counterpart refused to sanction Acts drawn up by men in their own name, as though they would make Scotland a republic.

Elizabeth was probably the only English sovereign up to her time who did not eye the crown of Scotland as a perquisite for herself: her strength lay in her concentration on being Queen of England. She never evinced any interest in the permanent union of Scotland and England, or in the future of Protestantism in either. Her horizon was bounded by her life span, a sphere that sufficed Elizabeth, who could not think of England as apart from herself or herself apart from England.

Elizabeth and Cecil knew all about the undercurrents speeding the Scots queen to return to her native land with her rich French dowries. For one thing she could not marry without the consent of the Scots Estates. For another, negotiations for the Spanish marriage could not be carried out to a satisfactory conclusion while she was under the hourly surveillance of her inimical mother-in-law Catherine de Medici.

Lord James Stewart, soon to be created Earl of Moray, had more in common with his English cousin Elizabeth than he had with his half-sister Mary, for he was more Tudor than Stewart. Elizabeth and he were compatible with the compatibility of born rulers. Purposeful as steel, he was the formidable strong master his stormy country needed. But he, the eldest of James V's chance-bairns, bore the bastard's bar and the crown belonged to his sister, eleven years his junior, who was more French than Scots, a Roman Catholic queen come to rule over a stoutly Protestant people.

Scotland meant to Moray what England meant to Elizabeth, to Mary it meant a spring-board to greater things. Her brother knew it could not stand alone in the Europe of his day, it had either to belong to the Catholic bloc or the Protestant bloc, and he was determined it would be the Protestant bloc. That meant alliance with England, and succession, should Elizabeth have no heirs of her own, would consolidate alliance into perpetuity.

Nothing would induce Elizabeth to countenance an heir presumptive, least of all Mary of Scotland, because of the tacit encouragement that would give English Catholics to hasten their Protestant queen from her throne to make room for a Catholic successor. But she had to keep her options open because of the fear of her cousin contracting a marriage unfavourable to England. She therefore played the game at which she was the best hand living, deferred the issue with a chain of half-promises and impossible stipulations when Moray and Mary's envoys came posting down to England, and of loving intentions she did not mean to implement when she wrote to her sister queen.

It was granted by Mary and her advisers that if she were to be named as the Queen of England's successor, it was only reasonable that the Queen of England should be allowed some say in whom she should marry. By this time only Mary of the parties involved knew that her secret negotiations to marry the King of Spain's son had been terminated by his father, known as Philip the Prudent, who did not wish to excite the enmity of England. The Queen of England was asked to name the partner she considered most suitable for the Queen of Scots.

Elizabeth's suggestion was the offer of her own discredited lover, Sir Robert Dudley. Nor was she put out when she heard that Mary's instant reaction to the insult was to call him Elizabeth's groom. Instead, Robert Dudley at last received his peerage from his sovereign. To prove her sincerity, and make him more honourable a match, she created him Earl of Leicester in front of Melville, Mary's envoy, but somewhat spoiled the effect by tickling the new earl's neck when she told him to rise. Mary asked Melville on his return what he thought of the English queen's intentions towards herself, and he replied with Scots directness, 'Neither plain dealing nor upright meaning, but great dissimulation, enmity and fear.'

Elizabeth, still unaware that the Spanish alliance would not come to pass, sent up to Scotland her young cousin Darnley, elder son of the Scots Earl of Lennox who had been exiled twenty-one years ago from his native land for treachery. Through his mother, Mary's aunt, Darnley was near to the English throne. Elizabeth's purpose for this move was probably twofold: to remind Mary there was another candidate for the succession should she prove troublesome, and to distract her cousin from the Spanish alliance by sending to Scotland someone Elizabeth could recall when she chose. Darnley, born in England, was subject to the English queen, not the Scots.

He was very personable, this young man bred at the cultivated English court. Unbearded, he looked younger than his nineteen years, he was three years younger than Mary, with hair the rich yellow of buttercups, the Stewart height and the Stewart long face and lily-white skin. Through wintry weather on rough roads, he outrode his retinue so that he could reach the Scots queen on St Valentine's Day.

Mary liked her cousin Darnley more than she expected to like someone sent by Elizabeth, and the more she saw of him the more she liked him. When one more bid to reopen the negotiations for her marriage to Don Carlos failed, she dispatched her Secretary of State to England to gain Queen Elizabeth's consent to the Darnley union and to harp on the old string of the succession now made doubly sure since Darnley himself was connected to the throne.

News reached Scotland that neither Queen Elizabeth nor the English Council would sanction the marriage. Darnley sent an impertinent answer instead of obeying his peremptory recall, and Mary married him. It was her first irrevocable mistake. The tragedy for her was it would not have been a mistake if Darnley had been other than the poltroon and coxcomb she was warned he was.

She had procured the unanimous consent of her nobles for the marriage. Moray remarked afterwards that seeing the other lords had all voted in favour of it, he thought it best to do the same. But he climbed down from the fence a little later to appear on Elizabeth's side, with some of the other noble signatories.

The revolt became known as the Chase-About-Raid. With energy and resolution Mary pursued the rebels from place to place, doubling back to try to catch them. They with their scanty forces, vainly waiting for Elizabeth's promised help of soldiers and ammunition, kept on the run until they were able to slip over the Border.

Moray made for the English court, but Elizabeth had no use for losers, particularly when she was chiefly responsible for their not having won the game. They had led her to believe Mary's rule in her realm was weak, whereas the Scots queen had carried all before her. Elizabeth found herself in the position she most dreaded, having shown her hand. The French and Spanish ambassadors alleged in their masters' names that the English queen had been the cause of the rebellion, and that her only delight was to stir up dissension among her neighbours. Assistance to rebels constituted declaration of war by England against the Queen of Scots, when the French would need no bidding to go to her aid and send troops again to Scotland. A scene was hastily improvised where Moray, clad in penitential black, was brought into her presence and swore on his knees in front of the ambassadors that the Queen of England had neither aided nor promised them support. She wrote to Mary that she only wished she could have been there to hear how roundly she had rated him.

Randolph, the English ambassador to Scotland, kept Cecil well informed with details of the Scots queen's misery in her marriage, which must have read like an object lesson to Elizabeth. All Edinburgh knew it had been the King and Queen when they were first married, then His Majesty and Hers, now he was known as 'the Queen's husband'. He was riotous, and drinking heavily. He insulted the Queen at a banquet when she tried to restrain him. He neglected his wife by spending his time with his own associates and Douglas kinsmen—the Douglases would be enemies of the ruling Stewarts to the clap of doom. What he—and they—wanted was the crown-matrimonial, but the Queen, now her eyes were opened, refused to gratify him, as she refused to pardon the rebel lords now in England. She had called a parliament when they were to be forfeited, Moray and all.

Mary made an Italian, David Riccio, one of her musicians, her secretary because she could trust him. The King and Randolph said he was the Queen's paramour and it was he who was advising the Queen not to give him the crown-matrimonial which would secure the crown for him and his heirs in the event of her death. She was with child, which meant her life was chancy. Riccio, with the consent of the King, was to have his throat cut. The King had made a bond with Moray and the rebel lords to return to Scotland and back him. Since the Queen would not cancel the parliament that was to forfeit them, the King would—with them behind him.

Moray, when he arrived in Edinburgh and saw his sister, swore by his God he had known nothing of the murder of Riccio until

166

his arrival. As Elizabeth and Cecil had both heard of the plot, and Moray had been in close touch with Darnley's associates during these past months, it is difficult to believe his protestation. The best that can be said for him is that, knowing of the plot, he would not have been a party to the manner in which it was carried out, which was that her secretary was hacked at in a small turret room before Mary, who did everything in her power to save him. There could be only one reason why he was taken in the presence of the Queen and that was in the hope she would have a miscarriage, when the throne would be vacant for the crown-matrimonial.

Mary did not have a miscarriage but outwitted the murderers, who woke up to the disagreeable realization that their prisoner had flown in the night to strong friends, with their trump card the King up her sleeve.

She went to the stronghold of Edinburgh Castle for her lying-in. The correspondence between the two queens at this time was at its kindliest, free of the dissembling insincerities of the past. Elizabeth admired a winner. She sent a message to Mary, wishing her short pain and a happy hour.

Sir James Melville carried the triumphant news to London, covering the 391 miles between the two capitals within five days. Elizabeth was dancing and merry after supper when Secretary Cecil whispered in her ear news of the prince's birth. Instantly, as though touched by frost, her mirth shrivelled. Her cry, 'The Queen of Scots is lighter of a fair son, and I am but a barren stock', has been interpreted as proof that Elizabeth was incapable of bearing children. It could also have been the involuntary cry of a thirty-three year old spinster.

She was told her godson was a fine boy, stout and hearty, and sent a merry message with her costly present of a gold font that if it were too small by the time it arrived Mary must keep it for her next.

Mary's son was born on 19th June 1566. On 29th July 1567 he was crowned James VI of Scotland. Within little more than thirteen months his father had been murdered, his mother had married the Earl of Bothwell, the man all believed to be the main perpetrator of the murder, their forces had been broken and his mother carried to a damp castle on a lonely island where she was forced to sign a deed of abdication in her son's favour, and appoint his uncle Moray Regent.

Elizabeth's reaction to the news of these startling events was characteristic. She did not herself write to Mary after the death of her 'slaughtered cousin', but employed Cecil to enlarge upon her perplexity being such 'that we cannot find the old way which we were accustomed to walk in by writing to you with our own hand'. Her perplexity reached incredulity when she heard Mary had left her mourning chamber in Holyrood House a week after the murder and travelled to Lord Seton's residence, some miles out of Edinburgh, with her ladies and nobles, where she held court untrammelled by woe. Cecil penned urgently that the Queen of England exhorted, counselled and begged the Queen of Scots to take this event so to heart that she would not fear to proceed even against her nearest. Mary's nearest was then the Earl of Bothwell whom, when he was acquitted by the unanimous verdict of a jury packed with Darnley's enemies, Mary's friends and the accused's henchmen, the Queen of Scots had married.

But when Elizabeth learnt that the Scots lords had imprisoned their queen, were talking of deposing her and crowning her baby son in her stead, even of killing her, she exclaimed that the usage and proceedings of the Scots lords against their queen over-passed all. She and Mary belonged to the most exclusive guild in the world, that of crowned heads, which did not admit the right of subjects to attempt anything against the sacred person of their sovereign. Cecil, Leicester and the English ambassadors and envoys plying between England and Scotland all might want England to give the Scots lords full-blooded support, but they had to obey their queen.

Elizabeth's pale face was oval, and had lost the shadowless egg-shell look it had had at her coronation. Above her high cheek-bones her eyes were wary, and already the face in which they moved was informed with a growing confidence.

She grieved and wept bitterly when Kat Ashley died. Her Kat had been with her since childhood and they had been separated only by her own or her young charge's duress. Elizabeth took to heart this irrevocable parting with the woman who had been her lady governess. Indiscreet Kat had done everything to further Thomas Seymour's suit with the Princess Elizabeth. But when the Princess was queen she had gone on her knees to implore her in God's name to put an end to disreputable rumours because her affection for the married Dudley, a man very much of Seymour's calibre, threatened to sully her honour.

Elizabeth's relationship with her Master of the Horse had much of the tug-of-war that protracted relationships do tend to have. The strain on the rope was always there. It would be reported that the Queen had fallen into some misliking with the Lord of Leicester, and therewith he was much dismayed, but Cecil for one refused to make a flame of that sparkle. Leicester became violent with jealousy when she singled out a handsome young courtier for her favour. She declared she was sorry for the time she had lost on him, at which Cecil commented to a friend, 'And so is every good subject.' My Lord would retire in dudgeon, and it was the Queen who would have to be the suitor. Sometimes there were tears on both sides, but the estrangement was always healed, with Leicester resuming his former position.

Elizabeth had advised the Scots lords, before they deposed their queen and crowned her baby son, to consider how to stay where they were. How could they hope to hold a woman not yet twenty-five a prisoner all her life? When she heard that, after less than a year's captivity, her sister queen had escaped, she had the satisfaction of having been proved right, and wrote with her own hand congratulating Mary on the joyful news. She offered to mediate between the Scots queen and her subjects, by which Elizabeth meant Moray and the Scots lords. If Mary agreed, Elizabeth promised to persuade or compel (the English queen knew her strength) Mary's subjects to do likewise. But Mary must not call for aid from France (Elizabeth had not rid Scotland of French troops to have them returned). 'Those who have two strings to their bow,' she wrote to the Scots queen, 'may shoot stronger, but they rarely shoot straight.'

Before the letter could be dispatched the news reached the English court that the Scots queen had disembarked from a fishing-boat with a small party on the Cumberland coast. Elizabeth, when she read the piteous letter of her very faithful and affectionate good sister and cousin and escaped prisoner, Maria R., who had arrived on her shores with nothing in the world but the clothes in which she had fled from Scotland, at once thought of bringing her to court and treating her with all honour.

It was Cecil who pointed out that for the English queen to receive the Scots queen, with 'her appetite to the Crown', would be tantamount to acknowledging her as heir. There was too the question of the murder of Elizabeth's near kinsman and subject, Darnley—could the Scots queen be admitted into the presence of the English queen before a full and searching inquiry had been made into that untimely matter?

As the Archbishop of Canterbury, Dr Parker, remarked when he heard who was now in their midst, 'I fear that our good queen has the wolf by the ears.'

Chapter Twelve

As Mary Tudor was responsible for saving her sister Elizabeth's life, so Elizabeth was responsible for saving that of her cousin Mary Stewart for nineteen years. Elizabeth's was spared for a reign of forty-four years, which has gone down in history as glorious, and Mary Stewart's for miserable captivity which culminated in her execution.

The ill-starred Queen of Scots was her own predicament. She could not be allowed to repair to France, where she would be a constant threat to England. Nor could she be permitted even limited freedom as a private individual in England, with her unassailable right, in Roman Catholic eyes, to the English throne. Nor dare she be returned to Scotland with Elizabeth's help, where she could involve both countries in the religious wars that were trailing their devastation across the Continent.

The rights and wrongs of keeping her prisoner were not questioned. What was best for England justified every and any expedient. The siftings, the plausibilities, the double-dealing to lend a semblance of legality, the cruel cat-and-mouse proceedings, all were necessary for England to prevent bringing France or Spain or both against Elizabeth in Mary Stewart's defence.

Even as a prisoner Mary Stewart was a perpetual danger. The headlong Catholic Earls of Northumberland and Westmoreland both lost their lives, as did their followers, in a precipitate attempt to rescue her, and for plotting against his country and sovereign the Duke of Norfolk was beheaded. Both Houses of Parliament petitioned that the Scots queen should share his fate, but, although touched and moved by her people's loyalty, Elizabeth asked how she could put to death the bird that to escape the hawk had fled to her for protection.

As the hawk could be none other than Mary's most relentless enemy, her half-brother Moray, whom Elizabeth admitted into the audience, which she denied the hunted bird, her simile is not so tender as it sounded. She was now the possessor of the famous pearls Mary had brought from France, twenty-five of which were the colour of and as large as black grapes. For these Catherine de Medici had been prepared to pay their value, but Moray gave them to Elizabeth at bargain price.

Elizabeth had been on the throne for seventeen years before the extreme penalty was exacted because of religion when two Dutch anabaptists were burned at Smithfield. Her policy of toleration covered many shades of belief, only the zealot found himself without, for the zealot does not compromise. And Elizabeth's Church was largely a compromise Church, Protestant in dogma with a hierarchical organization, making use of Roman Catholic liturgy translated into English.

The Puritan looked upon his queen as his dear natural sovereign who did not go far enough in the right direction, the extreme Catholic bore allegiance to Mary Stewart not her cousin. He called for the mass, the Puritan for a return to the primitive Church purged of ceremonial and vestment.

It has been truly said that Elizabeth had all the right men round her, Mary Stewart all the wrong. But it was not the men round Elizabeth who made her reign what it was. It was she who was its dominance and their inspiration. She might swear and shout like a man, but because she, their lion-hearted queen, was a woman afraid to have one of her teeth pulled, her Ministers held her in protective reverence.

Sir William Cecil became Lord Burleigh when she raised her Secretary of State to the peerage; she made him her Lord Treasurer, which meant he devoted his sound and deep judgment to the public economy. When he was invested Companion of the highest Order in England, she herself buckled the garter about his knee.

A charmed orbit of courtiers circled round the glittering queen. Tall, young and handsome for the most part, each of her votaries strove not only to keep but to better his proximity, his only bond with his fellows the jealousy excited by the rising of a new star on their mistress's horizon.

She knew to look behind her cushion to find her adorers' poems, and carried their letters in the capacious 'pouch' dangling at her side. It was a scintillating circle, intimate with nicknames, the sparkle of compliments, the flash of repartee and a woman's salutary wit. In her withdrawing chamber, where she sat with her ladies, her very presence supplying light and warmth to the galaxy of her worshippers, she could retire from the rigour of the

Council table, the facts of dispatches, the endless playing of one ambassador against another.

Into this inmost circle of the chosen there darted not a courtier blessed with handsomeness and graced with gifts but a small, under-sized man, his face blemished with smallpox and a nose so big it was a deformity. A king's son, the Duke of Alençon had come from France to fling himself at the English sovereign's feet. She who liked well a precipitate wooer gave him the fond name of Frog, and smiled on his suit. The Spanish ambassador marked that she enjoyed nothing better than to bask publicly in her royal suitor's adoration. He wrote love letters before he saw her that would have softened a frozen rock, and after they met others so passionate they were enough to set fire to water.

As Philip of Spain reached his pinnacle of power, England's friendship was as essential to France, torn with religious strife, as France's was to an England aware of Spain's growing antagonism towards her.

Catherine de Medici's bait for perpetual union with England was her boy sons. Each was suggested in turn, and with each Elizabeth toyed and stalled, the difference in the ages of the prospective bride and bridegroom widening as a younger brother was brought forward to fill the place vacated by the elder when he married elsewhere.

French ambassadors did gallant juggling with any disparity which really was not there at all, seeing Her Majesty, from her charms of mind and person, appeared younger than she really was, and Monseigneur the Duke, because of his manly bearing and sprouting beard, was so much older than his years—if only they could be certain of Her Majesty remaining in the mind to marry.

Elizabeth was forty-five on Alençon's first visit to England, and she must have known that as far as marriage was concerned this was her swan song. Her suitor, less than half her age and with every disadvantage except birth, had a Frenchman's adult adroitness at making love, which carried Elizabeth through the next crisis-packed years, so that at times she could not have told if this were merely a game she, skilled with practice, was playing.

All the young men in the inner circle round the Queen were against her marriage to the French prince, as was the not-so-young Leicester, which was natural enough. The French realized it was he, so close to her he knew the high beating of her heart, who counted. Alençon's confidential friend broke the news to

173

her that Leicester, who they knew would go to any lengths to prevent the marriage, was himself a married man and had been for more than a year.

Elizabeth may have known of an earlier alliance he had contracted, but she was a woman of the world and may have chosen to shut her eyes to what her favourite repudiated. She did not know of the second, and the outrage she felt was such that she wanted to commit him to the Tower. It was her loyal Lord Chamberlain who counselled against such an action, which would cause irretrievable damage to herself who alone had the power of arbitrary arrest. He held no brief for Leicester, a man he despised and distrusted, but he pointed out it was a lawful marriage and lawful marriage had always been accounted honourable.

The two women who made cuckolds of their husbands were known at court as Leicester's Old Testament and his New. Both were kinswomen of the Queen on her mother's side. The sniff of poison always clung to Leicester. Lord Sheffield 'parted beds' with his wife when he learnt of her intrigue, but before he could bring his wife's lover to book he died. The Earl of Essex also died, but the father of his widow was the Puritan Sir Francis Knollys. The marriage of his daughter to the Queen's favourite might be secret, but he saw to it that it was legally performed before witnesses chosen by himself.

Fishing in other nations' troubled waters was legitimate employment. Burleigh had informers in every court, spies watching every foreign port. They all harboured their enemies' malcontents, and did everything they could to mine and sink as long as nothing appeared on the surface. Philip lied through his ambassadors when he said that no Spaniards were in Elizabeth's Ireland, and Elizabeth lied to his ambassadors when she said she knew nothing about English pirates seizing rich Spanish merchant ships at sea and bringing them to England with their unlawful cargo. The sea-rover Drake, in whose current expedition she was the largest investor, could be relied upon if taken to deny with his last breath that his queen knew anything about his buccaneering exploits. It was noticed that Ireland cost the Queen more vexation than anything else: 'The expense of it pinched her; the ill success of her officers wearied her; and in that service she was hard to please.'

The Netherlands were Philip's most fishable waters. He had unloosed in 1567 what became known as the Spanish Fury when ten thousand Spanish veterans occupied the Low Countries to subdue once and for all the most intractable of his far-flung dominions. Religion never obscured Elizabeth's judgment as it did his. What did it matter to his master, she demanded irritably of a Spanish ambassador, if the Netherlands went to the devil in their own way?

The fall of peaceful, prosperous cities, their garrisons slaughtered, the women who had helped to man the defences torn to pieces, the senseless killings and brutalities, were a fiendish lesson of what could happen to England—if Spain struck. The branching masts of new ships began to line the dockyards at Chatham as Walsingham's spies brought news of the army and fleet Philip was preparing, an army and a fleet which could be turned against England once he had enforced his claim to Portugal and its colonies.

Elizabeth sent aid to her co-religionists in the Netherlands, but it was with reluctance, although her Councillors, stouter Protestants than she, tried to urge her to greater generosity. But she had no wish to invite war with Philip over the inhabitants of the seven northern States, who to her were an impossible, fanatical people. Instead of coming to terms with Philip, now he had succeeded in conciliating the south, they were demanding preposterous peace conditions as though they were the victors.

In the year 1580, when Philip overran Portugal and its colonies, Francis Drake was bound for England. He had brought home treasure before but nothing like this, for he had been where he had never been before. He had sailed on the sea he had sworn to sail on when he had sighted it on an earlier voyage from the top of a lofty tree to which Negro slaves, escaped from their Spanish masters, had led him. His sailor's blue eyes had feasted on it as it lay glittering in its immensity to the south—the Pacific Ocean.

No danger threatened the Spanish there. Its ports were unfortified, its ships unarmed. Drake swept the coast northwards on his star-charted voyage round the world. He seized ships and treasure as he sailed, annexed California, and added a valuable cargo of spices to his gold and silver and fabulous jewels.

France could not view with equanimity that the whole of the Iberian peninsula was now Spain's, as well as part of Italy, the Netherlands, the entire New World, the East Indies and numerous settlements in Africa. Nor could England.

It was a period of acute danger for her with Jesuit priests

stealing into the country, hiding in the houses of the faithful, heartening the fearful. 'Holy, peaceable, and sweet endeavours of orderly men,' their missionary work was described by those who sent them. 'A sort of hypocrites, naming themselves Jesuits, a rabble of vagrant friars newly sprung up and running through the world to trouble the Church of God,' was the English verdict. And in her rigorous imprisonment the aging Mary Stewart wrote in her broken handwriting to prince and king, the Pope, ambassador, emissary and nuncio, to her Guise kinsmen in France and her son in Scotland, and to her sister queen, Elizabeth of England, who named her the daughter of discord.

The marriage negotiations with Alençon were revived.

It had pained Catherine de Medici that she could not imbue her favourite child Henri with ambition to win Queen Elizabeth as his bride. But male Medicis were short-lived and, now Charles IX was dead and her most propitious son reigned as Henri III, she had to place all her considerable weight behind Alençon, her youngest, for the new king married a portionless princess of his own age.

By this time Alençon was in the Netherlands with the Protestant rebels who, the French hoped, would make as much trouble for the Spaniards as possible. Not that Henri or his mother openly countenanced French embroilment, but Alençon was better anywhere than in France plotting with the Huguenots against them. For this maverick son and traitorous brother to be consort to the firm Queen of England was a prospect dazzling not only for him but for France.

To the people of England the union of their Queen to a Frenchman was as abhorrent as had been Mary Tudor's to a Spaniard, and they loved Elizabeth as they had never loved Mary. Her Council sat discussing the marriage for eleven hours without stirring from the room. Burleigh wrote out their opinions under the two headings Perils and Remedies: the Perils outnumbered the Remedies. One ran, 'In years the Queen might be his mother. Doubtfulness of issue more than before. Few old maids escape.'

Every year since her coronation Elizabeth had been pressed by her faithful Commons and Lords to marry. Now when she asked for their opinion she was incensed to be told they were against it.

When all that was left of the Alençon negotiations were memories, and the beautiful banqueting pavilion, with its three hundred glass windows and ceiling painted with all the glories of the firmament built to entertain the embassade from France, Elizabeth could give a great clap on the shoulder of one who had advocated the French alliance and say, 'I will never marry; but I will ever bear goodwill and favour to those who have liked and furthered the same.'

In the golden month of September Drake rode on the tide into Plymouth Sound. His queen's instructions were explicit: he was to be allowed to abstract most secretly ten thousand pounds of his plunder so that, should his sovereign be forced to return the spoil, he would still have his reward.

Mendoza, the Spanish ambassador, clamoured for an audience. She, even she, could not deny that this man Drake was a robber. She, even she, would be forced to meet Spain's most vigorous demands for his disgrace and the restoration of his contraband to its lawful owners. But he was left to chatter with frustration. Her Majesty, he was told, could not speak to him since she had not yet received a letter of apology from his master regarding his interference in Ireland.

In April of the following year, when the French embassade was on its way to England to complete the negotiations for their prince to marry the English queen, it was made clear as daylight that the first Englishman to circumnavigate the globe was not going to be sacrificed on a Spanish altar. Her Majesty dined in state on board the *Golden Hind*—never since the days of Henry VIII had there been such a banquet—and knighted its captain on his own quarter-deck, blithely telling him as he knelt before her she had a sword ready to cut off his head.

Elizabeth went to incredible lengths not only to further but to seal the Alençon marriage. When she induced him to accompany her to St Paul's Cathedral to propitiate her Protestant subjects, she kissed him during the service in full view of the congregation. As she walked with him in the gallery at Greenwich, the French ambassador asked if he could tell his sovereign that the marriage would take place. For reply she kissed her suitor on the lips, the English signal that they were affianced, took a ring from her finger and put it on one of his saying, 'You may tell His Majesty that the Prince will be my husband.'

Burleigh was the only one who saw the hand she was playing. 'God be thanked!' he exclaimed when he heard about the ring incident. 'Her Majesty has done her part. Now Parliament must do theirs.' For three years the Queen had gained time, and the marriage terms could always be raised until the French king was bound to refuse them. The return of Calais was one impossible condition which so insulted the French they were on the verge of severing diplomatic relations.

Alençon tore off the ring Elizabeth had given him when he heard that, although her affection for him was undiminished, she must sacrifice her own happiness to the welfare of her people. The women of England, he declared, were as changeable and capricious as their own climate, or the waves that encircled their island. He told her he would sooner be cut in pieces than not marry her and so be laughed at by the world. When he burst into tears she gave him her handkerchief.

She felt played out as she waited for the winter winds to allow him to depart, mollified by promises of money to finance him in the Netherlands and with the prospect that, if he returned in six weeks, conditions to marry him might be more favourable. She was forty-eight now, and confided to a trusted male friend that she hated the idea of marriage more every day; she had reasons against it she would not divulge even to a twin soul—if she had one.

Undoubtedly she used Alençon to achieve her own ends, which she did with masterly success, out-manœuvring everyone on the field, but it is difficult to believe that she did not feel affection for her Frog Prince. Two years later, when he died in France in disgrace, her grief made her feel as forlorn as a widow.

'We all do what we can to persuade Her Majesty from any progress at all, only to keep at Windsor, or thereabouts,' runs a letter from Leicester, 'but it disliketh her not to have change of air.' A nobleman honoured to be allowed to entertain the Queen trusted Lord Burleigh would see that Her Majesty's tarrying with him would not exceed two nights and a day, for that was all his long preparation for her could last.

Not only was she lodged, banqueted and entertained but she departed laden with gifts. We read of one host who presented her with a gown of embroidered cloth of silver, a black network mantle bright with pure gold, a white taffeta hat that bloomed with flowers and a golden jewel set with rubies and diamonds. Nor could she grace his lordship more than when she removed from his table a salt, a spoon and a fork of fair agate.

The spectacles and transformation scenes to enchant her beggar description. Tritons towed a fully rigged pinnace bearing musicians across a crescent-shaped lake constructed for the royal occasion, nymphs emerged from a cave to the sound of heavenly music although no musicians were visible, a marvellous mermaid, eighteen feet long from top to tail, swam and frisked, and pagan gods and goddesses chanted the praises of their sovereign. Perhaps the most wonderful of all was Arion with music following him all the way as he rode his dolphin to and fro across the lake, for his mount housed unseen a six-voice choir and an orchestra.

Elizabeth's relationship with Leicester was too close to be sundered even by her discovery that he was a married man. It was to withstand a strain as heavy if not heavier. The ties that united them were now too interwoven to constitute a tug-of-war. Instead of the wear and tear of passion, their association had settled into a durability that had nevertheless a certain chivalric quality, so that his image was never shrouded for her by his growing obesity, and to the last he felt for her the awe that she was his queen.

She did not want him to leave her after all preparations were made in the fateful year of 1585 for him to lead an English force into the Netherlands. She had been low since August, when she made a treaty with the rebel States to give them armed assistance in exchange for the ports of Flushing, Brill and Rammikens. It was a treaty she had never wanted to sign with those whom she called an ungrateful multitude, a true mob, but it was thrust upon her by hard necessity.

Twice she had been offered the sovereignty of Holland, Zeeland and Utrecht, and twice she had refused what her father would have grasped with both hands. Elizabeth was not even tempted. To accept would mean open war with Philip, and not for anything on the map would she expose England to that.

To send a force into the Netherlands was not in her eyes a declaration of war, but it depressed her to act against the grain. She undertook to maintain on foreign soil an army of 5,000 English foot soldiers and 1,000 horse. The expense alone was enough to alarm her. But Philip's generals had recovered for him the central provinces of the Low Countries, and in the month she made her treaty with the States Antwerp had fallen. She had no alternative except to buttress the rebels. No longer could she count the French king as an ally: his unhappy country was riven with civil strife.

It was called the War of the Three Henris in France. Now

Alençon was dead, the heir presumptive to Henri, the last of the Valois, was his brother-in-law Henri of Navarre, of the House of Bourbon. But no member of the powerful Guise family, Catholic to a man, could be expected to acknowledge the leader of the Huguenot party as a successor to the throne of France. Instead Henri of Guise backed Navarre's uncle the Cardinal of Bourbon, who had remained Catholic and had dissociated himself from his apostate family. Round him a Catholic League formed, with Philip of Spain as one of its supports. Between his two namesakes wobbled the feeble Henri III, who first recognized Navarre as his successor, and then allowed himself to submit to the Catholic League.

Elizabeth's hopes were pinned on her co-religionist Navarre, but if the Spanish army were allowed to subjugate the entire Netherlands, they would sweep over the border into France to link up with the Guise and overwhelm Navarre. Then the might of Spain reinforced by the might of France would be turned against Elizabeth.

In 1585 Philip placed an embargo on all English ships in Spanish ports and seized an English corn fleet to prove he was in earnest, an action which raised the indignation of Englishmen and their queen to fever-heat. Drake was ordered to sea. He left hurriedly, with twelve companies of soldiers on board twenty-eight vessels, before the Queen's caution could trim his sails. By the time he returned the following year he had sacked San Domingo and Cartagena, what he called singeing the King of Spain's beard. England was challenging the supremacy of Spain both at home and abroad.

It was Drake's opinion that the Spanish fleet should be destroyed in its home waters before it could reach England. He knew, Elizabeth knew, her Councillors knew, England was the reason for the King of Spain's Armada. A Scots captain counted twenty-seven galleons at Lisbon, and they were not ships but floating fortresses. Eyes trained to detect every reference to what was known in Spain as 'The Enterprise of England' sifted through all the deciphered letters and scraps of paper which reached the country. The Queen of Scots was moved to a still safer prison—as always in the depths of winter when there was less danger of rescue during transit. For a year she had been cut off from all communication with the outside world. No letters or tidings reached her, no whispers of promised relief penetrated to her, no pledges to quicken the over-stored spirits of this Catholic heir apparent with her potentialities, her unremitting claims and unceasing demands.

Leicester sailed in December and arrived in Flushing in January. Before the end of the month Elizabeth learned that scarcely had he landed when he allowed himself to be inaugurated, with lavish ceremonial, the Governor-General of the United Provinces.

The news acted on her like a stimulant. She was no longer the ailing queen he had left. She uncoiled like a python.

This upstart, this creature she had raised out of nothing, who had not only slighted but broken her express commands, a subject who had accepted for himself what she, his queen, had refused for herself, would learn how easily the hand which had exalted him could beat him down to the dust. In the very place where he had assumed his office of sovereignty he was to renounce the title as publicly as he had assumed it.

Her Councillors knew the disastrous effect such a scene would have both in the Netherlands and at home, but Elizabeth was beyond listening to them. The odious Lady Leicester further enraged her by preparing to leave England with a train of ladies and gentlemen, rich coaches, litters and side-saddles that surpassed anything in the Queen's possession. Such ill-considered presumption was peremptorily forbidden. Lady Leicester remained where she was nursing her chagrin, and Leicester's brother wrote him that the Queen's extreme rage against him increased rather than diminished.

Burleigh told the Queen that he would be forced to leave her government if she persisted in her plan to make a public shame of Leicester. She railed at him, but in the end he was not called upon to resign office. The States, having failed to force the Queen of England to take a decisive stand on their side, sent submissive answers to her angry demands, and Leicester's contrite letters assured her all he hoped for now was to be employed in her stables to rub her horses' hoofs. By summer she was writing to her Rob, 'Now will I end, that do imagine I talk still with you and therefore loath to say farewell. . . . As you know—Ever the Same. E.R.'

The year 1586 was a year of letters. When the hopes of the Queen of Scots were at their lowest, the unlooked for happened. In January her loyal servants discovered letters for her hidden in a barrel of beer, and she found herself linked to her supporters through one Gifford. She accepted his credentials without hesitation and lavished rewards on him and on the brewer who supplied beer to her household.

At once she sent to the French ambassador for all the foreign correspondence that had been accumulating for her while she was incommunicado, using the same unconventional mail-bags when the barrels were returned empty to the brewer. Twenty-one packets reached her, with their references to the Enterprise of England secreted in as many ciphers as there are minutes in an hour.

There were in England eager Catholic youths and priests who would stop at nothing, ready to deliver the Scots Queen. As she sat with her secretaries preparing missive after missive, inditing and directing, she and they were unaware that each letter before it reached her from her ardent young confederates, every letter that left her hands, was read by those who watched the plot they themselves were fomenting, waiting until the six English gentlemen who were to assassinate Queen Elizabeth should be named.

Mendoza heard from the captive Queen of Scots that she intended to bequeath the English crown to the King of Spain. She had learned that her son, for an English pension, some dubious promises of the English succession and a gift from Elizabeth of a dozen bloodhounds, had repudiated all further dealings with his mother and entered into a separate treaty with the Queen of England.

It was news so ominous that at first Mary could not believe it. ' A mother's curse shall light upon him,' she wrote. 'I will deprive him of all the greatness to which he can pretend.' But even as she penned the words, she must have known that nothing she could say, write or do could dislodge her son wedged on the throne of Scotland.

He was nineteen now, the child she had left a cradled infant in harried Scotland, who grew from a terrorized bairn king, seized first by one and then another faction of men all intent to use him for their own purposes, recording his detestation of Roman Catholicism and growing in political significance every year of his life. The letters his mother sent him when he was a little boy, her gifts of ponies and saddles, never reached him because she could not bring herself to address him as king.

To Mary, this unknown child was the son she had borne, flesh of her flesh, from whom she looked for love and obedience and deliverance. To him she was an unremembered mother, whose name he had heard from his earliest years defamed and stigmatized, whose shame and dishonour he had been burdened with by kirk and tutor: an unknown woman who wanted to share his throne with him, a would-be rival to his power.

Elizabeth had once called James VI of Scotland 'that false Scots urchin' when he displeased her, but with his weather eye cocked on the English succession, he did not by choice place himself on her wrong side. When the trap was sprung on his mother, all his honour required of him was to demand that her life be spared.

And that was what Elizabeth's Councillors, what both Houses of Parliament, were determined should not happen this time. Ever since she had come to England plots had gathered round the Queen of Scots like wasps in a nest, and each and every time Queen Elizabeth turned aside their petitions that the queen wasp should share the same fate as her fellow conspirators. But this occasion was different, on this occasion the Queen of Scots was brought to trial and with one assent found guilty.

Yet it was happening all over again. Her fourteen confederates were hanged on gallows of extraordinary height in St Giles's Fields that Elizabeth's loyal subjects could all watch the traitor's death of men who would have murdered their beloved Queen. But when in November a deputation from both Houses waited on Elizabeth and grimly told her that by no other way or means whatsoever could true religion, her life and the realm be secure other than by the speedy execution of the Queen of Scots, she replied at length, praying them in conclusion to accept her thankfulness, excuse her doubtfulness, and take in good part her answer—answerless.

The dogged Burleigh's answer to the answerless was to prevail upon Elizabeth that the sentence on the Queen of Scots should be drawn up and made known, which he achieved by the beginning of December. At the same time the death-warrant was engrossed, waiting for Her Majesty to sign, for without her signature there could be no execution. That was how her Councillors saw it. The Queen of Scots had been found guilty of being privy to conspiracy and of imagining and compassing Her Majesty's death. Just condemnation called for just execution, and just execution demanded the legality of the Queen's signature, otherwise it was assassination, which was without the law.

Assassin or assassins could be hired, but who would be the hirers? Certainly no officer of the Crown, however high or low, for he could be repudiated by the Crown after the work was done.

Elizabeth, however, viewed it in a different light. Burleigh, Walsingham, all of them wanted the dispatch, had always wanted the dispatch of the Queen of Scots, why then could they not see to it? They were men, and this was men's work. It was not a woman's to be burdened with the opprobrium of the world for signing away the life of a queen royal and anointed as Elizabeth was royal and anointed. To put her hand to such a deed was to rend the sacrosanct.

All through December she delayed. She kept more to herself than was her wont, and was said to sit speechless for a great length of time until she broke her own silence by muttering, 'Strike, or be stricken, strike or be stricken.'

By January the highly charged atmosphere was combustible. There was talk of an abortive plot against the Queen's life which involved the French ambassador and his secretary. Alarm followed fast on alarm: the Queen of Scots had broken out of her prison, London was on fire, at that very moment thousands of Spaniards were landing in Wales. The Queen was told, what she had to face, that the suspense was intolerable, and it was dangerous to prolong it because of the temper of the people.

On 1st February she signed the warrant. Walsingham, her Secretary of State, was ill and the second Secretary, one William Davison, was summoned to bring it to her. Her voice was light, her remarks inconsequential. She read it over before drawing her beautiful signature, dropping the document on the floor after she was done and signing the others he had brought.

Early in the morning of 8th February 1587, the Queen of Scots was beheaded on a scaffold in the great hall of Fotheringhay Castle, where she had been held for her trial. In London the bells of every church in the city pealed as though for a wedding, and did not cease from their clamour until the next day.

The execution appalled the world. A Frenchman or a Spaniard would have understood if the Scots queen had met a stealthy end, by poisoning or suffocation with a pillow, but this open death of scaffold, axe and block revolted and sickened them. It was an act of barbarity to inflict upon one who had been Queen of Scotland and Queen of France, and the grandeur with which Mary Stewart met so ignoble an end clothed her with martyrdom. 'I never saw a thing more hated by little, great, old, young and of all religions than the Queen of Scots' death,' wrote the English ambassador in France, 'and especially the manner of it. I would to God it had not been in this time.'

All her life Elizabeth had been sensitive to public opinion and concerned that people should think well of her. As a girl of sixteen she had written to Protector Somerset an outraged letter regarding the false rumours flying about that she was with child by my Lord Admiral—'rumours that be greatly both against my honour and honesty, which above all things I esteem'. The enormity of her prisoner Mary Stewart's beheading as though she were a common criminal overpowered her long before she could learn of the reaction of foreigners. Instinctively she knew what that would be and as instinctively she disclaimed all responsibility for it. Publicly and privately she washed her hands of it.

Davison had betrayed her, all her Councillors had betrayed her. She had signed the warrant but told him to keep it in his hands, he had no right to show it to other Councillors, she had not meant to let it go forward, she had never meant it to go forward. How dare Burleigh hasten to dispatch what he—what they all knew she had never wanted done, thus in their wickedness encroaching upon her power and prerogative, and making her an object of hatred and calumny to the whole world.

The Scots' reaction to the slaughter of their rejected queen was instant and fierce. All their age-old hostility to and hatred of the English accoutred them. They cried for war on the old enemy. Placards set up in the streets lampooned the King and his ministers who had made an alliance with Jezebel, the English whore. Elizabeth, when she wrote to James vindicating herself, was answered secretly by one of his chief ministers that if she could but give some proof that what had happened was without her sanction, the King would love her above all princes and the league with Scotland would still stand.

Burleigh, forbidden to go near his mistress, was aghast to learn that the Queen had been told she could, without trial, have Davison hanged. Burleigh needed no one to name for him the Justice she had gotten that from. The Queen herself was saying that Mr Justice Anderson had told her that her prerogative was absolute, and now she intended to hear what the other judges had to say. Urgently her Lord Treasurer wrote a letter in cipher warning the judges to be very careful how they replied. He would rather not live than see a woman of such wisdom as she be wrongly advised, for fear or other infirmity, that her prerogative was above the law.

Davison was not hanged. He was tried in the Star Chamber, ordered to pay a fine of ten thousand marks and committed to the Tower during the Queen's pleasure, which lasted eighteen months, by which time England had withstood invasion. His fine was remitted and, although he never regained his office, he retained his fee as Secretary to the end of his story.

Her young cousin Robert Carey was to remember that up to near the end of her life, he never heard his sovereign fetch a sigh but when the Queen of Scots was beheaded.

Chapter Thirteen

Elizabeth was in her fifty-fourth year when Mary Stewart met her doom. She still retained that splendour of figure and form upon which foreign ambassadors had expatiated when, over a quarter of a century before, they described her to their royal masters who were her suitors, but the long face was more angular. There was something now of a shining, strong bird about her appearance, with her hooded lids, the high bridge of her thin nose, prominent cheek-bones and beady black eyes.

The violence of her cousin's death caused a reverberation abroad over which England had no control. The dead Queen of Scots was more potent to move the King of Spain to action than the living one had ever been. Philip had little incentive to mount an invasion against England to place Mary Stewart upon Elizabeth's throne, but now she was dead he could claim it for himself and his heirs. The Queen of Scots had bequeathed to him all her rights in England and Scotland, and he himself was descended, through both his father and mother, from Edward III's son, John of Gaunt. The fact that James VI of Scotland was a heretic conveniently obliterated him from the line of succession as far as Philip and Roman Catholics were concerned.

Now with his invincible Armada at full strength, the King of Spain was strong enough to move against the Queen of England from whom he had suffered every affront that shameless double-dealing could pay him. He was kept up to date by his advisers about conditions in her realm. Her fleet was riddled with dry rot, not four ships in it were seaworthy, and English Roman Catholics were daily praying and looking to him for deliverance from her yoke. The sentence of her excommunication was reissued to put heart into them.

The Spaniards could not believe what was taking place before their very eyes. A few months after the murder of the Queen of Scots, on the full spring tide when sun and moon pull together, English ships sailed into fortified Cadiz harbour and destroyed thirty-three store-ships without which no fleet could sail.

'Just look at Drake!' cried Pope Sixtus V. 'Who is he? What forces has he?'

The Spaniards could tell him. They called him El Draque, The Dragon, for this was no man but a devil. He could unfurl or furl the winds as he chose, for he was in league with a spirit, a familiar whom he could summon at will. What else could explain that the next thing the Spaniards knew he had seized Cape St Vincent just as their fleet was trying to assemble at Lisbon? He had a magic mirror in his cabin which revealed his enemy's ships and all that went on aboard them. There he was riding at anchor off Lisbon and they could do nothing to him. Even when his craft were becalmed, their long-ranging guns kept the heavy Spanish galleons at bay. When the Spaniards sailed as fast as they could to the Azores to protect a carrack, a large treasure ship fitted for fighting homebound from the East Indies, El Draque was entering Plymouth Sound with it in tow. The treasure was valued at £114,000.

Every nugget, every jewel, every doubloon was needed. Elizabeth was alarmed at what the Netherlands was costing her. The maintenance of her army there was running at the rate of £126,000 a year, with nothing to show for this enormous outlay, neither victory nor triumph, but maladministration and corruption. It was a sieve that spent as it received to no purpose. Never again, she vowed, would she allow her money to be misappropriated as it had been in the Netherlands.

Only because he had to make good the losses Drake had inflicted on his Armada was Philip, incensed beyond endurance by what had happened at Cadiz, restrained from sending it across that year.

Elizabeth had to prepare for war at sea and invasion on land, but she kept a skinflint's grip on the money-bags. 'Sparing and war have no affinity together,' groaned her admiral, Lord Howard of Effingham. Spanish strategy was obvious to every Englishman. When the formidable galleys did sail from Lisbon, Philip's General Parma would be waiting in the Netherlands with a second army and transports. The Armada would cover its crossing, and both armies attempt to land in England together.

The year 1588 broke like dawn upon the faces of Englishmen, for it had long been foretold that it was to be a year of wonders for their country. And their country was under arms. Two armies were raised, one at St James to protect the Queen, and the other at Tilbury to resist the invaders should they land. The same joyousness brightened the faces of the soldiers as brightened that of the sailors: they marched to Tilbury, dancing and leaping as they came, calling out brave words to the bystanders. The Tilbury army was smaller than that of St James and was under the command of Leicester, who made a better lieutenant-general in England than he had a profligate governor-general in the Netherlands.

Such faith had Elizabeth's seamen in their craft that they had no doubt they could beat the Spanish Armada however powerful. 'God bless them!' exclaimed one, 'they are such worthy ships.' Hawkins tested out four of the largest vessels by riding them in the Sound during a prolonged violent storm, and they felt it no more than if they were still at Chatham. 'I do thank God that they be in the state that they be in,' Lord Howard wrote to Burleigh; 'there is never one of them knows what a leak is.' He was one English Catholic who was certainly not looking to the King of Spain for succour.

Philip was spending three hours each day on his knees before the Sacrament. In July the Armada at last sailed, sped on its way by prayerful Spaniards walking in procession, undertaking austerities, fasting and devotions.

It was first sighted on the 19th by watchers on the Lizard at three o'clock in the afternoon. Nearer and nearer it came, the great Armada, forming a crescent whose horns were at least seven miles apart. Built high, the vessels were like floating castles, the sea their moat, and looked as impregnable. Inevitable as fate they came under full sail, but seemed to creep 'as the winds laboured and the ocean sighed under the burden of them' noted Camden, the historian.

Instead of attacking the English fleet as it lay, helplessly crowded to leeward in the harbour, the Spanish ships anchored outside Plymouth at nightfall.

July that summer was stormy. When the moon rose in a sky wild with rack and lit with its eerie light the unfamiliar scene, the Spaniards saw the enemy had worked themselves out of Plymouth Sound against the wind and were behind them.

The engagements were running battles that lasted ten days. The English might find the ponderous Spanish galleons difficult to sink, but they could not be handled like the slender nimble enemy. Compared with them, the swiftest vessels of the Armada appeared to be at anchor. Nor had the men aboard learnt their profession in the demanding school of piracy on the high seas. The Spanish ships were under-manned, for only a quarter of the force they carried were mariners. Primarily they had been built, protected by their guns on tiers, for the transport of troops, with their horses and stores, rather than for naval warfare, and the enemy saw to it they were given no chance to grapple and board, or land on hallowed English soil.

By the 28th the battered Armada drove on without further fighting to cast anchor in the sanctuary of Calais roads. So far they had lost only three vessels, but they were amongst their finest, and they had been unable to inflict any damage on the darting enemy ships.

That night the English launched the most dreaded engine of naval warfare amongst the galleons closely packed in the roads— eight fireships. In their panic the Spaniards cut their cables and stood out to sea. Morning revealed them scattered without formation along the coast, each a target.

The battle of Gravelines lasted for eight hours, until the English exhausted their ammunition. On the whole the weather had favoured the Spaniards, now it changed and the fated ships had to contend with fierce contrary winds as they made for home round the north of Scotland. Only about half of those the English chased as far as the mouth of the Tyne ever reached Spain.

The news percolated through to Philip before the remnants of his Armada limped home to shadow still further the darkness of defeat. 'In God's actions,' he said, 'reputation is neither lost nor gained; it is best not to talk of it.'

England did not talk of her glorious victory, she sang with thanksgiving to God who had delivered them, who had shown to the world that He favoured Elizabeth of England, branded by her enemies as heretic and bastard and so unfit to rule, and that Protestants were His Chosen People.

In the midst of the exaltation of triumph a bell knelled. Never had Elizabeth and Leicester been closer. He had been ill, which always made her tender towards him and because she too had ailed he wrote 'to know how my gracious lady doth', for her health was the chiefest thing in the world to him. He was on his way to Buxton to try the waters, and signed his letter 'this Thursday morning ready to take my journey'.

He died before he could reach his destination on 4th September, his birth month and hers, when both were fifty-five. He was so wrapped up with her life that with his death a part of herself seemed to die. Green wounds, she had said, scarce abide the toucher's hand. She shut herself up with her grief for so long that Burleigh had to order the door to be forced.

Throughout her life of three score years and ten it was remarked the Queen looked younger than she was, but at the beginning of that November we catch a terrifying glimpse of her through the eyes of an enemy. It was before the great day of national thanksgiving at St Paul's, a day which had no peer for jubilation unless it was that of her coronation, when a Spanish agent saw her. He reported to Mendoza in Paris, 'The Queen is much aged and spent and very melancholy. Her intimates say this is caused by the death of the Earl of Leicester.' He himself did not believe that. His pen is corroded with the acid of hate as it writes, 'It was the fear she underwent and the burden she has on her.'

The defeat of the Armada was the climax of her reign. For thirty years she had ruled, and it is these thirty years which globe the Elizabethan age rather than the fourteen that were to follow. They were the seed-bed for the extraordinary flowering of English poetical genius. Spenser, the first of the great modern poets, was a boy of six when she came to the throne. Her reign cradled Marlowe, whose 'mighty line' broke through the stilted metres of his forerunners; Donne, whose explorations of the language were as daring as Drake's voyages; immortal Shakespeare, whose *Twelfth Night* the Queen translated to her foreign guest when it was acted before her on her last Christmastide; rare Ben Jonson.

She outlived not only her senior statesmen but most of her contemporaries, and her Young Men, who were middle-aged when she was elderly. The men who had borne with her the heat of the day were true Elizabethans rather than the untried generation sallying forth, over-confident, to inherit a world they had had no hand in fashioning. The burden was still on her. The years up to the Armada had been years of comparative peace, those that followed years of war.

The high voice was louder and shriller now, and she flew out with blows at her maids of honour. Much has been made of her rages, attributed to the frustrated jealousy of a spinster, when she found one or other with child. But her maids were girls in their teens, and expected to live up to their name in the most sought-after service, with its brilliant marriage prospects, which only influence could attain for them. Certainly their sovereign would not allow at her court unlicensed behaviour of girls for whom she was responsible to their families, or of their partners in transgression, who found themselves in the Tower or the Fleet.

'She certainly is a great queen,' the far-sighted Pope Sixtus V had declared when he first occupied St Peter's Chair, 'and were she only a Catholic she would be our dearly beloved. Just look how well she governs! She is only a woman, only mistress of half an island, and yet she makes herself feared by Spain, by France, by the Empire, by all.'—'She alone is a king!' exclaimed Henri of Navarre when he was Henri IV of France. 'She alone knows how to rule!'

It was her timely help which enabled him, a Huguenot, to uphold his legitimate claim to the throne of France against the power of the Catholic League when he was left the sole survivor of the three Henris. The year after the Armada the assassin's dagger cut short the life of Henri III, the last of the Valois, in swift retribution for the murders of Henri of Guise and his brother. The penniless new king, without a crown or a capital city, retired into Normandy and appealed to Elizabeth.

She had to respond with loans, arms, ammunition and a small army, for the Catholic League placed at the King of Spain's disposal the resources of all the seaport towns under its control. If the Channel provinces fell into Philip's hands, they would be used as a base against England.

Henri's cheerful letters, lavish with gratitude and promises of repayment, never concluded without supplication for more. Elizabeth saw her opportunity to win for England what she had long coveted, a secure foothold on the other side of the Channel. For all the assistance she was giving him, without which he would have been lost, Henri must cede to her Brest or Marlaix, Rouen or Havre. But Henri had a country to win, and the total self-absorption of the born sponger who believes his thanks are more than enough. He was aware she dare not withdraw her troops, instead she was forced to send reinforcements to her army in Brittany.

He, who wore his religion as lightly as he wore his heart, went his own way, and in 1593, without even consulting her, turned Catholic to unite his people, thus checkmating the Catholic League. Five years later he made a separate peace with Philip of

Spain despite his treaty obligations with England and the Nether-lands. Elizabeth called him the Antichrist of ingratitude.

Nor did her Dutch protégés prove any more satisfactory. Her small English contingent helped them in four campaigns to expel the Spanish almost completely from the seven northern provinces. Because of the poverty of their soil, their inhabitants took to the sea, and the less wealthy area in Europe became the most pros-perous. Elizabeth, selling lands and jewels to pay for her wars, applied for repayment of the sums owed to her but, as with individuals so with nations, the more capable the Dutch were of reckoning, the more reluctant were they to do the addition.

With jealous distrust Elizabeth watched her allies develop into the carriers of the world. They even made money out of supplying at enormous profits their and her Spanish enemies with the munitions which were to be used against themselves. No sea was now big enough to contain the so-called English and Dutch allies: whenever they were within striking distance there was collision.

The Queen might still be paramount, but the men round her were changing. Burleigh died in 1598 at the age of seventy-eight. They tried not to mention him at Council meetings when she was present, for she would turn her face away and weep. She had once told him she did not wish to live longer than she had him with her. She had five years more to sojourn without her Alpha and Omega.

He had brought up his favourite second son 'as near as like unto himself' to fill the position of Secretary of State. Robert Cecil was a humpback and it was thought because of his deformity the fastidious Queen would exclude him from so high an office, which called for close attendance upon herself. But Elizabeth was made of sterner stuff and two years before Burleigh's death, at the age of thirty-three, the son received the great post against all comers. There was no malice when Elizabeth, with her inveterate love of nicknames, called him her pygmy, only unconscious appraisement of one who could never wear his father's mantle.

'Serve God by serving the Queen,' Burleigh enjoined him in a postscript to one of his last letters, but there was not the sanctity round the Queen for Robert Cecil or the men of his generation that there had been for their parents. He was to write to his brother with some querulousness, during the winter in which she died, that the Queen ought to realize she was old, and that there was no contentment to a young mind in an old body.

There was something in her Secretary's attitude towards her which made Elizabeth react fiercely against him during the last days of her life. She was shrewd enough to guess, when she felt time beginning to creep at her gate, that her Secretary of State was in secret correspondence with James of Scotland regarding the succession, thus assuring himself of a privileged position at the new court. When she refused to move from the cushions on the floor and he told her, 'Madame, to content the people you must go to bed', her smile was cutting with scorn as she replied, 'Little man, little man, the word *must* is not used to princes. If your father had lived ye durst not have said so much.'

Her brother-in-law and one time suitor died in the same year as Burleigh. Philip of Spain planned every detail of his own entombment, even to the black cloth to drape the church of Escurial which was the eighth wonder of the world and had taken him thirty years to build. The stench of his sores overcame his doctors and, crippled with gout, he died in agonizing pain but, true to the mother who bore him seventy-two years before, no word of complaint passed his lips.

His dying advice to his son was to make peace with England, even at the cost of opening to her the trade of the Spanish Empire, advice which, like many a son before and after him, Philip III did not take. It seemed as if neither Spain nor England could deal the other the *hors de combat* blow, but the newly acceded king could attack England through her Achilles heel, Ireland.

Philip II had had his Netherlands, Elizabeth her Ireland. Its inhabitants bore no loyalty to the English queen, whom they called the hag, forcing a hated religion upon them. They were Catholics who looked to the Pope as their head and to Spain for friendship—and aid. Celts, they were a different race from the English, and the maladministration of Elizabeth's Deputies made rebels of a people whose reckless bravery in battle was matched only by their lack of discipline.

In the year Philip II died the Earl of Tyrone inflicted a crushing defeat on English troops at Yellow Foot, near Armagh. The news appalled Elizabeth and her Councillors as much as it encouraged the Irish when it spread through their country. Recently established English colonizers were driven out of Munster, and the midlands rose. Dublin, the seat of government, was threatened.

The fear of Spain's sending reinforcements to the rebels became an imminent possibility. Tyrone must be overthrown, before the

English were completely expelled, and the country reconquered. The question was who should lead the army from England. Elizabeth, with her sound judgment of the right man, was for sending Lord Mountjoy, but her young favourite, the Earl of Essex, by vetoing every possible name raised in Council, nominated himself.

Her Young Men of an earlier period could jockey each other for position, hope for and aim at the highest offices in the land, live extravagantly at their sovereign's expense and die in her debt to the tune of £56,000, but she was their sun upon which they were dependent for light and warmth and everything that made life worth the living. Never had they dreamt of making her the constellation and themselves the sun as did young Robert Devereux, who inherited the earldom of Essex at the age of nine.

The odium Elizabeth felt for his mother did not fall on her son. She had been fond of her lively young cousin in the days when she was Lettice Knollys who became the Countess of Essex. Her husband, a good servant of the crown, succumbed with severe abdominal pains, asserting he had been poisoned. It was when Elizabeth learned that Leicester had secretly married his widow that her dislike fastened on one whose growing arrogance served to harden rather than soften it.

Gossip was always a busybody where Leicester was concerned. It was hinted when he brought to court the tall young boy with his idyllic good looks that he was his father, not his step-father. It was recalled that the late Earl of Essex had borne 'a very cold conceit' towards Robert, his wife's first-born, and lavished his affection on the second son Walter.

Elizabeth made Robert Master of the Horse when he was only twenty-two, and Knight of the Garter within the year. When he left for Ireland ten years later he was a Privy Councillor, Master of the Ordnance and Earl Marshal of England.

That the Queen loved him was obvious to all. With his mother's red hair he was like the son she had never had, the son she might have borne had she married Leicester. She spoilt him as a mother does spoil a cherished one and only child, but she was by no means blind to his faults and tried to curb and discipline him as a father would. She swore she would break him of his will and pull down his great heart, which he inherited from his mother's side, not realizing as she spoke that his mother's side was also hers.

The Queen's bounties came too soon and too fast: they were

not the cause, but revealed the flaws in a character that seemed the essence of chivalry. He played havoc with the hearts of her maids of honour, one of whom he made pregnant, and offended the Queen when he married Walsingham's widowed daughter. He, so supple and beholden when first he entered the inner circle round his sovereign, could boast, now he was nearer her than any other, that he was doing the Queen good against her will. He never saw or thought of her except in relation to himself; she was the Queen, but even a queen was only a woman.

He could brook neither opposition nor rivalry, and the court of the Queen of England flourished with rivals, which meant wherever he went there were broils. 'God's death!' Elizabeth exclaimed angrily when she heard he had been wounded in a duel he himself had provoked, 'it is fit that someone or other should take him down and teach him better manners, otherwise there will be no rule with him.' But his was a nature not to be ruled.

To the people he was 'great England's glory and the world's wide wonder'. He might have captured Cadiz from the Spaniards single-handed in 1595 for the glory that was his on his return 'with the bright gleams of his valour'. Even the Spaniards praised his courtesy and generosity to the inhabitants of the seized town. The people at home did not know that while the army was looting the city, an outward-bound merchant fleet, which would have replenished Elizabeth's depleted coffers, was lying unprotected in the harbour. When the English went to capture it they found nothing to capture—the Spaniards had set it on fire rather than let it fall into their hands.

Essex was warned before he set out for Ireland to use his power of conferring knighthoods with the utmost discretion, and only where there was notable service. His indiscriminate dubbing in France and later before he returned from Cadiz had cut Elizabeth to the quick, making a scoff in the world of what was her most intimate prerogative, which she herself guarded jealously.

He took horse at Seething Lane in March 1599 to ride through London on his way to Chester with what looked like an endless train of noblemen and gentlemen. After providing him with everything he had demanded and the largest army to leave England during her reign, Elizabeth and her Council could only wait for the harvesting of their efforts.

But Ireland was not Cadiz. No joyful throwing his hat into the sea here at the order to enter the harbour, no scornful fanfares of trumpets in reply to Spanish cannon. 'Ireland,' as a Venetian ambassador once remarked, 'may well be called the Englishman's grave.' 'What can you expect from an accursed country but unfortunate news?' Essex himself was to demand.

His first and supreme object when he arrived was of course to attack Tyrone in Ulster. To her bewilderment Elizabeth heard he was undertaking a campaign in Leinster—it was explained to her the main operations in Ulster had been postponed until June, when the grass had grown and cattle for feeding the army were fat.

To Elizabeth the Leinster expedition was like the track of a ship at sea—the rebels merely opened before the passage of Essex and closed behind him. From Leinster he was lured into Munster, where at no time had there been any suggestion of his going. June, the month for the postponed Ulster campaign, came and went. Everyone at court heard of the Queen's caustic remark that she was allowing Essex a thousand pounds a day to go on progress. In July he arrived back in Dublin with a tired army whose one conquest had been an insignificant castle.

The uneasy news was brought to England that instead of fighting Tyrone Essex was parleying with him. Elizabeth wrote her Commander that to trust this traitor upon oath was to trust a devil upon his religion. He was ordered to proceed against him without delay, and on his duty not to return without permission.

He received 'an express letter from the Queen, all written with her own hand' absolutely prohibiting him from making another knight. She had heard of the gross abuse of his power since his arrival, and this was not the misguided action of over-chivalric youth. It had a much more sinister aspect. The knights he was creating with such prodigality would in the very nature of things tend to bear allegiance to the man who had raised them rather than to their sovereign queen he represented. Despite her letter, he dubbed a further thirty-eight in August and September.

The one thing Essex could not digest was that his lack of success was due to himself. It was his enemies at home, Raleigh, Cecil, Cobham, Grey, Howard, who were fomenting all this trouble between him and the Queen. It was because of what they were distilling in her ear that she was writing these stinging letters to him—'You had your asking; you had choice of times, you had power and authority more ample than ever any had, or ever shall have.'

The Queen was in her bedchamber attended by her waiting-women as she dressed one morning towards the end of September. She was sitting at her mirror, her grey hair about her face, when the placid tenor of everyday was shattered as Essex, still in his riding-clothes, his face bespattered with mud, rushed into the room to fall on his knees before her and cover her hands, with kisses.

Even in such untoward circumstances, Elizabeth was mistress of the situation and answered his torrent of words quietly. He was heard thanking God when he left that though he had suffered much trouble and storms abroad, he had found a quiet calm at home.

He never saw the Queen again after the day of his return. She said a little later to the French ambassador that it was not her intention, but that of a Monsieur d'Essex, speaking the name with such passion she seemed to spit it, to pardon the Irish rebels; she would show him that he had no power. If it had been her own son who had committed a like fault, she would have put him in the highest tower in England.

But Essex was not her own son and instead of the highest tower in England he was placed in the custody of a Councillor friend in York House in the Strand. He was not to be charged with treason, although Elizabeth had more than an inkling of his secret pact with Tyrone, which she kept from her Council, hoping for the sake of those good things in him he would reform. His colleagues in Ireland had not allowed him to return to England with three thousand of the army as he had wished, but he had brought with him a competent number of choice fellows. London was full of them and deserters from the army in Ireland, their words frothing on their lips as they drank to their hero's health and damnation to his enemies, while every day the citizens looked for his release.

The Queen was very merry. Someone looked through a window and saw her dancing the Spanish Pavin all by herself except for Lady Warwick and a man who was playing the pipe and tabor. A foreigner watched the English queen enter the Presence Chamber at Nonsuch Palace in Surrey 'alone without escort, very straight and erect', and describes her with German thoroughness. 'She was most lavishly attired in a gown of pure white satin, gold-embroidered, with a whole bird of paradise for panache, set forward on her head studded with costly jewels; she wore a string of huge pearls about her neck and elegant gloves over which were drawn costly rings.' Luckily the sixty-six year old object of his gaze did not know he was under the impression she was 'already seventy-four', although she would have forgiven him everything because she seemed to him very youthful still, no more than twenty.

We have several descriptions of Elizabeth as she approached her seventieth year, most of them by foreigners, and more than one declared she looked no more than twenty. Perhaps the secret lay in the observance of the Duke of Stettin's Secretary that the Queen of England did not look ugly even in her old age when seen from a distance. The straightness and erectness Thomas Platter noticed when he saw her at Nonsuch lent youth to her figure, and she had been wearing wigs for some time, usually a darker red than the russet of her earlier days. While every description of her glitters with the jewels she wore.

The despairing Essex, his unwise family, his well-wishers and friends could not understand why the Queen, to whom he had meant so much, made no move to forgive and restore him to her side. It was Sir John Harington, one of her Young Men, who discerned the imbalance in the prisoner's attitude. 'The Queen,' he said, 'well knoweth how to humble the haughty spirit, the haughty spirit knoweth not how to yield.'

In March he was allowed to remove to his own house under the care of a keeper, in June he was suspended from his various offices, in July the keeper was removed and he was free to go anywhere save to court. But to be debarred from court was to Essex to be debarred from paradise, and if he were not in paradise he was in very hell. Paradise then must be taken by force; his addled brain returned to the treason that had inflamed it in Ireland.

She had made him gifts in the past of £300,000 and that Michaelmas she did not renew his lease of the custom on sweet wines. An unruly horse, she said, must be abated of its provender that he may be more easily and better managed. His dutiful letters had moved her because she had thought they had been written in the abundance of his heart. Now she found their purpose was that she might renew the lease of what was the mainstay of his estate.

Towards the end of the year the ruined Essex was talking so wildly of the Queen that good men hastened from him not to return, saying he was not in his right mind. His home became open house for 'swordsmen, bold confident fellows, men of broken fortunes, discontented persons, and such as saucily used their tongues in railing against all men'.

The revolt took place in February on a quiet Sunday morning when peaceful men were at church. He led a troop of some two hundred sprigs of the nobility and young gentlemen up Ludgate Hill and along Cheapside. He, who thought himself held so dear, expected the City would rise for him. Not the meanest artificer or prentice came over to him. When he went to the house of a sheriff, to be supplied with the promised arms and men, the sheriff left by the back door. An armourer said he had no weapons for him. 'Not for me, Pickering?' he asked, the sweat pouring down his face.

The Queen was playing the virginals one morning later in February, Raleigh and some other men standing about her, when she gave permission for a messenger to enter her presence. On his knees, he announced that sentence on the Earl of Essex had been carried out. The deathly stillness in the room was broken as the Queen began to play again. She was to tell the French ambassador in great grief that she had put up with but too much disrespect to her person, but she had warned him that he should not touch her sceptre.

Lord Mountjoy took the place of Essex in Ireland. Elizabeth kept in the closest touch with him, writing to him with her own hand. A Spanish army of 5,000 veteran troops landed at Kinsale, but instead of Irish confederates they found the English, who surrounded them and to whom they had to surrender. At the time of Elizabeth's death, the rebel Tyrone was still strong enough to make his submission conditional on a free pardon and restoration of his estates. This was the first effective conquest of Ireland which was to have what could be called an Irish peace for close on forty years.

No conflagration makes so dazzling a spectacle of the sky as sunset. Elizabeth was loved by her people, received the acclamation she always received, could bring tears to the eyes of her faithful Commons when they heard her tell them with touching simplicity, 'Though God hath raised me high, yet this I account the glory of my crown that I have reigned with your loves.' But a sunset despite its brightness heralds the chill of night and for another dawn men were turning to look towards the Border.

She still could hunt, and rode ten miles on horseback on a single day. In September, when she celebrated her last, her sixty-ninth, birthday, a visitor saw her walking about her garden as vigorous as though she were eighteen; she loved flowers as much as she loved jewels. Cecil could report she 'was never so gallant many years, nor so set upon jollity', and a courtier, 'We are frolick here at court.' Her doctors said she might live for several years, and pronounced her as having a sound and perfect constitution. Little more than a month before her death, she gave audience to the new Venetian ambassador, and the last picture we have of her is painted in brilliant colours.

He describes her clad in taffety of silver and white trimmed with gold, her dress somewhat open in the front, showing her throat encircled with pearls and rubies down to her breast, her hair 'of a light colour never made by nature', an imperial crown on her head and great pearls like pears round the forehead. She spoke to him with spirit, but when he congratulated her on her excellent health and paused for her assent, she remained silent.

She had outlived her generation and her day, and her world was beginning to echo. The coronation ring she had worn for forty-three years had grown into her finger and the symbolism when it had to be sawed off filled her with horror. She never recovered from the death of the Countess of Nottingham, one of her few surviving relatives, at the end of February.

Her astrologer warned her to beware of Whitehall, so the court moved to Richmond in January on 'a filthy rainy and windy day' when she caught cold. 'She grew worse,' said her young cousin Robin Carey, 'because she would be so.' Richmond might be the warmest of her palaces, but it was the sharpest season many could remember, yet Elizabeth went about in 'summer-like garments', affirming she did not believe in furs to withstand the cold of winter. She refused to be doctored, and told the Archbishop of Canterbury and Cecil, when they urged her to take medicine, that she knew her constitution better than they did.

They tried to persuade her to leave the cushions on the floor. She said if they saw such things as she saw when she was in bed they would not prevail on her to lie on it. One of her ladies in waiting relates that, being pulled to a standing position by force, she stood for fifteen hours, when she was lifted into bed.

The stories that she had lost her wits were discounted by those about her. They were spread by Cecil lest he was unable to extract her acquiescence that the son of Mary Stewart, James VI of

Scotland, should succeed her. The French ambassador wrote at the last, 'She is said, moreover, to be no longer in her right senses; this, however, is a mistake; she has only had some slight wanderings at times.'

An abscess burst in her throat, and she felt better, but it was still sore. Within flight-shot of her death, several members of the Privy Council gathered round to ask her to lift her hand if she agreed that the King of Scotland should succeed to the English throne. She raised her hand.

Between two and three on the morning of 24th March 1603, when her ladies approached the great bed, they saw her as if asleep with her head cradled on her right arm.

A hundred and eighteen years span the reigns of the five Tudor sovereigns, and on her last progress from Richmond to Westminster Abbey that April day in 1603 Elizabeth travelled the same road as had the first in the springtide of 1509. To house the dynasty of which he was the begetter, Henry VII raised what has been called the loveliest building in the world, when he built the chapel where he rests beside his queen, dwelling 'more richly dead than he did alive in Richmond or in any of his palaces'.

Only the prodigious body of Henry VIII does not lie there, for he chose to be buried beside his wife Jane Seymour in St George's Chapel at Windsor. But it is the resting-place of the son she bore him, and of his two daughters by Katherine of Aragon and Anne Boleyn, his three children who all reigned after him and whom he could remember, when he closed his eyes on the world, with their bright hair.

Bibliography

BAGLEY, John. *Henry VIII and his Times.* Batsford, London, 1962.

BESANT, William. *London in the Time of the Tudors.* Black, London, 1904.

BIGLAND, Eileen. *Henry the Eighth, 1491–1547,* 'Kings and Queens' Series. E.U.P., London, 1937.

BINDOFF, S. T. *Tudor England.* Penguin Books, 1950.

BURNET, Gilbert, Bishop of Salisbury. *The History of the Reformation of the Church of England,* vol. iii. O.U.P., London, 1829.

CHAPMAN, Hester. *The Last Tudor King.* Cape, London, 1958.

CHAPMAN, Hester. *Two Tudor Portraits.* Cape, London, 1960.

CHAPMAN, Hester. *Lady Jane Grey.* Cape, London, 1962.

D'AUVERGNE, E. B. *The English Castles.* Warner Laurie, London, 1908.

DUNLOP, Ian. *Palaces and Progresses of Elizabeth I.* Cape, London, 1962.

EMMISON, F. C. *Tudor Secretary: Sir William Petre at Court and Home.* Longmans, Green, London, 1961.

FERGUSON, Charles. *Naked to Mine Enemies: The Life of Cardinal Wolsey.* Longmans, London, 1958.

FROUDE, James Anthony. *The Reign of Edward VI.* Dent, London, 1909.

GOULD LEE, Arthur. *The Son of Leicester.* Gollancz, London, 1964.

JENKINS, Elizabeth. *Elizabeth the Great.* Gollancz, London, 1950.

JENKINS, Elizabeth. *Elizabeth and Leicester.* Gollancz, London, 1961.

JORDAN, W. K. *Edward VI: The Young King: The Protectorship of the Duke of Somerset.* Allen and Unwin, London, 1968.

LOTH, David. *Philip II of Spain.* Routledge, London, 1932.

MACKIE, J. D. *The Early Tudors.* O.U.P., Oxford, 1952.

MACLAURIN, C. *De Mortuis.* Cape, London, 1930.

MCNALTY, A. S. *Henry VIII: A Difficult Patient.* Christopher Johnston, London, 1952.

MURE MACKENZIE, Agnes. *Scottish Pageant.* Oliver and Boyd, Edinburgh and London, 1946.

NEALE, J. C. *Queen Elizabeth I.* Cape, London, 1934.

POLLARD, A. F. *Tudor Tracts: 1532–1588.* Constable, London, 1903.

POLLARD, A. F. *Henry VIII.* Longmans, London, 1905.

PRESCOTT, H. F. M. *Mary Tudor.* Eyre and Spottiswoode, London, 1952.

READ, Conyers. *The Tudors.* O.U.P., London, 1936.

SAVAGE, Henry. *The Love Letters of Henry VIII.* Allan Wingate, London, 1949.

SCARISBRICK, J. J. *Henry VIII.* Eyre and Spottiswoode, London, 1968.

SCHENK, W. *Reginald Pole, Cardinal of England.* Longmans, Green, London, 1950.

SHARPE, Reginald R. *London and the Kingdom* (from Guildhall Library). Longmans, London, 1894.

SIMPSON, Helen. *The Spanish Marriage.* Peter Davies, London, 1933.

SMITH, Lucy Baldwin. *A Tudor Tragedy.* Cape, London, 1961.

STANLEY, Arthur Penrhyn. *Historical Memorials of Westminster Abbey.* Murray, London, 1882.

STRICKLAND, Agnes. *Queens of Scotland and English Princesses.* Blackwood, Edinburgh and London, 1850.

STRICKLAND, Agnes. *Lives of the Bachelor Kings.* Simpkin, Marshall, London, 1866.

STRICKLAND, Agnes. *Lives of the Tudor and Stuart Princesses.* Bell, London, 1888.

STRICKLAND, Agnes. *Lives of the Queens of England.* Nash, London, 1905.

TIMBS, John. *Curiosities of London.* Virtue, London, 1878.

Index

Henry VIII's daughter by Anne Boleyn: birth, 27; proclaimed Princess of Wales, 28; health, 31, 57, 79, 125–6, 201–2; education, 39, 57, 58, 84–5; declared illegitimate, 38, 43; in disfavour with her father, 57; in Thomas Seymour's household, 78; sent from household, 79; attempt to implicate her in treason, 83–4; allowed to visit Edward, 96–7; congratulates Mary on foiling her enemies, 117; enters London with Mary, 118; Mary's attitude changes towards her, 121; suspected of implication in Wyatt's rebellion, 123; imprisoned in Tower, 126–128; sent to Woodstock, 129; returns to court and meets Philip of Spain, 137; rejects marriage proposal, 143–4; tacitly admitted in Mary's will as her successor, 150; enters London as Queen, 155–156; takes middle road in religion, 156–7; dread of war, 158; redeems debased currency, 159; her triumphant progresses, 159; exploits her marriage proposals, 161, 173, 176–8; involves England in Scotland's affairs, 162–3; offers Dudley to Mary Stewart as husband, 164; sends Darnley to Scotland, 164–5; abandons Mary Stewart's unsuccessful rebels, 166; hears of the birth of Mary Stewart's son, 167; hears of the murder of Darnley, 167–8; shocked by news of Mary Stewart's marriage to Bothwell, 167, 168; learns of Mary Stewart's escape from her rebel Lords, 168; and that Mary has taken refuge in England, 169; the captive Mary Stewart dangerous potential, 171; hand in glove with Drake, 174, 177; aids Protestants abroad, 178, 179, 192; learns of Spain's planned invasion, 180–1; and of Mary Stewart conspiracy, 183; urged to sign Mary Stewart's death warrant, 183; reluctantly signs it, 184; tries to disclaim responsibility, 185; shocked by condemnation of Mary Stewart's execution, 185; her glory in defeat of Armada, 190; poetic genius flowers in her reign, 191; the Protestant allies she has aided default, 192–3; her favourite Essex bungles Irish campaign, 197; Essex executed after abortive rebellion, 200; conditional submission of Ireland, 200; death in her seventieth year, 202; appearance of (as a child), 38, 48, 57; (as a woman), 118, 158, 168, 187, 191, 198, 201; character of, 39, 49, 57, 96–7, 128, 156–7, 158–9, 160–1, 172, 191–2, 200–1. *Relations with Dudley, Robert, Earl of Leicester:* the same age as, 158; makes him Master of the Horse, 158; attraction and divergence of their characters, 158; her favours stir up gossip, 159–60; scandal of his wife's death, 160; creates him Earl of Leicester, 164; outraged to learn of his secret marriage, 174; her distress when he has to leave to lead her army into the Netherlands, 179; her rage when he accepts the Governor-Generalship, 181; his death and her grief, 191. *Relations with her half-brother Edward:* fond of, 48; with him when they learn of their father's death, 66; intimacy denied to her once he is King, 88; allowed to come to court, 96–7; receives Hatfield manor from him, 105; tries but fails to see him during last illness, 105. *Relations with Essex, Robert Devereux, Earl of:* fond of, 191; heaps honours on, 195; allows him to lead army into Ireland, 196; incensed at his failure and suspected parleying with enemy, 197; places him in custody, 198; refuses to forgive,

Henry VIII's daughter by Katherine of Aragon: birth, 3; education, 7, 11, 58; abortive betrothal to Dauphin of France, 7, 9; health, 17, 21, 23, 32, 35, 40, 46, 57–8, 85, 134, 137–8, 144, 150; suggested betrothal to King of France, 14, 16; chance encounter with her father, 23; Anne Boleyn's dislike of her, 22; hears of Anne Boleyn's coronation, 23–4; separated from mother, 21; dispossessed, 28; birth of half-sister Elizabeth, 27; refuses to declare herself illegitimate, 28–9; forced to attend on Elizabeth, 29; refuses to take Oath of Supremacy, 32; Chapuys, Spanish ambassador, her only friend, 33; rejects Anne Boleyn's overtures, 35, 36; grief-stricken at mother's death, 35; learns of Anne Boleyn's execution, 37; restored to partial favour with father, 37; affection for infant Elizabeth, 39; submission exacted from her by her father, 40–1; restored to favour, 42; affection for stepmother, Jane Seymour, 42, 45; godmother to half-brother Edward, 47; chief mourner at Jane Seymour's obsequies, 48; submits to suggested marriage with Philip of Bavaria, 51; affection for Anne of Cleves, her father's fourth wife, 53; dislike of Katherine Howard, her father's fifth wife, 53; with Edward when he recovers from illness, 54; affection for Katherine Parr, her father's sixth wife, 56; difference in religion only friction between her and Edward, 71, 94; protests against religious intolerance, 77; anguish over new anti-Catholic acts, 85; blamed for revolt, 86–7; affection for Jane Grey, 93; accuses Council of breach of faith, 94; flaunts her prohibited Catholic faith, 95; wins short-lived battle over the Council, 97; visits Edward who is ill, 103–4; treated with deference by the Council, 103; becomes Queen, 117; enters London in triumph, 118; desires marriage with Philip of Spain, 121; distrusts Protestant Elizabeth, 122; allows her to leave for Hatfield, 122; envoys to negotiate marriage to Philip arrive, 122–3; three rebellions spring up, Wyatt's threatens London, 123–4; rebellions crushed, Wyatt taken prisoner, 124; Elizabeth implicated, Mary saves her life, 125–6; marriage to Philip of Spain, 132; her kinsman, Cardinal Pole, arrives, 135–6; Pope grants absolution to apostate England which is now Roman Catholic land, 136; believes herself pregnant, 135–8, 149; pregnancy proves false, 138, 150; Philip leaves her, promising early return, 139; Protestants persecuted as religious hatred spreads, 139–40; her unpopularity increases, 144; Spain and France at war, 146; Philip returns only to seek England's aid, 146–7; England joins in Philip's war, 148; Philip leaves her again having achieved his end, 148; heartbroken by loss of Calais, 149; hopes in vain for Philip's return, 149; leaves Crown in will to successor according to the law, 150; death, 151; appearance of: (as infant and girl), 4, 10, 23; (as a woman), 40, 77, 118, 133, 143, 146, 149; character of, 16, 17, 28, 40–2, 58, 95, 128, 150. *Relations with Dudley, Earl of Warwick and Duke of Northumberland*: his rise to power augurs no good for her, 94; contends with him, 95; her victory shortlived, 97; he pays her homage, 103; sends for her to visit her dying brother, 115; in arms against her, 115; has Jane